MYSTERY TRAIN

Images of America
in Rock 'n' Roll Music

GREIL MARCUS

E. P. Dutton & Co., Inc. New York   1975

Every effort was made to obtain permission to use the lyrics quoted in this book. Some lyrics appear without acknowledgement because we received no reply from the proprietors.

Library of Congress Cataloging in Publication Data

Marcus, Greil.
Mystery train.

Discography: p.
1. Rock music—United States—History and criticism.
2. United States—Popular culture. 3. Rock musicians—
Biography. I. Title.
ML3561.R62M35   784   74-20813

Published simultaneously in Canada by Clarke, Irwin & Company Limited,
Toronto and Vancouver
ISBN: 0-525-16328-X
ISBN: 0-525-16328-4

Designed by The Etheredges

MYSTERY TRAIN

To Emily and Cecily

CONTENTS

AUTHOR'S NOTE

Writing these opening notes reminds me of the prefaces to the American history books that were written during World War II, when the authors, looking back for the meaning of the Revolution or the Civil War or whatever, drew modest but determined parallels between their work and the struggle. They were affirming that their work was part of the struggle; that an attempt to understand America took on a special meaning when America was up for grabs. Those writers were also saying—at least, this is what they now say to me—that to do one's most personal work in a time of public crisis is an honest, legitimate, paradoxically democratic act of common faith; that one keeps faith with one's community by offering whatever it is that one has to say. I mean that those writers were exhilarated, thirty years ago, by something we can only call patriotism, and humbled by it too.

Well, I feel some kinship with those writers. I began this book in the fall of 1972, and finished it late in the summer of 1974. Inevitably, it reflects, and I hope contains, the peculiar moods of those times, when the country came face to face with an obscene perversion of itself that could be neither accepted nor destroyed: moods of rage, excitement, loneliness, fatalism, desire.

Like a lot of people who are about thirty years old, I have been listening and living my life to rock 'n' roll for twenty years, and so behind this book lie twenty years of records and twenty years of talk. Probably it began when a kid pushed a radio at me and demanded that I listen to a song called "Rock Around the Clock," which I disliked at the time and still do. I know the music came together for me in high school, thanks to my cruising friend, Barry Franklin. We spent years on the El Camino, driving from Menlo Park to San Francisco to San Jose and back again, listening to Tom Donahue and Tommy Saunders on KYA, trying to figure out the words to "Runaround Sue" and translating "Little Star" into French. Later, we followed the sixties trail to college, Beatle shows, and Dylan concerts.

About a month before the Beatles hit I met my wife Jenny, who confirmed my enthusiasms and who has always kept them alive; it means more to me to say that this book wouldn't have been written without her than to say that it couldn't have been.

The time I have spent talking rock 'n' roll with my friends Bruce Miroff, Langdon Winner, Ralph Gleason, Ed Ward, Michael Goodwin, and many more, has gone into this book; so has talk with my brothers Steve and Bill, with teachers and students, and with my daughter Emily, who picked "Mystery Train" as her favorite song at the age of two. My daughter Cecily is not as yet so discriminating, but I have hopes. As much as anything, rock 'n' roll has been the best means to friendship I know.

I have been writing about the music since 1966 —professionally, for publication, since 1968. Before I got up the nerve to see my efforts in print I put together a book of pieces by myself and some friends; one of them, Sandy Darlington, taught me a lot about music and a lot more about writing. After the book was finished I took over Sandy's music-space in the San Francisco *Express-Times*, then edited and inspired by Marvin Garson. Until the events of Peoples' Park sent it reeling into mindlessness, the *Express-Times* was the best underground newspaper in America, and I've always been proud to have been part of it. When it changed I moved across town to *Rolling Stone*, where I wrote and edited for a year. In 1970 I left, and ultimately ended up with *Creem*, a magazine that seemed like a place of freedom and was. *Creem* gave me the chance to try out many of the ideas that eventually found their way into this book.

There would be little to those ideas without the study I did in American political thought and American literature with three Berkeley teachers: John Schaar, Michael Rogin, and Norman Jacobson; they made me care about those subjects. And there are a few books that mattered a great deal to the ambitions of my own book, and to its content: D. H. Lawrence's *Studies In Classic American Literature*, Leslie Fiedler's *Love and Death In the American Novel*, James Agee's *Let Us Now Praise Famous Men*, Pauline Kael's *I Lost It At the Movies*, Alexis de Tocqueville's *Democracy In America*, and, in a way that is still pretty mysterious to me, Ernest Hemingway's short stories.

Mary Clemmey, Greg Shaw, Richard Bass, Pat Thomas, Ms. Clawdy, Bill Strachan of Anchor Press, Wendy Weil. Jenny Marcus, Peter Guralnick, Bruce Miroff, Bob Christgau, and Dave Marsh read every page of the manuscript, and made it far better than it would have been without their help.

Bob and Dave deserve special thanks. They have been part of my work from beginning to end; they encouraged it, at times inspired it, always cared about it. No critic could ask for better colleagues, and no one could ask for better friends.

And I owe as much to my editor, Bill Whitehead. Without his commitment to the book, mine would have faded out a long time ago.

What I have to say in *Mystery Train* grows out of records, novels, political writings; the balance shifts, but in my intentions, there isn't any separation. I am no more capable of mulling over Elvis without thinking about Herman Melville than I am of reading Jonathan Edwards (*not*, I've been asked to point out, the crooner mentioned in the Randy Newman chapter, but the Puritan who made his name with "Sinners In the Hands of An Angry God") without putting on Robert Johnson's records as background music. What I bring to this book, at any rate, is no attempt at synthesis, but a recognition of unities in the American imagination that already exist. They are natural unities, I think, but elusive; I learned, in the last two years, that simply because of those unities, the resonance of the best American images is profoundly deep and impossibly broad. I wrote this book in an attempt to find some of those images, but I know now that to put oneself in touch with them is a life's work.

Berkeley, August 9, 1974

PROLOGUE

OUR STORY BEGINS just after midnight, not so long ago. The Dick Cavett Show is in full swing.

Seated on Cavett's left is John Simon, The New York Critic. On Cavett's right, in order of distance from him, are Little Richard, Rock 'n' Roll Singer and Weirdo; Rita Moreno, Actress; and Erich Segal, Yale Professor of Classics and Author of *Love Story*. Miss Moreno and Mr. Segal adored *Love Story*. Mr. Simon did not. Little Richard has not read it.

Cavett is finishing a commercial. Mr. Simon is mentally rehearsing his opening thrust against Mr. Segal, who is very nervous. Miss Moreno seems to be falling asleep. Little Richard is looking for an opening.

Mr. Simon has attacked Mr. Segal. Mr. Segal attempts a reply but he is too nervous to be coherent. Mr. Simon at-

tacks a second time. Little Richard is about to jump out of
his seat and jam his face in front of the camera but Mr.
Simon beats him out. He attacks Mr. Segal again.

"NEGATIVE! NEGATIVE NEGATIVE NEGATIVE!" screams Mr.
Segal. He and Simon are debating a fine point in the history
of Greek tragedy, to which Mr. Simon has compared *Love
Story* unfavorably.

" 'Neg-a-tive,' " muses Mr. Simon. "Does that mean
'no'?"

Mr. Segal attempts, unsuccessfully, to ignore Mr. Simon's contempt for his odd patois, and claims that the critics
were wrong about Aeschylus. He implies that Simon would
have walked out on the *Oresteia*. Backed by the audience,
which sounds like a Philadelphia baseball crowd that has
somehow mistaken Mr. Simon for Richie Allen, Segal
presses his advantage. Little Richard sits back in his chair,
momentarily intimidated.

"MILLIONS OF PEOPLE were DEEPLY MOVED by my book,"
cries Segal, forgetting to sit up straight and slumping in his
chair until his body is near parallel with the floor. "AND IF
ALL THOSE PEOPLE LIKED IT—" (Segal's voice has now achieved
a curious tremolo) *"I MUST BE DOING SOMETHING
RIGHT!"*

The effort has exhausted Segal, and as he takes a deep
breath Little Richard begins to rise from his seat. Again,
Simon is too fast for him. Simon attempts to make Segal understand that he is amazed that anyone, especially Segal,
takes this trash to be anything more than, well, trash.

"I have read it and reread it many times," counters Segal
with great honesty. "I am always moved."

"Mr. Segal," says Simon, having confused the bull with
his cape and now moving in for the kill, "you had the choice
of acting the knave or the fool. You have chosen the latter."

Segal is stunned. Cavett is stunned. He calls for a commercial. Little Richard considers the situation.

The battle resumes. Segal has now slumped even lower
in his chair, if that is possible, and seems to be arguing with
the ceiling. *"You're* only a critic," he says as if to Simon.

"What have *you* ever written? What do you know about art?
Never in the history of art . . ."

"WHY, NEVER IN THE HISTORY!"

The time has come. Little Richard makes his move.
Leaping from his seat, he takes the floor, arms waving, hair
coming undone, eyes wild, mouth working. He advances on
Segal, Cavett, and Simon, who cringe as one man. The camera cuts to a close-up of Segal, who looks miserable, then to
Simon, who is attempting to compose the sort of bemused
expression he would have if, say, someone were to defecate
on the floor. Little Richard is audible off-camera, and then
his face quickly fills the screen.

"WHY, YES, IN THE WHOLE HISTORY OF AAAART! THAT'S
RIGHT! SHUT UP! SHUT UP! WHAT DO YOU KNOW, MR. CRITIC?
WHY, WHEN THE CREEDENCE CLEARWATER PUT OUT WITH THEIR
'TRAVELN' BAND' EVERYBODY SAY WHEEE-<u>OOO</u> BUT <u>I</u> KNOW IT
CUZ THEY ONLY DOING 'LONG TALL SALLY' JUST LIKE THE BEA-
TLES ANDTHESTONESANDTOMJONESANDELVIS—<u>I</u> AM <u>ALL</u> OF IT,
LITTLE RICHARD <u>HIMSELF</u>, VERY TRULY THE <u>GREATEST</u>, THE
<u>HANDSOMEST</u>, AND NOW TO <u>YOU</u> (to Segal, who now appears
to be *on* the floor) AND TO *YOU* (to Simon, who looks to
Cavett as if to say, really old man, this *has* been fun, but this,
ah, *fellow* is becoming a bit much, perhaps a commercial is in
order?), <u>I</u> HAVE WRITTEN A BOOK, MYSELF, I AM A WRITER, I
HAVE WRITTEN A BOOK AND IT'S CALLED—

"<u>HE GOT WHAT HE WANTED BUT HE LOST WHAT HE HAD!</u>
THAT'S IT! SHUT UP! SHUT UP! SHUT UP! <u>HE GOT WHAT HE
WANTED BUT HE LOST WHAT HE HAD!</u> THE STORY OF MY LIFE.
CAN YOU DIG IT? THAT'S MY BOY LITTLE RICHARD, SURE IS. OO
MAH SOUL!"

Little Richard flies back to his chair and slams down
into it. "WHEEEEE-OO! OOO MAH SOUL! OO mah soul . . ."

Little Richard sits with the arbiters of taste, oblivious to
their bitter stares, savoring his moment. He is Little Richard. Who are they? Who will remember Erich Segal, John
Simon, Dick Cavett? Who will care? Ah, but Little Richard,
Little Richard *Himself!* There is a man who matters. He
knows how to rock.

A phrase that Little Richard snatched off Erich Segal stays in my mind: "Never in the history—*in the whole history of art. . . .*" And that was it. Little Richard was the only artist on the set that night, the only man who disrupted an era, the only man with a claim to immortality. The one who broke rules, created a form; the one who gave shape to a vitality that wailed silently in each of us until he found a voice for it.

He is the rock, the jive bomber, the savant. "Tutti Frutti" was his first hit, breaking off the radio in 1955 to shuffle the bland expectations of white youth; fifteen years later the Weirdo on the Cavett Show reached back for whatever he had left and busted up an argument about the meaning of art with a spirit that recalled the absurd promise of his glory days. "I HAVE WRITTEN A BOOK, MYSELF, AND IT'S CALLED . . ."

Listening now to Little Richard, to Elvis, to Jerry Lee Lewis, the Monotones, the Drifters, Chuck Berry, and dozens of others, I feel a sense of awe at how fine their music was. I can only marvel at their arrogance, their humor, their delight. They were so sure of themselves. They sang as if they knew they were destined to survive not only a few weeks on the charts but to make history; to displace the dreary events of the fifties in the memories of those who heard their records; and to anchor a music that twenty years later would be struggling to keep the promises they made. Naturally, they sound as if they could care less, so long as their little black 45's hit number one and made them rich and famous. But they delivered a new version of America with their music, and more people than anyone can count are still trying to figure out how to live in it.

Well, then, this is a book about rock 'n' roll—some of it—and America. It is not a history, nor a purely musical analysis, nor a set of personality profiles. It is an attempt to broaden the context in which the music is heard; to deal with rock 'n' roll not as youth culture, or counter culture, but simply as American culture.

The performers that I have written about appeal to me partly because they are more ambitious and because they take more risks than most. They risk artistic disaster (in rock terms, pretentiousness), or the alienation of an audience that can be soothed far more easily than it can be provoked; their ambitions have a good deal to do with Robbie Robertson's statement of his ambitions for the Band: "Music should never be harmless."

What attracts me even more to the Band, Sly Stone, Randy Newman, and Elvis, is that I think these men tend to see themselves as symbolic Americans; I think their music is an attempt to live up to that role. Their records—the Band's *Big Pink*, Sly's *There's a riot goin' on*, a few of Randy Newman's tunes, Elvis Presley's very first Tennessee singles— dramatize a sense of what it is to be an American; what it means, what it's worth, what the stakes of life in America might be. This book, then, is an exploration of a few artists, all of whom seem to me to have found their own voices; it is rooted in the idea that these artists can illuminate those American questions and that the questions can add resonance to their work.

The two men whose tales begin the book—white country hokum singer Harmonica Frank and black Mississippi blues singer Robert Johnson—came and went before the words "rock 'n' roll" had any cultural meaning at all. Both men represent traditions crucial to rock 'n' roll, and both are unique. They worked at the frontiers of the music, and they can give us an idea of what the country has to give the music to work with—a sense of how far the music can go. Harmonica Frank sang with a simple joy and a fool's pride; he caught a spirit the earliest rock 'n' roll mastered effortlessly, a mood the music is always losing and trying to win back. Robert Johnson was very different. He was a brooding man who did his work on the darker side of American life; his songs deal with terrors and fears that few American artists have ever expressed so directly. In this book, Frank and Johnson figure as metaphors more than musical influences. Their chapters are meant to form a backdrop against which the later chapters can take shape, a framework for the images the other artists have made.

The Band, Sly Stone, Randy Newman, and Elvis are still vital performers. They share unique musical and public personalities, enough ambition to make even their failures interesting, and a lack of critical commentary extensive or committed enough to do their work justice. In their music and in their careers, they share a range and a depth that seem to crystalize naturally in visions and versions of America: its possibilities, limits, openings, traps. Their stories are hardly the whole story, but they can tell us how much the story matters. That is what this book is about.

. . . to be an American (unlike being English or French or whatever) is precisely to *imagine* a destiny rather than to inherit one; since we have always been, insofar as we are Americans at all, inhabitants of myth rather than history. . . .

LESLIE FIEDLER, "Cross
the Border, Close the Gap"

It's easy to forget how young this country is; how little distance really separates us from the beginnings of the myths, like that of Lincoln, that still haunt the national imagination. It's easy to forget how much remains to be settled. Since roots are sought out and seized as well as simply accepted, cultural history is never a straight line; along with the artists we care about we fill in the gaps ourselves. When we do, we reclaim, rework, or invent America, or a piece of it, all over again. We make choices (or are caught by the choices others have made) about what is worth keeping and what isn't, trying to create a world where we feel alive, risky, ambitious, and free (or merely safe), dispensing with the rest of the American reality if we can. We make the oldest stories new when we succeed, and we are trapped by the old stories when we fail.

That is as close as I can come to a simple description of what I think the performers in this book have done—but of course what they have done is more complex than that.

In the work of each performer there is an attempt to create oneself, to make a new man out of what is inherited and what is imagined; each individual attempt implies an ideal community, never easy to define, where that new man would be at home, where his work could communicate easily and deeply, where the members of that ideal community would speak as clearly to the artist as he does to them.

The audiences that gather around rock 'n' rollers are as close to that ideal community as anyone gets. The real drama of a performer's career comes when the ideal that one can hear in the music and the audience that the artist really attracts begin to affect each other. No artist can predict, let alone control, what an audience will make of his images; yet no rock 'n' roller can exist without a relationship with an audience, whether it is the imaginary audience one begins with, or the all-too-real confusion of the audience one wins.

The best popular artists create immediate links between people who might have nothing in common but a response to their work, but the best popular artists never stop trying to understand the impact of their work on their audiences. That means their ideal images must change as their understanding grows. One may find horror where one expected only pleasure; one may find that the truth one told has become a lie. If the audience demands only more of what it has already accepted, the artist has a choice. He can move on, and perhaps cut himself off from his audience; if he does, his work will lose all the vitality and strength it had when he knew it mattered to other people. Or, the artist can accept the audience's image of himself, pretend that his audience *is* his shadowy ideal, and lose himself in his audience. Then he will only be able to confirm; he will never be able to create.

The most interesting rock 'n' rollers sometimes go to these extremes; most don't, because these are contradictions they survive more than resolve. The tension between community and self-reliance; between distance from one's audience and affection for it; between the shared experience of popular culture and the special talents of artists who both draw on that shared experience and change it—these things

are what make rock 'n' roll at its best a democratic art, at
least in the American meaning of the word democracy. I
think that is true because our democracy is nothing if not a
contradiction: the creed of every man and woman for themselves, and thus the loneliness of separation, and thus the
yearning for harmony, and for community. The performers
in this book, in their different ways, all trace that line.

If they are in touch with their audiences and with the
images of community their songs hint at, rock 'n' rollers get
to see their myths and parables in action, and ultimately they
may even find out what they are worth. When the story is a
long one—a career—they find the story coming back to them in
pieces, which of course is how it was received.

Here is where a critic might count. Putting the pieces
together, trying to understand what is novel and adventur-
ous, what is enervated and complacent, can give us an idea of
how much room there is in this musical culture, and in
American culture—an idea of what a singer and a band can
do with a set of songs mixed into the uncertainty that is the
pop audience. Looking back into the corners, we might discover whose America we are living in at any moment, and
where it came from. With luck, we might even touch that
spirit of place Americans have always sought, and in the
seeking have created.

ANCESTORS

HARMONICA FRANK
1951

In 1951 Sam Phillips was the owner of a shoestring operation that cut records by young black blues singers in Memphis, Tennessee. A few years later he would shape the careers of such founding rockers as Elvis Presley, Carl Perkins, Roy Orbison, and Jerry Lee Lewis; today, he counts his money. But at least one writer has stepped forward to call him "America's Real Uncle Sam," a title he might like.

Phillips was raised on a plantation in Alabama; when he was a little boy an old black man would take him aside and sing him the blues, playing Jim to Sam's Huck. In the fifties, bored by the music business and itching for something new, it would be quite natural for Phillips to look for someone to complete a role that was sketched out in his own past. "If I could find a white man who had the Negro sound and the Negro feel," he was saying in those days (as Huck Finn met

11

the Riverboat Gambler), "I could make a billion dollars." Harmonica Frank Floyd, a white man in his early forties, who held a harmonica in one side of his mouth and sang out of the other, was Sam Phillips' first try.

Harmonica Frank was never famous. Born in 1908 in Toccopola, Mississippi, a short ways from Elvis Presley's birthplace in Tupelo, he was a drifter, who left home at the age of fourteen and bummed his way around the country for the next forty years, a man who came up with his own idea of the country's music, black and white.

In 1973, an old man, Frank wrote: "Just one thang I would love to say the first time I played a rock and roll tune on my oath I had never heard no one else do that type therefore I am almost sure I am the originator of rock and roll regardless of what you may have heard at the time I could not read or write music but now I can I am truly a hillbilly from the state of miss but have traveled all over played in old time vaudeville shows medicine shows on the streets barber shops court house lawns auctions sales woodman halls radios television you name it I've played it comedy fire eaters with carnivals tricks or magic so at least I'm an old showman picked cotton picked fruit dug mussel shells in Ark pan some gold in calif one time on KELW in Hollywood with Bustie steel and log cabin wranglers. . . .

". . . You see I played rock and roll before I ever heard of elvis presley I saw him in memphis before he ever made a record with sam phillips on north main in memphis tennessee. . . ." *

Frank cut many sides in 1951 for Phillips, who leased a few to Chess, the Chicago blues label. They didn't sell. Phillips put out two remaining tracks as a single on his new Sun label in 1954, just before Elvis Presley's first record was released, but the disc went nowhere.

Harmonica Frank's music was a joke, mostly, because there was a little more money for a street-singer who could make people laugh. Yet there was an edge to Frank's music, a

---

* From a letter Frank wrote to Greg Shaw.

fool's resistance to the only role he knew; and that, along with the vitality and invention of the sounds Frank made, was a key to the inarticulate desires shared by Sam Phillips and the impatient new audience whose presence he sensed. "Old Sam Phillips only had one thing to tell me," Harmonica Frank says today. "Said it over and over. 'Gimme something different. Gimme something unique.' "

In his own way Harmonica Frank was as much a maniac as Little Richard. He sounded like a drunken clown who's seen it all, remembers about half of that, and makes the rest up. He put together a style of country rock that did not really find an audience until years later, when Bob Dylan caught the same spirit and much of the sound with "Mixed-Up Confusion," his first single, a lot of the *Freewheelin'* album, and his "I Shall Be Free" songs. In a broader sense Frank can be heard every time a rocker's secret smile breaks open: when Randy Newman sings from the bottom of a bottle, or when Levon Helm gurgles "Hee, hee!" in the middle of "Cripple Creek," the Band's sexiest song.

Harmonica Frank was perhaps the first of the rock 'n' roll vocal contortionists—like Buddy Holly, Clarence "Frogman" Henry, and Bob Dylan—whose mission in life seemed to be the willful destruction of the mainstream tradition of popular singing and the smooth and self-assured way of life it was made to represent. Frank screeched, he bellowed, croaked, cackled, and moaned, carrying his songs and never mind about the tune. He was a noisemaker.

What matters about Frank is the sense of freedom he brought to his music: a good-natured contempt for conventional patterns of life combined with a genius for transforming all that was smug and polite into absurdity. The result was a music of staggering weirdness, dimly anchored by the fatalism of the blues and powered by the pure delight of what was soon to be called rock 'n' roll. Frank wasn't sexy, like the rockabilly singers who were to make Sam Phillips' fortune; he was more like a dirty old man. He was ribald, and he had flair. "I am," he growled in one of his numbers, "a howling tomcat."

His only Sun single was his best—"The Great Medical
Menagerist," a wonderful talking blues, backed by "Rockin'
Chair Daddy," a first-rate piece of nonsense that really does
set the stage for rock 'n' roll. Here he reaches for falsettos,
talks to himself, corrects himself, roaring into town

> *Rock to Memphis, dance on Main*
> *Up stepped a lady and asked my name*
> *Rockin' chair daddy dont have to work*
> *I told her my name was on the tail of my shirt!*

and pounding away to the finish: "Never been to college,
never been to school, if you want some rockin' I'm a rockin'
fool!"

"The Great Medical Menagerist" is simply a triumph.
Probably a miniature autobiography, it is a catalogue of all
the prim and decent people Frank made asses of, and of the
jobs his fun cost him. The first lines have the perfection of
myth:

> *Ladies and gentlemens, cough white dodgers and*
> *little rabbit twisters, step right around closely,*
> *tell ya all about a wonderful medicine show I*
> *useta work with. . . .*

"We have Doctor Donnicker here with us," he drawls,
too sly to believe, "The Great Medical Menagerist . . . *of the
World.*" That little pause charges the performance with wit
and even menace; Frank sings with a squeak. Frank barely
lets on that the menagerie is none other than Doctor Donnicker's audience, which is to say, his.

His most compelling record was "Goin' Away Walkin',"
one of the sides on Chess. It is a classic country blues, and a
kind of final statement. If the form is blues, though, the
spirit and the sound come from the high, lonely whine of the
white mountain music that goes back to the Revolution. The
notes seem to hang in the air like ghosts; the song is bitter,
unrepentant, and free. "I ain't gonna get married," Frank

Floyd sings. "I ain't gonna settle down. I'm gonna walk this highway, till my whiskers drags the ground."

That was his promise, and he kept it. Of all the characters who populate this book, only Harmonica Frank did more than keep the legend of Huckleberry Finn alive—he lived it out. He showed up, made his records, and lit out for the territory, banging his guitar and squeaking his harp, dodging Greyhounds and working the fields, setting himself free from an oppression he never bothered to define.

His humor, his cutting edge, came like Twain's from that part of the American imagination that has always sneered at the limits imposed by manners; the strain that produced both obscenity and the tall tale, two forms of a secret revolt against the Puritans who founded the country and against the authority of their ghosts. It is a revolt against the hopeful morality of Twain's aunts and the tiresomeness of Ben Franklin doing good and being right; a revolt against pomposity, and arrogance.

And this revolt is powerful stuff, after all. How long would Ahab have lasted if he'd been up against howling weirdo like Harmonica Frank instead of a dumb Christian like Starbuck?

A DIGRESSION THAT MAY PROVE
WORTHWHILE TO THOSE READERS
WHO DO NOT SKIP IT

Our latest Ahab almost had it both ways, because there was a lot of Harmonica Frank in Lyndon B. Johnson, once President of All the People; one of America's secrets is that the dreams of Huck and Ahab are not always very far apart. Both of them embody an impulse to freedom, an escape from restraints and authority that sometimes seems like the only really American story there is. That one figure is passive and benign, the other aggressive and in the end malignant; the one full of humor and regret, and the other cold and determined never to look back; the one as unsure of his own authority as he is of anyone else's, the other fleeing authority

only to replace it with his own—all this hides the common
bond between the two characters, and suggests how strong
would be a figure who could put the two together. For all
that is different about Ahab and Huck Finn, they are two
American heroes who say, yes, they will go to hell if they
have to; they will go as far as anyone can.

The obsessiveness and the wish for peace of mind that
most easily set Ahab and Huck off from each other—on the
surface, anyway—are cornerstones of how rock 'n' roll works
and what it is for, but we will find the two spirits together
more often than not.

LBJ had his year on the road, quitting college and hobo-
ing his way out to California, digging ditches and washing
dishes, finally coming home after having gone far enough to
say, years later, that any member of his generation that
hadn't been a communist or a dropout wasn't worth a damn.
Deeply contemptuous of Eastern gentility (and attracted by
it too), Johnson coupled a devastating talent for obscenity
that no Easterner could match with an image of himself as a
latter-day Pecos Bill; the American, Johnson might have
been telling us, is alive only as long as he is uncivilized. Thus
Johnson carefully received his guests on the toilet, because it
threw them off guard. Bob Dylan was pouting that even the
President of the Yew-Nited States had to stand naked, but
LBJ was way ahead of him: he forced heads of state to strip
for a swim and got the upper hand. He showed his scar and
the *New York Review of Books* never forgave him. He told
them his name was on the tail of his shirt.

But Johnson's best defense was his verbal obscenity,
that side of Huck that Twain left out of the book and kept
for himself.

Norman Mailer was the only one of Johnson's adver-
saries who understood this side of the man, and so he took
LBJ on with *Why Are We in Vietnam?* It was the most
gloriously obscene book Mailer could write, a book whose
hero was in fact a Texas Huck on his way to becoming a
Texas Ahab, changing fast from a reckless kid into a killer.

The job, Mailer knew, was to find the sources of Johnson's power—not merely his political power, but his personal strength. That meant Mailer had to understand the language LBJ really spoke, and then beat him at his own game. And so the obscenity of Mailer's book, at first so funny, so full of honest rebellion, becomes more and more cruel, until finally it is part and parcel with brutality, and murder.

But Mailer didn't win the fight with Lyndon Johnson. The richest, riskiest passages of his book cannot compare with Johnson's offhand remark, made when he was asked why he had not told the people more about Vietnam: "If you have a mother-in-law with only one eye, and that eye is in the middle of her forehead, you don't keep her in the living room." *

If anything could redeem the arrogant obsessions of the man who introduced us to the obscenity of the burnt baby, it was a style of personal obscenity. This allowed Johnson to transcend, for a time, the self-righteousness (and righteousness pure and simple) of those who vilified him with every obscenity at *their* command. After all, compared to the crowds who hounded him with their mechanical chants, Lyndon Johnson was a poet.

Perhaps, if the political language of America was as free as its secret language, LBJ could have made King Shit a title to be reckoned with. Perhaps, in the presidential election of our dreams, he could have beaten even Lenny Bruce.

And maybe he would have kept Harmonica Frank on retainer, down there on the LBJ ranch.

Harmonica Frank's music, like LBJ's language, has a spirit that occasionally emerges to redeem those impulses in American life that are cold, bitter, and corrupt—just as that book about a river and a raft was meant to displace Mark Twain's dread of what, hard into the Gilded Age, the country seemed eager to believe it was all about. The idea

* Cited in David Halberstam, *The Best and the Brightest*, (New York: Random House, 1972).

that the two Americas are separable, I suppose, is the heart
of our romanticism.

A good part of the impact of rock 'n' roll had to do with
its anachronistic essence, the way it seemed to come out of
nowhere—the big surprise that trivialized the events that
governed daily life. Rock 'n' roll gave the kids who had seen
no alternative but to submit to those events a little room to
move. Any musicologist, neatly tracing the development of
the music, can tell us that rock 'n' roll did not come out of
nowhere. But it sounded like it did. It was one of those great
twists of history that no one anticipated—no one, that is, except a few men like Sam Phillips, who were looking for it,
looking for something to break the boredom they felt when
they turned on the radio.

Harmonica Frank was part of Phillips' quest for the
weird, and weird it had to be if it was to crack the ice that
was seeping into Memphis in 1951. When Phillips looked at
his town he must have seen the thousands of good country
people, the people who worked hard and prayed harder, who
had migrated to Memphis after World War II. They wanted
a home that was safe, orderly, and respectable, and as far as
the old wide-open riverboat town was concerned, they were
perfectly satisfied to visit it in a museum. There was a sense
that life was set in a pattern; winding down.

"It seemed to me that Negroes were the only ones that
had any freshness left in their music," Phillips has said of
those days when he was looking for a white man. Maybe it
was a white man who sounded like a cross between a barn-
yard and a minstrel show—Harmonica Frank, say; maybe a
cocky kid, child of those new Memphians, who sang a new
kind of blues. Certainly it had to be someone who toyed with
race, the deepest source of limits in the South.

The alternative for Phillips, as a record producer, was
the white country music of the Carter Family, Jimmie
Rodgers, Hank Williams, Patsy Cline. But leaving aside the
fact that Phillips was not likely to make a billion dollars on it,
there was a problem with that music. It so perfectly ex-

pressed the acceptance and fatalism of its audience of poor
and striving whites, blending in with their way of life and
endlessly reinforcing it, that the music brought all it had to
say to the surface, told no secrets, and had no use for novelty. It was conservative in an almost tragic sense, because it
carried no hope of change, only respite. By the early fifties
this music was all limits. Country music was entertainment
that made people feel better, as all true American folk music
is before it is anything else, but at its deepest country music
was a way of holding on to the values that were jeopardized
by a changing postwar America. Country music lacked the
confidence to break things open because it was not even sure
it could find space to breathe. Hank Williams was eloquent,
but his eloquence could not set him free from the life he sang
about; he died proving it, overdosing in the back of a car, on
his way to one more show.

Phillips had not even worked out the sound he wanted; it
was music toward which he was only groping, and most important, ready to accept. Frank Floyd, a white man with
some life in him, whose music wasn't exactly blues but was
too strange to peddle as anything else, couldn't have sounded
less like Hank Williams (though he might have picked up
some of his twinkle from Jimmie Rodgers, whom he met on
the road years before). Maybe Frank's music was something
that would make people take notice if they heard him on the
radio, which they rarely did; whatever it was, it was music
to turn things around a bit—a clue to what Phillips was looking for, to what made rock 'n' roll happen and to what keeps
it alive.

What Phillips was looking for was something that didn't
fit, that didn't make sense out of or reflect American life as
everyone seemed to understand it, but which made it beside
the point, confused things, and affirmed something else.
What? The fact that there *was* something else.

What finally arrived was a music of racial confusion,
Huck and Jim giving America's aunt the slip, no dead-end
"white Negroes" but something new, men like Harmonica

Frank and Elvis Presley, whose styles revealed possibilities of
American life that were hardly visible anywhere else with an
intensity and delight that had no parallel at all.

The music unleashed by Elvis, Little Richard, and the
rest of the early rockers was a gas, and it was also unnerving.
I recall hearing Little Richard's "Rip It Up" for the first
time, loving the sound but catching the line, "Fool about
mah money dont try to save," and thinking, well, that *is* fool-
ish. Had Harmonica Frank's "Rockin' Chair Daddy" been on
my radio, I would have been appalled that anyone could skip
college *and be proud of it*.

I know that when Elvis was drafted I felt a great relief,
because he made demands on me. It was close to what I felt
when the politics of the sixties faded—an ambivalent feeling
of cowardice and safety. I loved his records—"Hound Dog"
was the first I ever owned; "All Shook Up" the first I bought;
and "(You're So Square) Baby I Don't Care" (the title may
sum up this dilemma) my first private treasure, a record I
loved that no one else seemed to like.

But I didn't like—that is, didn't understand—what the
Big E did to the girls I went to school with or the way he
looked on the cover of his first album, demented, tongue
hanging down his chest, lost in some ecstasy completely
foreign to me. What was this? Harmonica Frank wasn't the
source of this confused delight, not in terms of musicology
anyway, because almost no one ever heard him. But he was
in on it: he helped Sam Phillips open the doors the King
walked through. More than that, he was a harbinger of a certain American spirit that never disappears no matter how
smooth things get.

ROBERT JOHNSON
1938

When the train
Left the station
It had two lights on behind
When the train left the station
It had two lights on behind
Well, the blue light was my blues
And the red light was my mind.
All my love's
In vain.

ROBERT JOHNSON, "Love in Vain"

You know how it feels—you understand
What it is to be a stranger, in this unfriendly
land

BOBBY BLUE BLAND, "Lead Me On" *

It may be that the most interesting American struggle is the struggle to set oneself free from the limits one is born to, and then to learn something of the value of those limits. But on the surface, America takes its energy from the pursuit of happiness; from "a love of physical gratification, the notion of bettering one's condition, the excitement of competition, the charm of anticipated success" (Tocqueville's words); from a memory of open spaces and a belief in open possibilities; from the conviction that you *can* always get what you want, and that even if you can't, you deserve it anyway.

Most of the big shore places were closed now and there were hardly any lights except the shadowy, moving glow of a ferryboat across the Sound. And as the moon rose higher the inessential houses began to melt away until gradually I became aware of the old island here that had flowered once for Dutch sailors' eyes. Its vanished trees, the trees that had made way for Gatsby's house, had once pandered to the last and greatest of human dreams; for a transitory enchanted moment man must have held his breath in the presence of this continent, compelled into an aesthetic contemplation he neither understood nor desired, face to face for the last time in history with something commensurate to his capacity for wonder.

No one ever captured the promise of American life more beautifully than Fitzgerald did in that passage. That sense of America is expressed so completely—by billboards, by our movies, by Chuck Berry's refusal to put the slightest irony into "Back in the U.S.A.," by the way we try to live our lives—that we hardly know how to talk about the resentment and fear that lie beneath the promise. To be an American is to feel the promise as a birthright, and to feel alone and haunted when the promise fails. No failure in America, whether of love or money, is ever simple; it is always a kind of betrayal, of a mass of shadowy, shared hopes.

Within that failure is a very different America; it is an America of desolation, desolate because it is felt to be out of place, and it is here that Robert Johnson looked for his images and found them.

Robert Johnson was a Mississippi country blues singer and guitarist, born about 1910; he was murdered, likely by a jealous lover, in 1938. He died in a haze: if some remember that he was stabbed, others say he was poisoned; that he died on his hands and knees, barking like a dog; that his death "had something to do with the black arts."

Nearly forty years after his death, Johnson remains the most emotionally committed of all blues singers; for all the distance of his time and place, Johnson's music draws a natural response from many who outwardly could not be more different from him. He sang about the price he had to pay for promises he tried, and failed, to keep; I think the power of his music comes in part from Johnson's ability to shape the loneliness and chaos of his betrayal, or ours. Listening to Johnson's songs, one almost feels at home in that desolate America; one feels able to take some strength from it, right along with the promises we could not give up if we wanted to.

Like Charley Patton, Tommy Johnson, Son House, or Skip James—the men who worked out the country blues form in the late teens and twenties—Robert Johnson sang an intense, dramatic music, accompanied only by his guitar. He put down twenty-nine of his songs for the old Vocalion label in 1936 and 1937; his songs lasted, in the work of other bluesmen, long after Johnson was dead, and in the early sixties Johnson's original versions began to appear on albums. Today Johnson's presence can be felt behind many of the best modern guitar players; in a more subtle and vital way, his presence can be felt behind many of our best singers. And a good musical case can be made for Johnson as the first rock 'n' roller of all. His music had a vibrancy and a rhythmic excitement that was new to the country blues. On some tunes—"Walking Blues," "Crossroads Blues," "If I Had Possession Over Judgment Day"—Johnson sounds like a complete rock 'n' roll band, as full as Elvis's first combo or the group Bob Dylan put together for the *John Wesley Harding* sessions, and tougher than either. Johnson's way of looking at things, though, is just beginning to emerge.

I have no stylistic arguments to make about Johnson's "influence" on the other performers in this book, but I do have a symbolic argument. It seems to me that just as they all have a bit of Harmonica Frank in their souls, the artistic ambitions of the Band, Sly Stone, and Randy Newman can at times be seen as attempts to go part of the way into the America Robert Johnson made his own; that since his journey into that America knew few limits, his music can help us understand the limits of other artists and the risks they take when they try to break through them.

And as for Elvis Presley—well, his first music might be seen as a proud attempt to escape Johnson's America altogether.

Johnson's vision was of a world without salvation, redemption, or rest; it was a vision he resisted, laughed at, to which he gave himself over, but most of all it was a vision he pursued. He walked his road like a failed, orphaned Puritan, looking for women and a good night, but never convinced, whether he found such things or not, that they were really what he wanted, and so framing his tales with old echoes of sin and damnation. There were demons in his songs—blues that walked like a man, the devil, or the two in league with each other—and Johnson was often on good terms with them; his greatest fear seems to have been that his desires were so extreme that he could satisfy them only by becoming a kind of demon himself. When he sings, so slowly, in "Me and the Devil Blues,"

> *Early this morning*
> *When you knocked upon my door*
> *Early this morning*
> *When you knocked upon my door*
> *I said, Hello, Satan*
> *I believe it's time, to go*

the only memory in American art that speaks with the same eerie resignation is that moment when Ahab goes over to the devil-worshiping Parsees he kept stowed away in the hold of the *Pequod.* That is a remarkable image, but Johnson's images were simply part of daily life.

Me and the devil, was walking side by side
Oooo, me and the devil, was walking side by side
I'm going to beat my woman, until I get satisfied

It may seem strange that in the black country South of the twenties and thirties, where the leap to grace of gospel music was at the heart of the community, the blues singers, in a twisted way, were the real Puritans. These men, who had to renounce the blues to be sanctified, who often sneered at the preachers in their songs, were the ones who really believed in the devil; they feared the devil most because they knew him best. They understood, far better than the preachers, why sex was man's original sin, and they sang about little else.

This side of the blues did not come from Africa, but from the Puritan revival of the Great Awakening, the revival that spread across the American colonies more than two hundred years ago. It was an explosion of dread and piety that Southern whites passed onto their slaves and that blacks ultimately refashioned into their own religion. The blues singers accepted the dread but refused the piety; they sang as if their understanding of the devil was strong enough to force a belief in God out of their lives. They lived man's fear of life, and they became artists of the fear.

Or perhaps that is not the truth; perhaps Robert Johnson was very different from other blues singers. For all his clear stylistic ties to Son House, Skip James, and others, there are ways in which he stands apart. Part of this is musical—it has to do with the quality of his imagery, his impulse to drama, the immediacy of his singing and guitar playing—but mostly it is Johnson's determination to go farther into the blues than anyone else, and his ability, as an artist, to get there. Anyone from Muddy Waters to Mick Jagger to Michael Jackson could put across the inspired pornography of Johnson's "Terraplane [a good, rough car of the thirties] Blues"—

I'm gonna get deep down in this connection
Keep on tangling with your wires
I'm gonna get deep down in this connection
Keep on tangling with your wires
And when I mash down on your little starter—
Then your spark gonna give me fire

—but as for "Stones in My Passway," which was the other side of sex, no one has been fool enough to try.

Few men could brag like Robert Johnson: "Stuff I got'll bust your brains out, baby," he sang in "Stop Breaking Down Blues," "It'll make you lose your mind." Women crowded around him at the back country juke joints to find out if it was true, and no doubt it often was. But such tunes gave way to songs like "Phonograph Blues," where Johnson sings, with far too much emotion it seems, about his broken record player. "What evil have I done . . . what evil has the poor girl heard." That one line shows us how far he is trying to go.

The poor girl is the phonograph, softly personified; she refuses to play Johnson's wicked records and breaks down. With a blazing insistence, Johnson intensifies his personification, unveils his metaphors. At once, you see him struggling with his machine, and in bed with his girl. The records are his sins; the phonograph his sexuality. The song ends as a confession that the sins his records embody have made him impotent.

What Johnson found on his road was mostly this: ". . . the sense that life is essentially a cheat and its conditions are those of defeat, and that the redeeming satisfactions are not 'happiness and pleasure' but the deeper satisfactions that come out of struggle." So wrote Fitzgerald to his daughter, about what he had found in Lincoln and Shakespeare and "all great careers." His words make good company for Stanley Booth's: "The dedication [the blues] demands lies beyond technique; it makes being a blues player something like being a priest. Virtuosity in playing blues licks is like virtuosity in celebrating the Mass, it is empty, it means nothing. Skill is a necessity, but a true blues player's virtue lies in his acceptance of his life, a life for which he is only partly responsible. When Bukka White sings a song he wrote during his years on Parchman Prison Farm, 'I wonder how long, till I can change my clothes,' he is celebrating, honestly and humbly, his life."

When acceptance and celebration mean the same thing, or when the two words must fill the same space in the mind at once, we can begin to grasp the tension and the passion of Robert Johnson's music—because when one accepts one's life by celebrating it, one also asks for something more. In Johnson's blues the singer's acceptance is profound, because he knows, and makes us see, that his celebration is also a revolt, and that the revolt will fail, because his images cannot deny the struggles they are meant to master.

It is obvious that man dwells in a splendid universe, a magnificent expanse of earth and sky and heavens, which manifestly is built upon a majestic structure, maintains some mighty design, though man himself cannot grasp it. Yet for him it is not a pleasant or satisfying world. In his few moments of respite from labor or from his enemies, he dreams that this very universe might indeed be perfect, its laws operating just as now they seem to do, and yet he and it somehow be in full accord. The very ease with which he can frame this image to himself makes the reality all the more mocking. . . . It is only too clear that man is not at home in this universe, and yet he is not good enough to deserve a better.

PERRY MILLER, on the Puritan view of the world *

When Robert Johnson traveled through the Deep South, over to Texas and back to Memphis, into the Midwest and up to Chicago, across the border to Canada and back to Detroit to sing spirituals on the radio, to New York City (the sight of this primitive blues singer gazing up at the lights of

* From *The New England Mind: The Seventeenth Century* (Boston: Beacon Press, 1968).

Times Square is not only banal, it is bizarre), to the South
again, he was tracing not only the miles on the road but the
strength of its image. It was the ultimate American image of
flight from homelessness, and he always looked back: the
women he left, or who left him, chased him through the
gloomy reveries of his songs, just as one of them eventually
caught up. Like a good American, Johnson lived for the
moment and died for the past.

Sometimes the road was just the best place to be, free
and friendly, a good way to put in the time. In "Four Until
Late" there is even a girl waiting at the other end.

> When I leave this town,
> I'm gonna bid you fare, farewell
> When I leave this town,
> I'm gonna bid you fare, farewell
> And when I return again,
> You'll have a great long story to tell.

There is the grace and bitterness of "Rambling on My
Mind" (which Johnson played with his walking bass figure
that was to define Chicago blues, making the song sound just
like a man pushing himself down the highway, half against
his will); the slow sexual menace of "Traveling Riverside
Blues"; the nightmare of "Crossroads," where Johnson is sure
to be caught by whites after dark and does not know which
way to run; there is always one more "strange man's town,"
one more girl, one more drink; there is the last word of
"Hellhound on My Trail."

> I got to keep moving, I got to keep moving
> Blues falling down like hail, blues falling
> down like hail
> Blues falling down like hail, blues falling down
> like hail
> And the days keep on 'minding me
> There's a hellhound on my trail
> Hellhound on my trail, hellhound on my trail

It wasn't the open road, to say the least; more like Ishmael falling in behind funeral processions, because they made him feel more alive, and on good terms with death. You could imagine what the two travelers would have to say to each other: *This is no way for a young man to act!*

That spirit gives us what might be Johnson's most American image, these lines from "Me and the Devil Blues"— most American because, as a good, defiant laugh at fate, they are vital not only beneath the surface of American life, but on it. They are often called in as proof of Johnson's despair, and they are part of it, but also his most satisfied lines, a proud epitaph:

> *You may bury my body, down by the highway side*
> *Babe, I don't care where you bury my body when*
> *I'm dead and gone*
> *You may bury my body, ooooo, down by the*
> *highway side*
> *So my old evil spirit*
> *Can get a Greyhound bus, and ride.*

Robert Johnson had a beautiful high voice, a tragic voice when he meant it to be. In "Walking Blues" he wakes up to find that his woman has left him without even his shoes. He is plainly in awe of this woman ("Well!" he sings to himself, "she's got Elgin movements, from her head down to her toes . . . From her head down to her toes!"); when he says the worried blues are the worst he ever had, he's still too full of admiration for that woman to make you believe him.

So he will sing, with a distracted, comic determination:

> *Lord I—feel like blowin' my, old lonesome home*
> *Got up this morning, my little bunny ears was gone*
> *Now, up this light, ooooo, my lonesome home*

and then with utter grace his voice rises, almost fades away, and there is a soft moan that could echo in your heart for a long time, a melancholy too strong to step around:

Well, I got up this morning . . . all I had, was gone.

Johnson was in his mid-twenties when he sang these
songs (Don Law, the great recording engineer who handled
the sessions, thought of him as a teenager). Johnson didn't
have the worldly dignity of Son House or Skip James. Neither House nor James ever sound confused; they sing as men
who live deeply, but within limits. In Johnson's voice, there
is sometimes an element of shock—less a matter of lost innocence than of innocence willfully given up and remembered anyway.

Johnson seemed to take more pure pleasure out of making music than any other Delta singer; there is rock 'n' roll
fun in his guitar playing you can hear anytime you like. He
was, I think, working out a whole new aesthetic that rock 'n'
roll eventually completed: a loud, piercing music driven by
massive rhythms and a beat so strong that involvement was
effortless and automatic. Yet Johnson also had more to say
than other singers. His music was half seduction, half assault, meant to drive his words home with enormous force.
His technique was not only more advanced, it was deeper,
because it had to be.

Only his weakest songs move on an even keel; the greatest shudder and break and explode, or twist slowly around
quietly shaking strings into a kind of suspension, until Johnson has created a mood so delicate and bleak one feels he cannot possibly get out of his song alive. Johnson's most distinctive performances have the tension that comes when almost
everything is implied, when the worst secrets are hiding in
plain talk. With "Come on in My Kitchen" Johnson plays
out the sound of a cold wind on his guitar, and his voice
rides it; there is a stillness in the music. The loneliness is
overpowering and the feeling of desolation is absolute. The
most prosaic lines take on the shape of pure terror.

When a woman gets in trouble
Everybody throws her down
Looking for her good friend

None can be found.
You better come on, in my kitchen
There's going to be rain in our door.

It was songs like this one—the combination of voice,
guitar, words, and the mythical authority that comes when
an artist confirms his work with his life—that made Eric
Clapton see Johnson's ghost, and his own, in Jimi Hendrix's
death. "Eric wanted to do a Robert Johnson," one of Clapton's friends said when Hendrix died. "A few good years,
and go."

Johnson's music is so strong that in certain moods it can
make you feel that he is giving you more than you could have
bargained for—that there is a place for you in these lines of
his: "She's got a mortgage on my body, a lien on my soul." It
is no exaggeration to say that Johnson changed the lives of
men as distant from each other as Muddy Waters, who began
his career as a devoted imitator; Dion, who made his way
through the terrors of his heroin habit with Johnson's songs
for company; and myself. After hearing Johnson's music for
the first time—listening to that blasted and somehow friendly
voice, the shivery guitar, hearing a score of lines that fit as
easily and memorably into each day as Dylan's had—I could
listen to nothing else for months. Johnson's music changed
the way the world looked to me. Over the years, what had
been a fascination with a bundle of ideas and dreams from
old American novels and texts—a fascination with the fore-
boding and gentleness that is linked in the most interesting
Americans—seemed to find a voice in Johnson's songs. It was
the intensity of his music that changed fascination into commitment and a bundle of ideas into what must serve as a
point of view.

But commitment is a tricky, Faustian word. When he
first appeared Robert couldn't play guitar to save his life, Son
House told Pete Welding; Johnson hung out with the older
bluesmen, pestering them for a chance to try his hand, and
after a time he went away. It was months later, on a Saturday night, when they saw him again, still looking to be

heard. They tried to put him off, but he persisted; finally, they let him play for a lull and left him alone with the tables and chairs.

Outside, taking the air, House and the others heard a loud, devastating music of a brilliance and purity beyond anything in the memory of the Mississippi Delta. Johnson had nothing more to learn from *them*.

"He sold his soul to the devil to get to play like that," House told Welding.

Well, they tell a lot of stories about Robert Johnson. You could call that one superstition, or you could call it sour grapes. Thinking of voodoo and gypsy women in the back country, or of the black man who used to walk the streets of Harlem with a briefcase full of contracts and a wallet full of cash, buying up souls at $100 a throw, you could even take it literally.

If there was nothing else, the magic of Johnson's guitar would be enough to make that last crazy interpretation credible. But in a way that cannot be denied, selling his soul and trying to win it back are what Johnson's bravest songs are all about, and anyone who wants to come to grips with his music probably ought to entertain Son House's possibility. I have the feeling, at times, that the reason Johnson has remained so elusive is that no one has been willing to take him at his word.

Let us say that Johnson sought out one of the Mississippi Delta devil-men, or one of the devil-women, and tried to sell his soul in exchange for the music he heard but could not make. Let us say he did this because he wanted to attract women; because he wanted to be treated with the kind of awe that is in Son House's voice when he speaks of Robert Johnson and the devil; because music brought him a fierce joy, made him feel alive like nothing else in the world. Or let us say that the idea of the devil gave Johnson a way of understanding the fears that overshadowed him; that even if no deal was made, no promises passing from one to another, Johnson believed that his desires and his crimes were simple proof of a consummation quite beyond his power to control; that the image of the devil appealed to Johnson when he recognized (singing, "I mistreated my baby, but I can't see no reason why") that his soul was not his own, and, looking at the disasters of his life and the evil of the world, drew the one conclusion as to whom it did belong.

Blues grew out of the need to live in the brutal world that stood ready in ambush the moment one walked out of the church. Unlike gospel, blues was not a music of transcendence; its equivalent to God's Grace was sex and love. Blues made the terrors of the world easier to endure, but blues also made those terrors more real. For a man like Johnson, the promises of the church faded; they could be remembered—as one sang church songs; perhaps even when one prayed, when one was too scared not to—but those promises could not be lived. Once past some unmarked border, one could not go back. The weight of Johnson's blues was strong enough to make salvation a joke; the best he could do was cry for its beautiful lie. "You run without moving from a terror in which you cannot believe," William Faulkner wrote in one of his books about the landscape he shared with Robert Johnson, just about the time Johnson was making his first records, "toward a safety in which you have no faith."

We comfort ourselves that we do not believe in the devil, but we run anyway; we run from and straight into the satanic images that press against the surface of American life. I think of Robert Mitchum, the mad preacher in *Night of the Hunter*, with LOVE tatooed between the knuckles of his right hand, HATE tatooed between the knuckles of his left—and he seems, again, like the legacy of the men who began the American experience as a struggle between God and the devil, the legacy of a Puritan weirdness, something that those who came after have been left to live out.

The dreams and fears of the Puritans, those gloomy old men, are at the source of our attempts to make sense out of the contradictions between the American idea of paradise and the doomed facts of our history; they emerge when "solving problems" is not good enough nor even the point, when the hardest task is not to denounce evil, but to see it.

Unlike Fitzgerald's Dutch sailors, the Puritans did not take their dreams from the land; they brought them along. They meant to build a community of piety and harmony, what their leader, John Winthrop, called "a city on a hill"— an idea, in its many forms, that we have never gotten over, nothing less than America as the light of the world. They had a driving need to go to extremes, as if they could master God and the devil if only they could think hard enough; that, and a profound inability to make peace with the world as they found it. They failed their dreams, and their community shattered. "This land," Winthrop wrote before he died, "grows weary of her inhabitants."

The Puritans came here with a utopian vision they could not maintain; their idea was to do God's work, and they knew that if they failed, it would mean that their work had been the devil's. As they panicked at their failures, the devil was all they saw. Their witch trials were a decadent version of their America—schlock, as it were, but their biggest hit.

Their initial attempts to shape America, and their failures, set the devil loose in the land—as a symbol of uncontrollable malevolence, of betrayal, of disaster, of punishment. Just as the Puritans' failures and compromises anticipated our own, there is something in us that responds, not always quite consciously, to the original image of American failure—to the terror that image can speak for.

If the presence of that image has been felt from the Puritans' day to ours, it is, perhaps, because that image is a way of getting to the idea of an American curse. The image of the devil is a way of comprehending the distance between Fitzgerald's shining image of American possibility and his verdict on its result; it is a way of touching the sense (there in Fitzgerald's beautiful image of America as "an aesthetic contemplation [man] neither understood nor desired") that America is a trap: that its promises and dreams, all mixed up as love and politics and landscape, are too much to live up to and too much to escape. It is as if to be an American means to ask for too much—not even knowing one is asking for too much—and to trade away one's life to get it, whatever it is; as if this is what makes America special, vital, murderous, and noble.

The Puritan devil endures as a face on the betrayal of the promises we mean to keep; the Puritan commitment to extremes, the willingness to live in a world where the claims of God and the devil are truly at odds, has lasted as a means to comprehend the depths of the promise and the failure alike.

This world may have survived most completely in the tension between the blues and the black church. Robert Johnson inherited this world, and, as a black blues singer, he made a new kind of music out of it. The image of the devil was played out within the matrix of Johnson's struggle with women, and with himself. It was a drama of sex, shot through with acts of violence and tenderness; with desires that no one could satisfy; with crimes that could not be explained; with punishments that could not be escaped.

The most acute Americans, in the steps of the old Puritans, have been suspicious, probing people, looking for signs of evil and grace, of salvation and damnation, behind every natural fact. Robert Johnson lived with this kind of intensity, and he asked old questions: What is man's place in the world? Why is he cursed with the power to want more than he can have? What separates men and women from each other? Why must they suffer guilt not only for their sins, but for the failure of their best hopes?

This is a state of mind that gives no rest at all. Even if you have sold your soul to the devil, you cannot rest with him; you have to keep looking, because there is never any end to the price you have to pay, nor any certainty as to the form that price will take. Every event thus becomes charged with meaning, but the meaning is never complete. The moments of perfect pleasure in Johnson's songs, and the beauty of those songs, reminds one that it is not the simple presence of evil that is unbearable; what is unbearable is the impossibility of reconciling the facts of evil with the beauty of the world.

This shadow America comes to a verge with "Stones in My Passway." It is the most terrifying of Johnson's songs, perhaps because his desolation can no longer be contained in the old, inherited image of the devil—those lines from "Me and the Devil Blues" seem suddenly almost safe, comfortable, the claims of a man who thinks he knows where he stands. In "Stones in My Passway" terror is too ubiquitous to have a face: it is formless, elusive, overpowering.

A few months before he recorded "Stones in My Passway," Johnson sang these astonishing lines:

> *If I had possession, over Judgement Day*
> *If I had possession, over Judgement Day*
> *Then the woman I'm lovin', wouldn't have no right to pray*

No right to pray—that is a staggering demand to make on life; it is to ask for the same power the devil has over one who has sold his soul. "Stones in My Passway" is the song of a man who once asked for power over other souls, but who now testifies that he has lost power over his own body, and who might well see that disaster as a fitting symbol of the loss of *his* soul. There is no way to "know"; there are no Gothic images in this song. The idea simply takes shape as the song draws in all the echoes of hellhounds, devils, the weirdness of blues walking like a man, draws in those images and goes past them. If those images were a means to expression, they are no longer necessary—they are no longer good enough.

Because not even his body is his own, Johnson cannot satisfy his woman. Because that matters more than anything else in his life, that fact, as a symbol, expands to create more facts, more symbols. Finally, with stones in every passway and no way clear, there is a way in which the singer's life is resolved: he has seen all around his life, for as long as he can hold onto the image. Because the stakes of the song are so high, every word and every note is fashioned to carry the weight of what Johnson wants to say. The four knife-stroke notes that open the song are like a warning; the song is stark.

It communicates so directly any distance between the singer
and the listener is smashed.

> *I got stones in my passway*
> *And my road seems dark as night*
> *I got stones in my passway*
> *And my road seems dark as night*
> *I got pains in my heart—*
> *They have taken my appetite.*

The tune darts forward on a high, almost martial
rhythm; one shattering note freezes the music and the image
just before the last line of each verse. "Shock technique," a
friend called it.

> *My enemies have betrayed me*
> *Have overtaken poor Bob at last*
> *My enemies have betrayed me*
> *Have overtaken poor Bob at last*
> *And there's one thing certain—*
> *They have stones all in my passway.*

If the passway is in his body, immediately it must stand
for every invisible trap on the road; if the stones are at first
the most direct, physical description of the sexual collapse
that has made Johnson afraid to look his lover in the face,
those stones must be made to stand for the men who will
soon block the way to his lover's door.

> *I'm crying please—please, let us be friends*
> *And when you hear me howlin' in my passway, rider*
> PLEASE *open your door and let me in.*

The song is enormous. I cannot put it any other way.
The image of the words is subsumed into Johnson's singing,
his guitar, into the eerie, inevitable loudness of the song. The
music has its claims to make: no matter how long you set the
volume, the music creeps up louder, demanding, and the
only way to quiet this music is to shut it off.

I got three legs to truck on
Boys, please don't block my road
I got three legs to truck on
Boys, please don't block my road
But I been 'shamed by my rider—
I'm booked and I got to go.

"Stones in My Passway," like a few others of Johnson's songs—"Love in Vain," "Come on in My Kitchen," "Me and the Devil Blues"—is a two-minute image of doom that has the power to make doom a fact. One hardly knows if it is the clarity of the world Johnson revealed in his music, or Johnson's resilience as he made his way through that world that is most exhilarating; but that so many people—people who have never left the American mainstream that Johnson was never part of—respond to his music is perhaps not such a mystery. Because of our faith in promises, the true terror of doom is in the American's natural inability to believe doom is real, even when he knows it has taken over his life. When there is no way to speak of terror and no one to listen if there were, Johnson's songs matter.

What Robert Johnson had to do with other bluesmen of his time is interesting to me, but not nearly so interesting as what Johnson has to do with someone discovering him now, without warning and on their own. The original context of Johnson's story is important, and it is where his story is usually placed; but a critic's job is not only to define the context of an artist's work but to expand that context, and it seems more important to me that Johnson's music is vital enough to enter other contexts and create all over again. Off in the Netherlands to teach college, my friend Langdon Winner wrote back:

. . . the truth of the matter is that in my first months here I found out a lot more about America than I did about Holland. Hundreds of things which are second nature to us just do not play a part here. Dissatisfaction, for example. Dutch musicians know the techniques pioneered by America's black masters. But they are not interested in extremes of rage, ecstasy, dissipation, or religious enlightenment. And this sums up the place: While jazz has long been popular in the Netherlands, *the blues has never arrived.* How can you understand Aeschuylus, Augustine, Shakespeare, and Nietzsche if you can't listen to Robert Johnson in your own time?

Which is to say that if Robert Johnson is an ancestor, or even a ghost, he is really a contemporary.

It is the inescapable pull of Johnson's music that gives us Mick Jagger singing "Love in Vain" in the middle of a rock 'n' roll show—and a rock 'n' roll show is a celebration that is rooted in Little Richard's kind of revolt, or in Harmonica Frank's, far more than it is in Robert Johnson's. Robert Johnson is a presence these days, as rock 'n' roll fans find the world less of a home than it used to be, and yet accept more and more their inability to do anything about their displacement; Johnson is a sort of invisible pop star. He has caught up with us.

The music that is animated by Robert Johnson today is not really found in new rock 'n' roll versions of his songs; Johnson's spirit is not so easy to capture. All of Eric Clapton's love for Johnson's music came to bear not when Clapton sang Johnson's songs, but when, once Johnson's music became part of who Clapton was, Clapton came closest to himself: in the passion of "Layla" and "Any Day." Finally, after years of practice and imitation, Johnson's sound was Clapton's sound: there was no way to separate the two men, nor any need to. And perhaps to keep the story straight, there is, in "Layla," one lost echo buried under Clapton's screams and who knows how many guitars: "Please don't say/You'll never find a way/And tell me, all my love's in vain."

This music sounds like the real Delta blues to me, forty years after: Duane Allman's solos on Boz Scagg's "Loan Me a Dime"; Sly Stone's "Thank You for talkin' to me Africa"; Randy Newman's "God's Song"; much of the Rolling Stones' music from *Let It Bleed* on down; Bob Dylan's "All Along the Watchtower"; Eric Clapton's "Layla." If someone were to ask

me where Johnson's spirit had found a home, I would play
these songs.

All the beauty of the world and all the terror of losing it
is there in Eric Clapton's rock 'n' roll; Robert Johnson's
music is proof that beauty can be wrung from the terror itself. When Johnson sang his darkest songs, terror was a fact,
beauty only a glimmer; but that glimmer, and its dying
away, lie beneath everything else, beneath all the images that
hit home and make a home. Our culture finds its tension and
its life within the borders of the glimmer and the dying
away, in attempts to come to terms with the betrayal without
giving up on the promise. And so at the borders of Elvis
Presley's delight, of his fine young hold on freedom, there is,
in his "Peace in the Valley," a touch of fear, of that old
weirdness:

> *And I'll be changed*
> *Changed from this creature*
> *That I am* *

And at another frontier there is Robert Johnson, pausing
for a moment in "Hellhound on My Trail," frightened, running down his road, but glancing over his shoulder with a
smile:

> *If today was Christmas Eve, if today was Christmas Eve*
> *And tomorrow was Christmas Day*
> *If today was Christmas Eve*
> *And tomorrow was Christmas Day*
> *Aw, wouldn't we have a time, baby?*

* Copyright 1939 by Hill and Range Songs, Inc. Copyright renewed 1966 and assigned
to Hill and Range Songs, Inc. Used by permission.

INHERITORS

THE BAND
Pilgrims' Progress

The Band—four Canadian rockers held together by an Arkansas drummer—staked their claim to an American story from the beginning. The story had its veils, but the fact of the story was plain. "This is *it*," my editor Marvin Garson said in the spring of 1969, as he sent me off to cover the Band's national debut in San Francisco. "This is when we find out if there are still open spaces out there."

Marvin was a New Yorker; living in California sometimes made him talk like Natty Bumppo, but his words were accurate. By out there he meant right here, and he was talking about the Band because it was obvious they were committed to the very idea of America: complicated, dangerous, and alive.

Their music gave us a sure sense that the country was richer than we had guessed; that it had possibilities we were

43

only beginning to perceive. In the unique blend of instruments and good rhythms, in the shared and yet completely individual vocals, in the half-lost phrases and buried lyrics, there was an ambiguity that opened up the world with real force. The songs captured the yearning for home and the fact of displacement that ruled our lives; we thought that the Band's music was the most natural parallel to our hopes, ambitions, and doubts, and we were right to think so. Flowing through their music were spirits of acceptance and desire, rebellion and awe, raw excitement, good sex, open humor, a magic feel for history—a determination to find plurality and drama in an America we had met too often as a monolith.

The Band's music made us feel part of their adventure; we knew that we would win if they succeeded and lose if they failed. That was what Marvin Garson meant. It was a good feeling.

CROSSING THE BORDER

When the Band surfaced in 1968 with *Music from Big Pink*, they had been playing rock 'n' roll music for more than half as long as there had been such a thing. What mattered most, though, was that they had put in their years together, as a group. A rock 'n' roll group is a banding together of individuals for the purpose of achieving something that none of them can get on their own: money, fame, the right sound, something less easy to put into words. But what begins as a marriage of convenience sometimes takes on its own value. An identity comes into being that transcends individual personalities, but does not obscure them—in fact, it is the group, sometimes only the group, that makes individuals visible. The Beatles, after all, were the most satisfying and complex testament to the limits of self-reliance most of us have ever known; they were also proof of the limits of a common bond. Groups are images of community. That the Band had created itself through the years, and had come to our attention bent on demonstrating just what their years together had been worth, was perhaps the most potent image of all.

Like John Lennon and Paul McCartney, Booker T. & his MG's, Bob Dylan, and a few thousand others, drummer Levon Helm, guitarist Robbie Robertson, piano man Richard Manuel, bass Rick Danko, and organist Garth Hudson started out in the high school bands that appeared overnight in the flash of the first great rock explosion.* Still in their teens in the early sixties, they came together in Toronto as the Hawks, back-up band for Ronnie Hawkins, a small-time Arkansas rockabilly singer who had brought Levon north with him around 1958.

Hawkins, though he brushed the charts twice in 1959—with a Chuck Berry remake and his own "Mary Lou"—was too little and too late to pass for the next Elvis Presley; his task was to keep himself alive. In the U.S.A. he was one of too many; in Canada, where authentic American rockers were a solid commercial rarity, Hawkins could bill himself "The King of Rockabilly" and get away with it. Sometimes he liked to call himself "Mr. Dynamo." It was, as so many have testified, better than working.

Ronnie Hawkins was a windjammer in the grand style. He claimed to have picked cotton right alongside Bo Diddley; to have made the first rock 'n' roll record of all, back in 1952 (no one, so far as I know, has ever found it, but Hawkins, keeping his story straight, says it was the first version of "Bo Diddley"); to have passed up a chance for stardom when he graciously offered the sure-hit "It's Only Make Believe" to his old pal Conway Twitty; to know more back roads, back rooms, and backsides than any man from Newark to Mexicali. His singing was only fair, though in one sense it was quite distinctive: Hawkins is the only man I have ever heard who can make a nice sexy song like "My Gal Is Red Hot" sound sordid. "None of us rock 'n' rollers could understand all that fuss about Jerry Lee Lewis marrying a

---

* The names of those bands are too good to leave out: the Robots, the Consuls, Thumper and the Trombones (Robbie); Paul London and the Capters—what are "Capters"? Shouldn't it be "Copters"? "Captors"? (Hudson); the Rockin' Revols (Manuel); and the Jungle Bush Beaters. The last was Levon's original Marvel, Arkansas, outfit—and as the soubriquet of a bunch of Southern white boys chasing the blues across the tracks, it's rock 'n' roll poetry if anything is.

thirteen-year-old girl," he is reputed to have said. "All us Southern cats knew she was only twelve."

Hawkins was no fool; he needed a band to carry him, and when the razorbacks he had imported began to scatter, he and Levon recruited the Canadian kids one by one. As characters in the classic bildungsroman that tells of the wise old philosopher who initiates innocent young boys into the mysteries of life, Hawkins and his Hawks played their way through the collected works of Gene Vincent, Chuck Berry, Larry Williams, Fats Domino, and the rest, filling out their shows with tunes about the whores they met.

Robbie wrote his first song, "Hey Boba Lu," which Hawkins recorded; on stage, Manuel and Levon handled most of the singing. "When Ronnie sang," Robbie remembers fondly, "we had to count out the beat for him. It was, 'Oh, Carol—one, two, three, *four*—Don't let him steal. . . .' "

The Hawks were looking for their music. When Robbie was fifteen Levon took him into the South, with hopes of putting the Bush Beaters back together. That came to nothing, but the trip changed something in Robertson; just what it was is elusive even to him, but listening to the man retrace his steps, one gets the sense that an enormous creative ambition was set free when he discovered that the place that had put magic into his life was real. There had been the music, of course—rock 'n' roll from Memphis, rock 'n' roll from New Orleans—and Robbie already had the beginnings of his idea that the land makes the music. But there were also the family histories and local legends Levon had told him; the inexplicably exciting foreign names, suddenly right there on billboards and coming over the drifting Southern radio dial in between the fiddles and sermons, names like "Dr. Pepper" and "Ko-Ko bars"; there was the fact of seeing people, black and white, living out the sounds he had heard on his records. The reality only made the magic that much more fierce. Here was a different world, with more on its surface than Canada had in its abyss; you could chase that world, listen to it, learn from it. Perhaps you could even join it.

Before too long, Howlin' Wolf, Junior Parker, Bobby Bland, and other bluesmen were climbing the Hawks' charts, and Hawkins' repertoire no longer seemed so romantic. Robbie had tried to get Kenny Paulsen, Hawkins' original guitarist, to teach him how to play—Paulsen, with a good eye for the competition, told the kid to get lost—but now Robbie was in a position to feel the competition himself. For a white boy, that meant James Burton, star of "Suzie Q" and hero of Ricky Nelson's hits; Roy Buchanan, the lonesome master of the blues; Lonnie Mack, who sang from the church and played straight from the alley. To live up to all that Levon had shown him, and to satisfy his own brash self, Robbie had to be better than any of them.

He was listening hard to Wolf's guitarists: Willie Johnson on "How Many More Years" and Hubert Sumlin on "Wang Dang Doodle." Johnson and Sumlin had created a guitar style so chaotic and fast it demanded a rhythm section as quick as it was hard just to keep a performance from flying to pieces. There was none of the polite formality of a band setting up a solo, taking turns; there was no showcasing. Wolf's best records came on like three-minute race riots. The drums, bass, piano, and harp converged on the beat, hammering, shoving; for a moment they let the beat take the song, let you think you had the sides sorted out and the picture clear, and then the guitarist leaped in, heaved himself through the crowd like a tornado, and the crowd paid no attention and went right on fighting. This was the sound the Hawks were after, and on an unbelievably demonic recording of Bo Diddley's "Who Do You Love," they got it. Hawkins' vocal (his only real claim to greatness, but it will do) was one ghastly scream; Robbie fought back with a crazed, jagged solo that to this day has never been matched. It is still possibly the most menacing piece of rock 'n' roll ever made.

The Hawks, however, did not need their front man—fooling around in the studio after the dry sessions for Hawkins' *Mojo Man* LP, Levon took over the mike for Bobby Bland's hard-rocking "Further on Up the Road" and Muddy Waters' slow and sexy "She's 19," and the group left behind the most exciting white blues recordings since the early days of Elvis Presley. "White blues" doesn't really describe the music—though they were white, and the songs were blues—Levon's singing and Robbie's guitar playing fell into no genre. This wasn't like the early Paul Butterfield Band, or John Hammond, Jr., to be judged on how precisely the white music matched the sound of the black idols. The Hawks were a long way past questions of technique; the problem was to find out what they could do with that technique.

Unfortunately, they were making music in a vacuum; in America, those great sides were never released, not that they would have fit the commercial demands of the radio anyway. Like most of the best bands forming at the time, the Hawks were a walking jukebox that played only other people's hits, and the jukebox was a few years out of date to boot. Over in Hamburg, the Beatles too were jamming out five sets a night, as John Lennon shouted "Dizzy Miss Lizzy" with a toilet seat around his neck; Van Morrison and the Monarchs were peddling their Ray Charles imitations to homesick GIs in Germany; the Rolling Stones were up all night trying to figure out how Sonny Boy made his harp sound like that; Elvis was having fun in Acapulco; and Creedence Clearwater, calling themselves the Blue Velvets, were scuffling up and down the road from Sacramento to San Jose, fighting a battle of the bands with Peter Wheat and the Breadmen, while John Fogerty scribbled the bayou fantasies that would lift him out of a world he hated. In the early sixties, rock 'n' roll was a waiting game.

After a year or two apprenticed to Hawkins, Levon led the Band out on their own as Levon and the Hawks, sometimes as the Crackers, sometimes as the Canadian Squires. They traveled Hawkins' circuit of honky-tonks and dives—a tough, loud band that played, as Garth Hudson once put it, "for pimps, rounders, and flakeouts." "We had one thing on our minds," Robbie says. "Stomp."

They cut occasional 45's, whenever they found someone

to let them into a studio: "Go Go Liza Jane," the old folk
song; a good hard punch-out of a record called "Leave Me
Alone"; an odd, churchy paean to "this righteous land" with
the even odder title of "The Stones I Throw (Will Free All
Men)"—crude stuff, but hopeful. "Down in LA, you know
they got everything," Levon sang on "Uh-Uh-Uh." "Think
I'll move out there, become the new Southern King."

This was not earthshaking. By 1965 the Beatles and the
Stones were running the scene, and from their name to their
nightclubs, the Hawks were an anachronism. Still, they built
up a vague word-of-mouth reputation on the East Coast;
eager to take on the world with a new sound and perhaps
feeling a bit anachronistic himself, Bob Dylan got in touch.
The combination clicked: suddenly Dylan was singing like a
demon, and the Hawks—never introduced, always anony-
mous—twisted around him with a noise that not even they
could have been prepared for. The Hawks backed Dylan
through the rough, mean tours of 1965 and 1966, and the
Stones sat in the audience. The Hawks left the stage as the
best band in the world.

Levon, a pro when Bob Dylan was still hard at work
scaring his high school principal, did not go along; the
Hawks, after all, had been *his* band. But when the Canadians
followed Dylan to Woodstock once the tours were over,
Levon joined up again, and the Band made a second founding.

Out of all this they fashioned a music that sounded not
at all like what had preceded it; they seemed to draw less on
their old music than on the friendship they had discovered
making it. Calling themselves "The Band" was proof of their
arrogance, but there was a depth of experience in their music
that could not be denied, and the fans they won had no wish
to deny it. It was, in fact, precisely what a lot of people were
looking for.

In 1968 rock 'n' roll was coming out of its San Francisco
period—psychedelic music, rebel energy, Father-Yes-Son-I-
Want-To-Kill-You, drum solos, drug visions, bright and

happy dancing crowds—a fabulous euphoria in the middle of a war, innocence and optimism running straight into the election of Richard Nixon. It had been a fine time, with many chances taken and many chances blown, but it was over, it was soft underneath the flash and it had exhausted itself. There was a peculiar emptiness in the air, and in the music; *Sgt. Pepper*, generally enshrined a year earlier as the greatest achievement in the history of popular music—by some, in the history of Art—now seemed very hollow, a triumph of effects. The Yippies showed up to take over the politics of the decade, and defrauded them. There were heroes and heroines of the era just past who had only a year or two to live; some of the political heroes had already been murdered. We had gone too far, really, without getting anywhere.

With Bob Dylan, the Band had seen much of this world from the inside, seen it as it was born, even helped bring it into being; but they came through on the other side, in a place very much of their own making. They stepped out, very consciously, as an alternative.

The pictures inside *Big Pink*—of the Band, their friends and relatives, and their ugly but much-loved big pink house—caught some of what they had to say. Against a cult of youth they felt for a continuity of generations; against the instant America of the sixties they looked for the traditions that made new things not only possible, but valuable; against a flight from roots they set a sense of place. Against the pop scene, all flux and novelty, they set themselves: a band with years behind it, and meant to last.

Many young Americans had spent the best part of the decade teaching themselves to feel like exiles in their own country; the Band, particularly songwriters Robbie Robertson and Richard Manuel, understood this, and were sure it was a mistake. They had come here by choice, after all. They had fallen in love with the music, first as they sought it out on the radio and on records, later as they learned to play it, and, wonder of wonders, define it. Coming out of Canada into the land that had kicked up the blues, jazz, church music, country and western, and a score of authentic rock 'n' roll heroes, playing their way up and down the spine of the continent, they fell in love with the place itself.

They felt more alive in America. They came to be on good terms with its violence and its warmth; they were attracted by the neon grab for pleasure on the face of the American night, and by the inscrutable spookiness behind that face. American contradictions demanded a fine energy, because no one could miss them; the stakes were higher, but the rewards seemed limitless. The Band's first songs were a subtle, seductive attempt to get this sense of life across. Their music was fashioned as a way back into America, and it worked.

STRANGER BLUES

With *Music from Big Pink*, the Band gave us a rough moral drama. It had none of the mythic clarity of, say, John Ford's movies; it came through a modern haze, something like Robert Altman's *McCabe and Mrs. Miller*, obscure in its plots, dialogue hard to catch, communicating with a blind humor and a cryptic intensity nothing in rock 'n' roll has ever remotely touched.

They began with "Tears of Rage," an eerie invocation of Independence Day, dragging the organ and their secretive horns across a funeral beat, changing the Fourth of July into an image of betrayal, and of loneliness: America betrayed by those who would no longer be part of it. The Band made a claim to an identity others no longer wanted, and the album opened up from there. In its stories, its feel for place and language, its music, and most of all in its quest, this was an American mystery.

The liveliest songs (half Robertson's, half Manuel's, and all of a piece) shared an oddly familiar actor: the voice of "Lonesome Suzie," "Caledonia Mission," "To Kingdom Come," "We Can Talk About It Now," "Chest Fever," "The

Weight," and "Long Black Veil." * His part is taken by
Levon (gutty, carnal, bewildered, always hanging onto the
end of his rope), Rick Danko (quivering, melancholy, hesi-
tant), Manuel (the Band's great sentimentalist, devastated
and bursting with joy by turns), or the three of them at once;
but as I hear them now, years after I thought I knew this
record, the vocals, like the writing, complete a single story.

The hero of this story (such as I find him, and I ought to
note that I am setting the story down—or, if you like, making it up—simply as I hear it, without much regard for song
sequence, cross-checked lyrics, or other formalities) has *Big
Pink* pretty much to himself. He almost disappears on the
next album, *The Band*, returns with *Stage Fright*, loses his
voice on *Cahoots*, and perhaps hits the end of his road with
Richard Manuel's singing on a handful of the rock 'n' roll
classics that make up *Moondog Matinee*. To follow his trail is
to leave out a good bit of what the Band has done—wonderful tunes like "Get Up Jake" and "Strawberry Wine," and
their work with Bob Dylan. But there is a storyteller in their
music, and in one form or another, his tale is the one I'm
after, because it seems to be the one the Band tells best: The
story of the worried man.

"Delivered Under the Similitude of a Dream, Wherein
Is Discovered the Manner of His Setting Out, His Dangerous Journey, and Safe Arrival at the Desired Country," as
John Bunyan put it. That, really, is only the beginning of his
adventure.

He first appears on *Big Pink* as a wanderer, a quester,
hoping to brazen his way through a strange land and learn

* This last, a modern country tune in the guise of an old Kentucky murder ballad,
was not the Band's song, but it fits in perfectly with the rest. "Wheel's on Fire" and
"I Shall Be Released" (the former by Dylan and Danko and the latter by Dylan)
don't fit in, not because the lyrics are out of place but because as performances the
songs are not emotionally convincing, and the quality of emotion is what makes *Big
Pink* a great album, not merely an interesting one. The music and the singing sound
strained, contrived, probably because the Band felt obligated to replace the original
arrangements they had worked out with Dylan when the songs were first put down
on the famous Basement Tape. "Tears of Rage" is another Basement composition,
but it works, perhaps because it was so necessary to what the Band was after; but
the other two sound like filler on a record that needs nothing of the sort.

something. He lives by his wits, moving across the territory explored by Robert Johnson and Harmonica Frank, taking his spirit from the best of both men.

To use a dark old word the worried man would recognize, these two men are his familiars. Like Johnson, he is obsessed by choices he never asked for, because he sees too clearly to avoid the guilt and fear that worm out of the Bible he carries in his carpetbag; like Harmonica Frank, he is saved by his sense of humor, and he refuses to take his fears too seriously.

The combination gives us a resurrection shuffle: prophecy, cut with jive. "Been sittin' in here for so darn long, waitin' for the end to come along," he complains in "To Kingdom Come"—Judgment Day is supposed to deliver the answers he wants, but unlike some people he will meet in *Big Pink*, he can't hang around forever. He moves on, but before he is even out of the song a stranger appears to suggest that it might be wiser for him to turn back. " 'Tarred and feathered, thistles and thorns—One or the other,' he kindly warned." Well, that's not much of a choice—what else can you show me? The seeker knows the stakes are high, but he can't believe the game is fixed. He keeps looking, scared to death and full of optimism—careful to watch out for himself, once he's fallen into a trap. The devil might be anywhere—though, thanks to the touch of Harmonica Frank in the story, the devil comes on like the Headless Horseman—so the quester only wants to do the right thing; given the clutch of all-too-human doomsters that fly through the album, he'd better. "Time will tell you well," he offers hopefully, "if you truly, truly fell."

And so he dives headlong into a Gothic world of tricksters, fortunetellers, mummers, lunatics, witch doctors, cops, and lovers, struggling to find a home at the heart of that world. The music, like the character it shapes, is full of chance, uncertainty, and humor; the sound of *Big Pink* is one version of the quester's struggle, and of the world that makes his struggle interesting.

That sound is an uncanny blend of ancient folk songs,

New Orleans jazz, postwar blues, white gospel groups, the
Monotones, and Motown; and these sources are only a few of
the obvious, picked almost at random. Al Kooper, reviewing
Big Pink in 1968, heard the Beach Boys, the Association, the
Swan Silvertones (*black* gospel), Hank Williams, the Beatles,
Bob Dylan, and the Coasters. He's right, of course: *Big Pink*
music is as dense as it is elusive. All those people are in it,
and anyone's listening will turn up dozens more. The
richness of *Big Pink* is in the Band's ability to contain endless
combinations of American popular music without imitating
any of them; the Band don't refer to their sources any more
than we refer to George Washington when we vote, but the
connection is there. The Band's music on *Big Pink* is personal, their own invention, but not merely personal; it is an
unpredictable resolution of a common inheritance, something
we shared in pieces. This was a new sound, but you could
recognize yourself in that sound. *That* connection is what gives
this music its natural authority, and makes it so exhilarating.

There are times when Richard Manuel sounds like the
ghost of Johnny Ace (that sweet-voiced fifties R&B singer
who died in a game of Russian roulette)—Johnny Ace con-
demned to haunt a gloomy radio, from which "Pledging My
Love," the first posthumous rock 'n' roll hit, issues every
time you spin the dial. There are times when the tone is desperate, close to the panicky feeling Marving Gaye got on "I
Heard It Through the Grapevine." But more often than not,
the music is simply ominous.

This has to do, I think, with Robbie's hide-and-seek
guitar, Garth Hudson's slithery organ, and the Band's collective sense of timing—which is really a sense of freedom. In
most blues or rock bands, each musician has to give something up in order to make a performance work; the men in
the Band played and sang with second sight, and they made
no concessions at all. The beat is tough, but open; fast little
riffs shoot out from behind vocals without warning; vocals
twist around seemingly random chords. The parts combine
to pull the listener into a labyrinth, with no idea of what
might be lurking around the next turn.

When the music is most exciting—when the guitar is fighting for space in the clatter while voices yelp and wail as one man finishes another's line or spins it off in a new direction—the lyrics are blind baggage, and they emerge only in snatches. This is the finest rock 'n' roll tradition ("I learned the words to Little Richard's songs the best I could and what I couldn't figure out didn't matter," Robbie said once), but on *Big Pink* such a style also seems to link up with an older tradition: the instinct of the American artist to put his story in disguise, to tell his tale from the shadows, probably because that is where he usually finds it. Those who mean to seduce do not announce their intentions through megaphones.

On the other hand, those who are too subtle wind up plying their seductions in the mirror. If *Big Pink* wasn't good to hear from a distance, no one, certainly myself included, would ever bother to get close to it. The first virtue of the album is that the danger, promise, and craziness of the quester's adventure come across directly in the *music*; not only can't you understand the words, you don't have to. Garth Hudson's satanic organ playing (straight out of *Sunset Boulevard*, with Erich von Stroheim at the pipes) is the key to "Chest Fever"—the words couldn't be, no one has ever deciphered them anyway. You don't need to analyze the lyrics of "The Weight" to understand the burden Miss Fanny has dropped on the man who sings the song; as Jon Carroll has written, Levon Helm is the only drummer who can make you cry, and drums are all he needs to get across the weary, fated sense of a situation that simply cannot be escaped. We never find out who Miss Fanny is, let alone what the singer is supposed to do for her; but the music, not to mention the singing, is so full of emotion and complexity it makes "the weight"—some combination of love, debt, fear, and guilt—a perfect image of anyone's entanglement.

So the story is revealed, and concealed, in flashes, dreams, pieces of unresolved incident, rumbles of doubt exiting through a joke. Yet if the music is part of the story, it is also the landscape against which the story takes place.

Blurred at the edges and unsure of its center, this America is
still a wilderness—the moral, social wilderness that is left
even when the natural wilderness is gone. Excited and intrigued by the place for just that reason, the worried man has
to get on without maps.

He has, however, brought along a lot of time-honored,
prudent advice; unfortunately, it's never equal to the impru-
dent dilemmas life persists in forcing upon him. "Be careful
what you do, it all comes back on you," he says, poking his
head out of the mad confusion of "To Kingdom Come" (re-
calling, perhaps, a Sunday School lesson); but a few songs
later, stuck in "The Weight" and surrounded by the suddenly comic riddles first set out in Robert Johnson's "Me and
the Devil Blues," this is not quite good enough. Miss Fanny
has given him his job, packed him off "with her regards for
everyone," and since that phrase is as mysterious to him as it
is to us, all he can do is stick out his hand and hope that
whoever grabs it will eventually let go.

> *I picked up my bag, I went looking for a place to hide*
> *Then I saw Carmen and the devil, walking side by side*
> *I said, Hey, Carmen, come on, let's go downtown*
> *She said, I gotta go, but my friend can stick around.**

The sound of the quester's voice (whether it's Levon,
wrestling with "The Weight," or Manuel, in "Lonesome
Suzie") tells us that his first desire is simply to be left alone—
left alone by friends, enemies, neighbors, women, relatives,
dogs, good and evil—but he was born with his eyes and ears
wide open, and he misses nothing. He can't stop asking questions (which is not to say that there aren't times when he
wouldn't mind stopping—the golden calf that chases him
through "To Kingdom Come" is not his idea of a good time);
with nothing but the best intentions, he stumbles into everything in his way. And because he is fascinated by everything
the rest of us take for granted, he finds himself caught up

---

with his fellow men and women, and inevitably, their troubles become his own.

Looking for salvation, he ends up trying to save others: the women of "Caledonia Mission" (she lives hidden behind a wall, and the city has a lock on her gate), "Chest Fever" ("She drinks from the bitter cup," he declares; "I'm trying' to get her to give it up"), the daughter in "Tears of Rage," and many more. Whether he succeeds is never made clear, but what is clear is that his salvation is tied to theirs.

There is Lonesome Suzie, for one; an outcast, or maybe an aging spinster, in the timeless and mythical American town in which *Big Pink* seems to be set. She dearly needs a friend, and though he's not willing, he thinks, in Manuel's wonderful phrase, that maybe he can loan her one. But that, he knows, only makes him one of the confidence men his search has bound him to unmask, and so he gives in: "I guess just watching you/Has made me lonesome too."

The whole of *Big Pink*, and perhaps the best of what the Band has had to say over the years, seems to dovetail into those modest lines. The man who lives them feels like part of the crowd, and he is only too happy to fade into it; but he recognizes himself in everyone he meets, and so he is drawn out of himself and into the world. He takes his vitality from that paradox. To survive it, he can't afford to be anyone's fool; to make it worth his considerable trouble, he needs a talent for friendship that is as deep as it is broad. "Save your neck, or save your brother," he shouts a couple of years later in "The Shape I'm In," just out of jail and searching for his woman, "Look's like it's one or the other." But it's one more false choice, one more denial of the fraternity he feels in spite of himself, and he can't rest with it. Maybe that's why he sounds so desperate; even running for his life, his mind is on the people he leaves behind.

Now, taken all at once, this is a remarkable figure: the Band's recreation of an American original, the democratic man—trapped, against his better judgment, in a hilarious and scarified recreation of a very old American idea: this is a joint-stock world. A joint-stock world is open to devils and

angels alike; all barriers are betrayals, and the man who sees
only himself sees nothing at all.

This is the possibility the Band pursue through the tan-
gles of the country itself. The extraordinary diversity of the
place, and the claim of every man and woman to do just as
they please, make a joint-stock America both necessary and
hard to find; the man who looks for it has a right to be
worried.

America has a lot of mottoes—common slogans, because
they sum up how individuals act among themselves. "We
Must All Hang Together, Or We Shall All Hang Separately" is a sentimental favorite, but the edge goes to "Don't
Tread On Me"—which is to say that the man who wants to
hang together had best take care not to give the good people
he meets an excuse to string him up. America, as the quester
finds it in his songs, is not a very friendly place. It is suspicious of itself. Most people no longer even know that they
have brothers to save, and if they do, "brother" means men,
but not women; the young, but not the old; blues singers,
but not country singers; Northerners, but not Southerners;
whites, but not blacks; or a general vice versa. The man who
tells this story becomes who he is, the one who reaches out,
because he responds so deeply to the yearning for unity and
affection that these facts hide. Perhaps because he comes
from outside, he can see the country whole, just as those
who have always lived there see it only in pieces. His job, as
in "The Weight," no longer a matter of isolated predicament
but of vocation, is to drag that affection out into the open,
even if it comes hard, as his did.

The song for that is "We Can Talk About It Now," a
wonderful Richard Manuel tune that sounds like the best
merry-go-round in the world. Full of exultation, exhortation,
smiles, and complaints, it is the song of a man who has gone
far enough to have become a part of what he sings about.
"It's safe now," he says, "to take a backward glance."

> It seems to me, we've been holding something
> Underneath our tongues

I'm afraid if you ever got a pat on the back
It would likely burst your lungs
Whoa—stop me, if I should sound
Kinda down in the mouth
But I'd rather be burned in Canada
Than to freeze here in the south! *

If his quest has taught him anything, it is that if he wants to find a home in this country he will have to make it himself, and that means breaking through to the warmth others hide, just as Lonesome Suzie broke through to him. The pure joy of the music unveils the depth of emotion that's his to win; and that must have been the treasure he was after from the beginning, whether he knew it or not. He had to learn, in John Barth's line, that the key to the treasure is the treasure—that to be free is not to get what you want or to settle for what you've got, but to begin to know what you want and to feel strong enough to go after it. So now, out of the claustrophobia of *Big Pink*, he has a glimpse of what he wants. For a moment, to say yes is to say everything.

We can talk about it now
It's the same old riddle, always starts from the middle
I'd fix it but I don't know how
Well, we could try to reason
But you might think it's treason
One voice for all
Echoing around the hall, ECHOING, *echoing around the hall!* *

The song is loose and rangy, and the song has plenty of room in it: room for doubt, and room for doubt to turn into love without any explanation at all; room for arguments interrupted by a bottle, room for friends and strangers, room for escape and room for homecoming. For its moment, the song—a free and friendly conversation between the men in the Band and anyone who might care to listen—is that one voice.

The song creates, out of words and music, a big, open, undeniable image of what the country could sound like at its best, of what it could feel like. One good burst of rock 'n' roll blows the trail clean, and the people our man has seen and the places he has been look brand-new.

"Dontcha see," he shouts, in an extraordinary flash of vision, that seems to reveal the secret America holds, even as it hints at deeper secrets, "There's no need to slave."

"The whip," he sings, "is in the grave."

THIS RIGHTEOUS LAND

Those lines, I think, deserve a pause—there is no bottom to them. Nothing I know captures with such mystery and clarity the circle traced by American optimism, and by the dread that optimism leaves behind and inevitably meets again. You couldn't ask for a more perfect statement of the conviction that America is blessed, nor of the lingering suspicion that it is cursed. When the two ideas come together—in a story, a voice, or a group—all things seem possible. The lines touch both sides of the country's soul at once; the tension they create can push out the limits of what an artist can accomplish, for just so long as the spirit of the lines can support their contradictions. By contradictions I mean that a paradise is made out of a line that turns on the image of a whip; by spirit I mean the joy one feels when Richard Manuel shoots the line across Levon's drums—and the way Levon sounds like a man calling a town meeting to order with a gavel in each hand.

When the spirit fades, those lines will contract, and trap the man who sings them. But until then, what they bring is freedom, and the space to use it. The result is *The Band*.

That second album—arriving in 1969, soon after the group went out on the road on their own for the first time since Levon and the Hawks broke up—is the map *Big Pink*'s quester was missing. The new songs roll right over the sur-

face of American life, proof of how magnificent that surface
can be.

Turn the sound up, and the music rocks like "Blue-
Suede Shoes"; keep it quiet, and it sounds as folksy as an old
Charlie Poole 78. The good eye of the last record is still
working, but instead of probing the dark for phantoms, there
is a loving feel for detail, for nuance. With its warm, happy
vocals, and an irresistible snapping rhythm square in the
middle of almost every tune, *The Band* is the testament of a
man who has come up from a netherworld for a breath of air,
a man who can now afford to have himself a good, long look
around.

The worried man is a settler now, here to stay, complete
with wife and kids, and the album opens with his wife holding a gun on him. As he pleads and jokes with her, trying to
explain himself (No matter what you think, honey, I didn't
do it), he is drawn back to the days when all he wanted was a
place to come home to. He remembers his hard times, his
fears, how close he came to giving up the ghost; he thinks he
just may have to hit the road again if she doesn't put that gun
away. By the time his reverie is finished the fight is over—
still, he wouldn't mind knowing where she hid the pis-
tol. . . .

The song is called "Across the Great Divide," an appropriate beginning for an album Robbie once said the Band
could have called *America*—might as well kick it off right
there where the water runs both ways. But there is more to it
than that.

The Band give author's credit to the land because while
we usually read our own meanings into the landscape—when
we don't miss it altogether—they know that at our best we
live and speak according to the metaphors of the land. The
land—the image of a place like "The Great Divide," the
simple fact that there is such a phenomenon—attracts the
Band. The symbol seems full of meaning—the Great Divide
is where the two sides of the country separate, but it is also
where the two sides meet. If we look into this double meta-

phor, we can understand the ambitions of *The Band* clearly.
That first song and those that follow are meant to cross the
great divide between men and women; between the past and
the present; between the country and the city; between the
North and the South; between the Band and their new audience. The worried man steps back, once he has shown up to
play the theme song: he wants to celebrate the country he
has discovered, and he celebrates by letting the country
speak for itself, in as many voices as can be crammed onto a
twelve-inch disc. At home here now, the man from *Big Pink*
can sit back and listen with the rest of us.

The songs, all but one by Robbie, are classics now;
"Cripple Creek," "Rag Mama Rag," "The Night They Drove
Old Dixie Down," "King Harvest (Has Surely Come)" have
made up the heart of the Band's stage show for years. What
they say was clear the moment they were released, and I
have nothing to add to that. Their power, though, is too
great to take for granted.

The songs were made to bring to life the fragments of
experience, legend, and artifact every American has inherited
as the legacy of a mythical past. The songs have little to do
with chronology; most describe events that could be taking
place right now, but most of those events had taken on their
color before any of us was born. There is a conviction here
that every way of life practiced in America from the time of
the Revolution on down still matters—not as nostalgia, but
as the necessity of someone's daily life—and the music,
though it never bends to any era, never tries for any quaint
support of a theme, seems as if it would sound as right to a
gang of beaver trappers as it does to us. There is no feeling of
being dragged back into the past for a history lesson; if anything, the past catches up with us. Robbie put his stories on
the surface, but they hit home because they draw the traces
of that legacy out of each of us, bringing them to the surface
of our own lives.

"The Night They Drove Old Dixie Down," for one—
written for Levon, who sings it—is not so much a song about
the Civil War as it is about the way each American carries a

version of that event within himself. In this case it is a man named Virgil Kane, who makes no claim to speak for anyone else; but something in his tone demands that everyone listen.

In a few short verses, we learn a lot about him. He is a poor white farmer from the Confederate side of Tennessee, probably not more than twenty years old, a survivor of the attacks made by General Stoneman's cavalry on the Danville train he defended. With the war over, a glimpse of Robert E. Lee is worth as much to him as the memory of his brother, who died fighting for the sense of place Virgil Kane's war was all about. He wants us to understand that the war has cost him almost everything he has.

It is hard for me to comprehend how any Northerner, raised on a very different war than Virgil Kane's, could listen to this song without finding himself changed. You can't get out from under the singer's truth—not the whole truth, simply *his* truth—and the little autobiography closes the gap between us. The performance leaves behind a feeling that for all our oppositions, every American still shares this old event; because to this day none of us has escaped its impact, what we share is an ability to respond to a story like this one.

The scope of the album, words and music, is astonishing. In "King Harvest," probably Robbie's greatest song, we meet a man who might be Virgil Kane's grandson—or our contemporary, you can't tell. He works that same farm, but it fails and sends him into the bitter mills of the New South; when times are slow the mills shut down, and he runs into the arms of a union, hoping for one last chance. Yet wherever he is driven, he carries his roots with him like a conscience. He cannot escape the feel of the land any more than we can escape its myth.

"King Harvest" is the last number on the album; like "Dixie" or the desolate "Whispering Pines" (Richard Manuel's sole contribution), the song is optimistic only because it is so full of desire. It goes against the usual playful, rocking grain of *The Band*, giving the music the tension it must have if it is to work as a version of our own roots, of our own conscience.

The distance between those songs of struggle is marked by a set of easy, honest affirmations that can be summed up in a dozen lines, but perhaps best by this one: "Life has been so good to us all." Jawbone, the Band's unregenerate thief, would say yes to that; certainly the trucker and his semipro girlfriend down in Lake Charles would, along with the little boy and his grandfather in "When You Awake" and the tired sailors of "Rockin' Chair." Even the people scrambling into the storm cellar in "Look Out Cleveland" and the lover stuck with a woman who only wants to dance would show up to sign that pledge. The man who sings "King Harvest" is alone, and he probably could not agree.

With the last reservation ahead of us we ride down the Mississippi, out to California, through the Midwest to Virginia, back again to Canada. We listen to fiddles, what sounds like an amplified jew's-harp, a rock 'n' roll band, laughing horns, good guitar, yodels, sniggers, snorts, and moans; along with the people we meet we take satisfaction in whiskey, in the grinning joys of miscegenation, in Garth Hudson's mad piano, trickling through the fast steps of "Rag Mama Rag." From song to song paradise means good times— and good times are where you find them.

> Up on Cripple Creek she sends me
> If I spring a leak, she mends me
> I don't have to speak, she defends me
> A drunkard's dream if I ever did see one! *

Again and again, the music creates that moment of shared recognition first confirmed in "Dixie"—the songs catch it in sex, in work, in failure, in the weather, in the choice of an instrument, in names lifted from half-forgotten Westerns, in the emotion of a vocal, in a memory of family life. The shifts between the songs finally let us understand that the man who sings "King Harvest" wants nothing more from his life than to sing a song like "Rag Mama Rag"; we understand that the voice of "Rag Mama Rag" is real because it has been shaped by the terrors of "King Harvest," and knows a chance to dance them away for what it's worth.

The album tells no lies. It touches the size and the age of the country, takes in its fabulous multiplicity, but that repeated moment links us to each part of the story even as it knits the songs into one.

For as long as that moment lasts, the story seems complete. Every character, every place, every event in the music looms up at once. Crossing the great divide, the Band left community in their wake.

EVEN STRANGER BLUES

The problem with community, as the Band was to discover when they finally followed their records into the country, is that you have to live in it. They had, in fact, made those first two albums from a distance—isolated in the musicians' haven of Bearsville/Woodstock and walled off from the crowd by their manager, Albert Grossman. *Big Pink* had been out for almost a year and *The Band* was in the can when the group arrived in San Francisco to meet their audience for the first time—people had gathered from all over the West to celebrate *them*.

No matter how many rave record reviews the Band might have read, until they stepped onto a stage there was no way they could have understood how fierce and intense the expectations of their audience would be. Their music had cut even more deeply than they could have hoped—to many, *Big Pink* was one of the memorable events of their lives, and the stakes of that first night were as high as they could be.

After hours of delays, excuses, promises, and interminable tuning up, the Band came on with Robbie dazed and sick, dragging along a hypnotist to cure him. The hypnotist stood on the stage conjuring up spells while the Band fell apart before the crowd's very eyes. They struggled through a handful of weak, ragged tunes, and then they turned and ran. The crowd's hopeful energy had been suspended between disappointment and desire, and it collapsed into fury. The Band's first concert ended with an outpouring of anger and rage unlike anything I have ever seen at a rock 'n' roll show.

Perhaps the crowd's reaction was vicious, but it was certainly real—a good measure of how much the Band had to live up to. They had it all the next night, playing on and on with a wild, raucous delight that finally climaxed with Little Richard's "Slippin' and Slidin'," a number that the five had likely been playing—in afterschool pick-up bands, as the Hawks, up in Woodstock—since it came out in 1956. But we had loved the song as long as the Band had, and as Richard Manuel tossed off the unmistakable first notes of the tune the crowd began to dance and cheer. This was a common celebration now: as we made the old song new, what seemed most remarkable was the recognition that our links to the Band had been forged so long ago, and that our time together was just beginning.

Still, I think something of that initial disaster stayed with the Band. They made a number of cross-country tours after that, but if they never played as badly as they did that first night, they never played with the freedom of the show that followed either. Performing involved all the psychic risks they had faced and dodged in the adventures of *Big Pink;* performing also demanded new links, no matter how tenuous, to the America their audience lived in, which was very different from their own—a scary place, violent with blocked hopes and bad dreams, a place where roots were not enough, where a good concert by the Band was like shelter in the storm, a means to strength and pleasure. And they had aimed for more than that.

Sometimes, though, there was less. The Band began to hedge their bets. They called their next album *Stage Fright,* and both the new songs and the concerts of the time proved they meant it. *Stage Fright* was an album of doubt, guilt, disenchantment, and false optimism. The past no longer served them—the songs seemed trapped in the present, a jumble of desperation that was at once personal and social. The music at its best was still special, but in every sense, the kind of unity that had given force to those first two albums, and to the idea of the Band itself, was missing. Now, instead of hearing music that could not really be broken down, one picked at parts for satisfaction—Robbie's guitar and Garth's organ on "The Shape I'm In," Rick Danko's bass and fiddle on "Daniel and the Sacred Harp." Robbie had completely taken over the songwriting; the surprises of three voices wrestling for a lyric were abandoned for solo vocals. There was an edge of separation in the music: the worried man was back, drawing the shade on his window as the police wailed by in one tune, picked up for vagrancy himself in another, spinning a hilarious but ultimately unsettling tale of sin and damnation in a third. He still reaches out to others—*he* needs shelter now—but no one is there.

Facing an audience, the Band hid in their arrangements. The arrangements were tight, disciplined, precise; the open spirit of their music contracted. They were known to spend more time on testing the sound system than they did playing, but often they didn't play loud enough to come across. They presented perfect replicas of their records—to the point where Rick Danko would back off from the mike at the end of "When You Awake," imitating the studio fade—the surest way to please an audience without really moving it.

From the days when they had first paid out their money to hear Howlin' Wolf, there had been a side to the Band that was anarchic, risky, virtually out of control, and when they caught that spirit, they could take it farther than anyone else. Sometimes Robbie made his guitar sound like a musical equivalent of Jim Brown's big scene in *The Dirty Dozen*—that moment when he takes off on a broken-field run around a Nazi chateau, dropping a hand grenade down an air shaft every ten yards and grinning madly as explosions leap up behind him in sequence—but to bring such qualities into your music you have to touch such emotions in yourself. The Band saw chaos in the crowd, in the country, in the commercial pressures that were driving the five of them apart, driving at least one of them into dope and alcohol, and they stepped back.

Almost always, the numbers they had never recorded— Rick Danko's lovely country version of the Four Tops' "Loving You Has Made My Life Sweeter Than Ever," or their hard rock assault on Marvin Gaye's "Baby Don't Do It (Don't Break My Heart)"—were most vital, because you could hear them reaching for the songs and grabbing hold. But most of all they were looking for safety—they rarely cut loose, tried hard not to take chances. Their shows began to lose excitement, their music began to lose its drama, and the Band began to lose their audience.

Cahoots came out in 1971, but only the earlier songs gave any weight to the title—and the title was the best thing on the album. The songs were stiff and the music was constricted; all the humor and drive had gone. On *The Band* Robbie had breathed life into his characters in a line, and the singers made you care about them; here there were only abstractions and stereotypes, and the singers sounded as if they had no real connection to the words they were given.

The music no longer had any life of its own; it took its cues from the lyrics, and when the result wasn't flat, it was cute. "When I Paint My Masterpiece" was about an expatriate artist in Europe, so the tune featured a little Michel Legrand accordion; the utterly pointless "Shootout in Chinatown" came complete with Fu Manchu guitar, a touch so tasteless it verged on racism. The Band's ability to create a sense of place was reduced to a humorless presentation of fixed images. The failure of language made even the good ideas of the lyrics unsatisfying—made the truth sound false.

That sense of struggle and reward that bled through *Big Pink, The Band,* and *Stage Fright,* the balance always changing, had collapsed into a nostalgic pastoralism in which few who had felt the strength of their best songs could believe. The last cut on *Cahoots,* a tribute to the white gospel communities of the South, was as sentimental in its performance as it was honest in its intent; hearing it after the strained failures of the rest of the album, I couldn't help but think of the studio happy ending that was tacked onto Fritz Lang's *You Only Live Once*, wherein Henry Fonda, having died tragically in the last shot, suddenly ascends to heaven with a bewildered smile on his face. *Cahoots* was a commercial disaster; the Band retreated even further, playing only an occasional concert, making no tours at all.

In the last week of 1971 they arranged a special set of shows in New York, and with a horn section unlike anything ever heard in rock 'n' roll to force their music past itself, the Band broke through and said their piece once more. Out of those nights came a magnificent live album, *Rock of Ages*—a claim that their music was meant to last, and certainly the best of it will. But as I listened to the live records when they were released in 1972—so full of playfulness and bite, blazing with soul and love—I was struck by how long it had been since the Band had put out a single new song that mattered.

The Band's vision of the country had darkened as they moved farther apart. If they were to keep the group they had made, they could not ask too much of it. The music seemed to say that they had lost their trust in the country, in themselves, and in each other—that they had to fight harder than they were able to touch the spirit that had made their work worth doing in the first place. Like most good American artists, and like their worried man, they had been romantics, but not fools; when the romance began to go, their talent for asking the right questions went with it. They still looked for community, but like many who cannot find it, they fell back into an even deeper privacy than they started out with. Because their dreams were too real and too beautiful to give up, they felt a sense of guilt; their withdrawal—a separation from the country, from their audience, and from each other—was a betrayal of those dreams.

They had closed out *Stage Fright* with a queer song that had all the warmth of *The Man Who Corrupted Hadleyburg*, which it resembles: "The Rumor." The old quester who sings it is afraid now, and his voice is muted—no one else speaks at all. He sings to a crowd he has long since joined,

but the bonds between them—of loyalty, affection, fascination—have faded away. When the singer first came to the
country, he found it poisoned by suspicion and shame; he
meant to change it, but instead, the country changed him.

Someone in the crowd has been harmed: "His name
abused, his privacy refused." Why he has been harmed is not
spelled out, probably no one really knows, and the mystery
deepens the malevolence of the scene. "Feel the good," the
seeker calls out, "hang down your heads/Until the fog rolls
away—Let it roll away." He means it, but the words no
longer mean what they might have, because the community
can never be what it was. "He can forgive—and you can
regret—but he can never, never forget." Not even the victim
is known—the victim might be anyone, as might be the vil-
lain.

When the worried man looks into the crowd, as he
must, for he has nowhere else to go, the people he sees will
seem different to him, as he will to them. The whip will
hang over them all.

Perhaps. The last song on *Rock of Ages* was the old
Chuck Willis/Jerry Lee Lewis hit, "(I Don't Want To) Hang
Up My Rock and Roll Shoes," and it capped a New Year's
Eve night when the Band and their fans had put themselves
back in touch with each other. But as the Band left the stage,
Robbie says, they felt a common sense of depression—no,
they didn't wanna, and they weren't gonna, but the song,
like so many, was complex in its context. The Band knew
that when Chuck Willis's version was on the radio, he was in
the grave; that while Jerry Lee kept his rock 'n' roll shoes, he
lost his rock 'n' roll audience. The song was not a curse, but
it wasn't the simple affirmation they had bargained for either. It simply raised questions they could not answer, about
the cheers that had ridden them off the stage; reaching for
the past had forced them to think about what they had left to
do.

Many months later, in the fall of 1973, an article appeared in *Playboy*, measuring Richard Manuel for a straight-

jacket; at the same time, the Band released *Moondog Matinee*, a collection of some favorite oldies. Manuel had been in bad shape for a long time; he had not finished a song of his own for years, but this was his album.

He sang about giving up the bottle in "Saved," deepened his hopes with "A Change Is Gonna Come," and slowly pulled down his mask with "The Great Pretender." If that last had been more than a little overblown when the Platters first sang it in 1955, one would have thought that after nearly twenty years there would be nothing left of the song but nostalgia. Manuel transformed it into the truest kind of soul music; his singing made the Band's more predictable rockers sound tame by comparison.

The best of the album took the Band's tale back to its beginnings, and eased their special voice into its parts. "Third Man Theme," their little instrumental, had a quiet affection in its modesty and humor—the music asked for good times, perhaps for less than before, perhaps not. The finest cut of all, Manuel's gentle, utterly despairing version of Bobby Bland's "Share Your Love," was as lonesome a song as any can be. As he sang, surrounded again by the old sympatico of the Band, it seemed like the last word of that worried man. Share your love with me, share your love with me—what had he ever said but that, what else had anyone ever said to him?

THE WEIGHT

"It was a rowdy life," Robbie once recalled, thinking back over the years before *Big Pink*. "The places we played had tough audiences. They would throw things at you; they were rednecks. Fighting plays a big part in their life, you know—fighting and woman-stealing. And you fall in, you just do what the custom is. If they take off their shoes, you take off your shoes.

"We were all so young—we were sixteen, seventeen years old at the time. We played in joints. That's what they were. Some of it was great and some of it was scary and some of it was horrible, and some of it was very valuable to us, to this day.

"You see—instead of throwing a knapsack over your back and getting out on the highway, to learn about life, we were able to do it together. We were protected by one another. We were secured by one another."

Those are fine words. They tell us that the Band sought in America what they found among themselves: that their music and their stories were not only a version of America, but a reflection of their own unity. All those years on the road had given them their values; in a sense, community was only a projection of comradeship.

The group was its own joint-stock world, but it could not survive the honest demands of the greater joint-stock world that was the country itself. Every song on the first two albums had been written before the Band had played a single show in public; once they began to tour, the group, as men who contributed what was special about themselves to something bigger than any of them, began to fall apart. Richard Manuel never wrote another song; the singers stopped calling out to one another across the verses; the uncanny sense of timing that had made the Band's early music move disappeared altogether. As the Band stepped back from their audience, you could feel the friendship go out of their sound.

In order to save the group, Robbie took it over. He took it over as lyricist, manager, strategist, savant, visionary, and spokesman. No one else in the Band ever gave an interview; after a time, the rock press began to celebrate Robbie as a genius and the Band as his foil, and the other members were not asked to talk. And yet, because the group was no longer truly whole, Robbie could not really draw on it; since his links to the country and to his audience were no longer strong, he could no longer see the country or his audience clearly. *Moondog Matinee*, for all of its satisfactions, had the melancholy tinge of a reunion—a feeling that became all the more unsettling when one realized the five men saw each other all the time.

Friendship, in the end, is not community, though it was the Band's sense of friendship that let them embody community—in their stories, in their music, in their ambitions. Friendship can be the means to community. But if one does not live in the world, then one will feed off the small world of friendship until there is nothing left.

When I went up to Woodstock to talk to Robbie late in 1972, he was ready to leave. The Band had been hiding out there for years, their houses squirreled off in the Catskills; I had never seen that part of the country before, and I understood how one could read its signs as a promise of peace of mind. Woodstock itself looked like the usual American idea of community—quaint, tasteful, small, homogeneous—but in fact it was more like a private club, inhabited by musicians, dope dealers, artists, hangers-on. The town made me nervous; it seemed like a closed, smug, selfish place.

I asked Robbie about his favorite cities. Montreal and New Orleans, he said, and he began to talk about the cultural confusion that he thought gives those cities their spirit—the mix of languages, customs, religions, music, food, architecture, politics. You could spend your whole life in one of those cities and be surprised every day. He had a house in Montreal—that was his wife Dominique's hometown—and they were going back. What that would mean for the future of the Band I didn't ask; the pastoral traps of Woodstock had already taken too much of the soul out of the group. That they had protected each other years ago was only half of their best music—the other half came from what they had protected themselves against: those rowdy audiences, scattered all over the country in dance halls and bars. "They take off their shoes, you take off your shoes"—in those days, the Band could not afford to keep their distance. They learned to lean on each other and to listen to the crowd; that, in a queer way, brought their commitment to friendship and their feel for community together.

Before I left Woodstock I sat and talked for a long time with Dominique Robertson. She told me about the struggles of the Quebec Separatist movement and what that fight

meant to her, that she had tried to find someone to talk to
when Trudeau imposed a terror on the people after Separat-
ists kidnapped a government official, that no one in Woodstock had any idea there really was a world different from
their own. There's nothing here but dope, music, and
beauty, she said; if you're a woman, and you don't use dope
and you don't make music, there's nothing here at all.

The Band did leave; they moved to Los Angeles, and
early in 1974 they set out on a grand tour with Bob Dylan.
With Dylan, they were once again the best rock 'n' roll band
in the world; their own sets had all the old limits, and not a
song was less than four years old. Still, there was a joy in
their faces as they played that I had not seen since that great
night in San Francisco, and it made me wonder if the Band
might not have as much ahead of them as they have already
left behind.

America is a dangerous place, and to find community
demands as much as any of us can give. But if America is
dangerous, its little utopias, asking nothing, promising
safety, are usually worse. "Look at all this," Dominique said,
taking in her house, the trees, the mountains. "It's beautiful.
It's everything people ought to want, and I hate it." Then
she grinned. " 'This country life is killin' me,' " she sang,
turning a song we had both heard too many times on its
head. "I gotta find my way back to the city, and get some
corruption in my lungs."

SLY STONE
The Myth of Staggerlee

I named my son Malik Nkrumah Staggerlee Seale. Right on, huh? Beautiful name, right? He's named after his brother on the block, like all his brothers and sisters off the block. Stagger*lee*.

Staggerlee is Malcolm X before he became politically conscious. *Livin' in the hoodlum world.*

You'll find out. Huey had a lot of Staggerlee qualities. I guess I lived a little bit of Staggerlee's life too, here and there. That's where it's at. You move yourself up from a lower level to a higher level. And at one time brother Eldridge was on the block. He was Staggerlee.

"Staggerlee shot Billy . . ." Billy the *Lion.* "Staggerlee had a sawed-off shotgun and a Model A Ford and he owed money on that as well; his woman kicked him out in the cold 'cause she said his love was growin' old. Staggerlee took a walk down *Ramparts Street,* down where all them baaad son-of-a-guns meet. By the Bucket o' *Bluuuuuud.*" You know, the main drag? That's from

75

Louisiana, Ramparts Street? Yeah, this is where Staggerlee's history is. Staggerlee is all the shootouts that went on between gam-
blers, and cats fightin' over women—the black community.

Staggerlee shot Billy, you know? "Shot that poor boy dead."
Two black brothers fightin' each other. Billy the Lion was bad too.
"Staggerlee walked into a bar and ordered . . . just to get a bite to
eat. And he wound up with a glass of muddy water and a piece of
rotten meat. He asked the bartender, did he know who he was?
And the bartender says, 'I heard o' you across the way,' he says,
'but I serve *bad* son-of-a-guns *three* times a day.' " *Everybody's* bad,
you see?

Something else, huh? That's *life*. And all the little Staggerlees,
a *lot of 'em*! Millions of 'em, know what I mean?

And so I named that brother, my little boy, Staggerlee, because . . . that's what his *name* is.

BOBBY SEALE, from a jailhouse
interview with
Francisco Newman, 1970.

STAGGERLEE

Somewhere, sometime, a murder took place: a man called
Stack-a-lee—or Stacker Lee, Stagolee, or Staggerlee—shot a
man called Billy Lyons. It is a story that black America has
never tired of hearing and never stopped living out, like
whites with their Westerns. Locked in the images of a thousand versions of the tale is an archetype that speaks to fantasies of casual violence and violent sex, lust and hatred, ease
and mastery, a fantasy of style and steppin' high. At a deeper
level it is a fantasy of no-limits for a people who live within a
labyrinth of limits every day of their lives, and who can
transgress them only among themselves. It is both a portrait
of that tough and vital character that everyone would like to
be, and just another pointless, tawdry dance of death.

Billy died for a five-dollar Stetson hat: because he beat
Staggerlee in a card game, or a crap game; because Stack was
cheating and Billy was fool enough to call him on it. It happened in Memphis around the turn of the century, in New
Orleans in the twenties, in St. Louis in the eighties. The

style of the killing matters, though: Staggerlee shot Billy, in the words of a Johnny Cash song, just to watch him die.

Sometimes it was a cautionary tale, as in Mississippi John Hurt's version, recorded in 1929.

Po-lice officer, how can it be
You can 'rest everybody, but cru-el Stagolee
That bad man, Oh, cru-el Stagolee

Billy the Lion tol' Stagolee
Please don't take my life
I got two little babes, and a darlin' lovely wife
That bad man, Oh, cruel Stagolee

What I care about your two little babes
Your darlin' lovely wife
You done stole my Stetson hat
I'm bound to take your life
That bad man, Oh, cruel Stagolee

Boom-boom, boom-boom, went a .44
Well, when I spied ol' Billy the Lion
He was lyin' on the floor
That bad man, Oh, cruel Stagolee

Gentlemens of the jury, what you think of that
Stagolee shot Billy the Lion 'bout a five-dollar Stetson hat
That bad man, Oh, cruel Stagolee

If that was something like the original idea of the story, it didn't hold up very long. Usually, no white sheriff had the nerve to take Stack on, and he got away. When he didn't—when he was caught and hung—it was only for a chance to beat the devil. The song carried Staggerlee down to hell, where he took over the place and made it into a black man's paradise.

Innocent Billy was no longer seen as a helpless victim, but as a hapless fool. Staggerlee's secret admirers came out of the woodwork; the women (all dressed in red) flocked to his funeral (it was the best money could buy). Stagolee was a winner. "GO!" shouted Lloyd Price, caught up in the legend, "GO! GO! Staggerlee!"

Nobody's fool, nobody's man, tougher than the devil
and out of God's reach—to those who followed his story and
thus became a part of it, Stack-o-Lee was ultimately a stone-
tough image of a free man.

In the blues, Stack changed names, but little else. He
was the Crawling Kingsnake; Tommy Johnson pouring
Sterno down his throat, singing, "Canned heat, canned heat
is killing me"; Muddy Waters' cool and elemental Rollin'
Stone; Chuck Berry's Brown-Eyed Handsome Man; Bo
Diddley with a tombstone hand and a graveyard mind; Wil-
son Pickett's Midnight Mover; Mick Jagger's Midnight
Rambler.

Stack rode free as the Back Door Man in the deadly
electric blues of Howlin' Wolf (" 'Cuse me for murder/ First
degree/ Judge's wife cried, Let the man go free!/ *I am* . . ."),
and gave up the ghost, proud never to rest easy, in "Going
Down Slow." Stagolee was a secret, buried deep in the heart
as well as ruling the streets: in Bobby Marchan's "There Is
Something on Your Mind," Stackerlee crawled out of a man
who only wanted love and pulled the trigger that turned love
into death. When the civil rights movement got tough, he
took over. And Staggerlee would come roaring back on the
screen in the seventies, as Slaughter, Sweet Sweetback, Superfly.

"Stagger Lee shot Billy. . . ." The line echoes from
Lloyd Price's rock 'n' roll hit through fifty years of black culture, passing, on its way back to its hidden source, thousands
and thousands of Staggerlees and Billys. There is an echo for
Jimi Hendrix, a star at twenty-two and dead at twenty-four;
for Sly Stone, "not," as was said of Bob Dylan once, "burning his candle at both ends, but using a blow torch on the
middle"; for young men dead in alleys or cold in the city
morgue; for a million busted liquor stores and a million
angry rapes. Stack and Billy merge into a figure innocent on
one level and guilty on another: into Robert Johnson, living
from town to town and woman to woman, driven and
searching for sin and peace of mind; into junkies twisted

from their last OD's; into a young George Jackson, drunk
and out for easy money, or his brother Jonathan, rising years
later with a gun in his hand. Look and you will see King
Curtis, stretched out dead in front of his house; Muhammed
Ali; Rap Brown, so bad that Congress passed a law against
him. Farther on are pimps like Big Red Little, Jack Johnson
in a car full of white women, Sportin' Life steppin' out. It is
an echo all the way back to the bullet that went through Billy
and broke the bartender's glass, a timeless image of style and
death.

SLY STONE

Born Sylvester Stewart in Texas, Sly Stone grew up in
Vallejo, California, a tough and grimy polyglot town on the
north end of San Francisco Bay. He picked up guitar and
drums as a kid, led his own gang into the streets, and played
his part in the high school race riots that were endemic in the
town. He made it into a few semipro bands in the early sixties; by the time he was nineteen, in 1964, he was producing
small hits by local white club bands for Autumn Records,
the label owned by the baron of San Francisco Top 40, Big
Daddy Tom Donahue. This put Sly right in the mainstream
of Bay Area rock 'n' roll; up until 1965, the local music scene
pretty much came down to Donahue's kind of radio and the
big package shows he and his partner, Bobby Mitchell,
booked into the Cow Palace.

There was no big money; in fact, a lot of what there was
never seemed to find its way from the distributors back to
the company. The music that was going to put San Francisco
on the rock 'n' roll map was taking shape; it would wipe out
the tight, commercial sounds Donahue and Sly were after—
that is, it would make them uncool.

Sly went to radio school and got a job on KSOL, the
number two black station in the area. Fast on the air, he was
a hit. A brilliant, kinetic DJ, he found the straight soul for-
mat a fraud on his taste, and salted it with Bob Dylan and

the Beatles. At the same time, he was pulling a band together. There were whites as well as blacks, women—who played real instruments—as well as men: "The Family."

By early 1967 the hippie bands of the Haight had the ear of the nation, and San Francisco geared up for the crunch of the Summer of Love. The first hip FM rock station, led by Larry Miller and a reformed Tom Donahue, was breaking the Top 40 monopoly. *Sgt. Pepper* was on the way, as was the Monterey Pop Festival. It was a genuinely exciting time.

And it was a very white scene. If the Jefferson Airplane had little to say to blacks, the fact that they and bands like them brought a white audience into the Fillmore ghetto every weekend seemed unimportant, even if racial tensions were beginning to emerge in the Haight. No one knew what to say about that, so no one said anything, except that they sure dug spades.

Black music, led by Aretha Franklin, Wilson Pickett, and Sam and Dave, had hit a commercial peak and was approaching an artistic impasse, as inspiration turned into formula. Otis Redding became the white hope of the new rock 'n' roll fans, and at Monterey they would cover him with glory because he said they were all right. But six months later he was dead.

A musical vacuum was opening up, and the racial contradictions of the counterculture were coming to the surface. There was no music to work out the contradictions, and no music to fill the vacuum.

It was at this point that Sly and the Family Stone emerged from the unhip white bars of Hayward and Redwood City—middle-class suburb towns—with a music they brashly called "a whole new thing," leaving behind (and picking up again on the radio) an audience of small-time boosters, bikers, college students, and the sons and daughters of transplanted Okies.

Sly had mastered the recording studio and a dozen instruments. He was tough and wily, already burned in the record business and determined never to let it happen again;

a man out to build something worth the trouble it would take. He was bursting with ambition and ideas, the wildest dresser rock 'n' roll had ever seen—which is saying something—an outrageous showman whose style was a combination of Fillmore district pimp gone stone crazy and Fillmore Auditorium optimism with a point to it. A cultural politician of the first order, Sly was less interested in crossing racial and musical lines than in tearing them up.

In the manner of the very greatest rock 'n' roll, Sly and the Family Stone made music no one had ever heard before.

In moments you could catch echoes of Sam Cooke, the Beatles, a lot of jazz, and even a little surf music. Not just the singers but the whole band seemed to find much of their inspiration in a few classic rock 'n' roll songs, building off the furious vocal lines of the Silhouettes' "Get a Job," the mad desire of Maurice Williams' "Stay," and the chaos of Stevie Wonder's preteen apocalypse, "Fingertips." The band dismissed the simple, direct sound of the black music of the day, from Stax to James Brown, but took advantage of its rhythmic inventions; the Family Stone had much of the exhilaration of the white San Francisco sound, along with the open spirit that sound was already beginning to lose. And there was a keen ear for the hook lines and commercial punch crucial to the charts of any rock era.

The whole was something other than its parts, perhaps because what came across was not simply a new musical style, though there was that, but a shared attitude, a point of view: not just a brand-new talk, but the brand-new walk of young men and women on the move.

There was an enormous freedom to the band's sound. It was complex, because freedom is complex; wild and anarchic, like the wish for freedom; sympathetic, affectionate, and coherent, like the reality of freedom. And it was all celebration, all affirmation, a music of endless humor and delight, like a fantasy of freedom.

They had hits: "Dance to the Music," "Stand!," "Everyday People," "Hot Fun in the Summertime," "Thank You falettinme be mice elf Agin." A smash with black kids and white, these records had all the good feeling of the March on Washington, and the street cachet that march never had.

Sly's real triumph was that he had it both ways. Every nuance of his style, from the razzle-dazzle of his threads to the originality of his music to the explosiveness of his live performance, made it clear he was his own man. If the essence of his music was freedom, no one was more aggressively, creatively free than he. Yet there was room for everyone in the America of a band made up of blacks and whites, men and women, who sang out "different strokes for different folks" and were there on stage to show an audience just what such an idea of independence meant. Vocals were demystified: everybody sang (even Cynthia Robinson, who screeched). When the band growled out "Don't Call Me Nigger, Whitey (Don't Call Me Whitey, Nigger)," they gave pleasure by using the insults for all they were worth, and at the same time showed how deeply those insults cut.

Sly was a winner. It seemed he had not only won the race, he had made up his own rules. Driving the finest cars, sporting the most sensational clothes, making the biggest deals and the best music, he was shaping the style and ambition of black teenagers all over the country—expanding the old Staggerlee role of the biggest, baddest man on the block. Sly was Staggerlee, and the power of the role was his, but he didn't have to kill anyone to get it.

RIOT

Motown raced to absorb Sly's new music, to catch up. They tightened his aesthetic and roared back up the charts with a revamped version of the Temptations and the new Jackson 5. Sly kept up the pace, breaking the color line at Woodstock and emerging as the festival's biggest hit. In early 1970 the band cut a new single, called "Everybody Is a Star," and it was their best—a lovely, awesomely moving statement of what the band was about and what it was for. A new album was on the way, Sly told an interviewer, "the most optimistic of all."

But something went wrong. Sly began to show up late for concerts, or not at all. That caused riots, including a very bad one in Chicago. Performances, when they came off, were often erratic, angry, or uncommitted. There was no new album; there was trouble with promoters; lawsuits; rumors of the band breaking up; rumors of bad dope, gangsters, extortion, death threats. Sly's manager said his client had a split personality.

Finally, in late 1971, the new record hit the stores. There was an American flag on the cover (flowers instead of stars) and happy pictures all over the rest of it (with odd, somber shots of Lincoln and the Gettysburg Address here and there). The album was called *There's a riot goin' on*, and the title cut was blank.

The record was no fun. It was slow, hard to hear, and it didn't celebrate anything. It was not groovy. In fact, it was distinctly unpleasant, unnerving. Many people didn't like it, wrote it off as a junkie bummer. If Robert Johnson were alive today there would be someone around to yell "Boogie!" at him.

There's a riot goin' on was an exploration of and a pronouncement on the state of the nation, Sly's career, his audience, black music, black politics, and a white world. Emerging out of a pervasive sense, at once public and personal, that the good ideas of the sixties had gone to their limits, turned back upon themselves, and produced evil where only good was expected, the album began where "Everybody Is a Star" left off, and it asked: So what?

The album contained, in a matrix of parody and vicious self-criticism, virtually all the images and slogans Sly had given to his audience. The new music called all the old music and the reasons for claiming it into question. Like *Bonnie and Clyde*, which angered critics in much the same way, *Riot* was, and is, a rough, disturbing work that can be ignored, dismissed, but never smoothed over.

Riot joined other pop reversals that confused and divided audiences and created new ones, pop acts that risked the destruction of the artist's audience. It was Sly's equivalent of Van Morrison's *Blowin' Your Mind*, his first solo album, where Van reached for the grotesque because it seemed the only rational description of everyday life; of Dylan's *John Wesley Harding*, in that Sly was escaping his own pop past and denying its value; of John Lennon's screaming break with the Beatles, though Sly worked with much greater sophistication and intelligence. Instead of merely orchestrating his confessions, Sly transformed them into a devastating work of art that deeply challenged anyone who ever claimed to be a part of his audience, a piece of music that challenges most of the assumptions of rock 'n' roll itself.

In an age when politics succeeds by confusing and obscuring matters of life and death, the strongest artists must claim those things as their own and act them out. Not many will ever have the nerve or the vision to do it, but at least for as long as it took to make *Riot*, Sly did.

Riot begins with a slow, stuttering beat, a chanting parody of "Stand!" As Sly comes in, wailing and groaning, half-satisfied, half-desperate, the question that comes through is whether it is worth standing up at all, or possible even if it is worth it. In another world, the man who sings this song did not merely "control the decisions that affected his life," to use a phrase from the decade this album left behind, he *made* them; now the words "control" and "decision" have lost their meaning. Tense, nervous, creepy, the song careens to an end, and it sets the tone. What follows is an expertly crafted and brilliantly performed review of folly, failure, betrayal, and disintegration—the confession of a man, speaking for more than himself, who has been trapped by limits whose existence he once would not even admit to, let alone respect: trapped by dope; by the weakness behind a world based on style; by the repression that sent black men and women into hiding, into exile, into the morgue; by the flimsiness of the rewards a white society has offered him. A testament to oppression, the music is, on first listening, itself oppressive.

The songs seem to wander, to show up and disappear, ghostly, with no highs or lows. At their kindest, they are simply ironic. Some, like "Africa Talks to You (The Asphault Jungle)," are morbid: chased into hiding by the band, Sly shouts back, "Timmmmmmberrr!" and the guitar mocks him into silence. "Brave and Strong" pleads for survival, but hints that only dope will get it.

Two tracks were released as singles—"Family Affair" and "Runnin' Away"—both were hits, and both had a deceptively easy movement. But the first was about finding your way back to mother and a marriage falling to pieces, and the second used a saucy girl chorus to drive nails into a fool.

The album found its end with "Thank you for talkin' to me Africa," a reversal of "Thank you fallentinme be mice elf Agin." There is no vocal music in rock 'n' roll to match it; the voices creep in and out of the instruments, cutting out in the middle of a line, messages from limbo, golem-talk. "I'm a-dyin, I'm a-dyin," you can hear Sly wailing, and the only way to disbelieve is to stop listening. The song gathers up all the devastation of the rest of the album and slowly drives it home, grinds it in, and fades out.

This music defines the world of the Staggerlee who does not get away, and who finds hell as advertised. There is an enormous reality to the music: a slow, level sense of getting by. It is Muzak with its finger on the trigger; the essence of the rhythms James Brown has explored without the compensations of Brown's showmanship or his badass lyrics. It is a reality of day-to-day sameness and an absence of variety— like prison—that requires, if one is to endure it, either a deadening of all the senses, or a preternatural sharpening of them, so that the smallest change of mood or event can be seized on as representing something novel or meaningful.

In this sense, and only at the farthest margin, the music is part of the way out of the disaster it affirms. If you listen, you get sharper, and you begin to hear what the band is hearing; every bass line or vocal nuance eventually takes on great force. The disaster gains an emotional complexity, and you enter it. Finally, *Riot* bears the same relationship to most music as George Jackson's *Soledad Brother* does to *Confidential*. The second is easier to get into, but nothing is there.

Stand!, the brilliant album that preceded *Riot* (and literally turned black music inside out with its flash and innovation), had all the drive and machinery of a big semi-truck; listening to it put you in the driver's seat, made you feel like you owned the road. *Riot* is about getting off the truck. The mood is one of standing still; of performing every act with the care of one who is not sure his mind and his body will quite connect; of falling apart; of running, looking back, realizing you can be caught.

> *Lookin' at the devil,*
> *Grinnin' at his gun.*
> *Fingers start shakin',*
> *I begin to run.*
>
> *Bullets start chasin',*
> *I begin to stop.*
> *We begin to wrestle,*
> *I was on the top.*
>
> "Thank You for talkin' to me Africa"

When the song was released a year earlier as "Thank You fallentinme be mice elf Agin," it had a snappy rhythm. It was a winner's song, and neither the music nor the vocals left any doubt as to who was going to stay on top. On *Riot* the song comes slowly, emphasizing the thud of the bass guitar. The words are buried in a slurred half-chant; when Sly sings, "Thank You falletinme be mice elf Agin," the contempt in his voice is inescapable.

Notice how the song reads. The words Sly wrote for *Riot* are some of the most imaginative and forceful in all of rock 'n' roll. The images are perfectly developed; the songs achieve a tense and eerie balance, as each element of the music seems to pull more than its own weight. Not one image, not one note, is wasted. Nothing is gratuitous.

One song, "Poet," was called pretentious, because it said such things as, "I'm a songwriter, oh yeh a poet." The

number is intentionally crude, but in the end such a song is
pretentious only if it is false. And although for rock 'n' roll
the terms themselves are probably false, the words of the
songs on this album are better "poetry" than anything the
"rock poets" have written. The rock poets are all of them
white, of course, because the rock 'n' roll audience—and rock
critics—often think in neat racial categories, and "black" does
not fit into the "poetry" category. When Bob Dylan quipped
that Smokey Robinson was America's greatest poet, most
people thought that was some kind of joke.

Of all the nonsense that has been written about the poetry of Neil Young, Paul Simon, or even Bob Dylan, no one
has ever said anything about Jimi Hendrix's "Little Wing."
The poetry question, especially when we are dealing with a
song, has to do with how a writer uses language—and his
music will be part of his language—to make words do things
they ordinarily do not do, with how he tests the limits of language and alters and extends the conventional impact of
images, or rescues resources of language that we have lost or
destroyed. The music on *Riot* mostly flattens out what Sly
wrote, hiding it, telling the truth, but not quite out loud.
The words peek out, and only occasionally, as with "Family
Affair," do they hit you in the face.

> *Lookin' at the devil,*
> *Grinnin' at his gun.*
> *Fingers start shakin',*
> *I begin to run.*
>
> *Bullets start chasin',*
> *I begin to stop.*

The poetry of those lines is the use of the words "start"
and "begin," which slow the usual pace of the violent images
Sly is presenting. The eye is working here, taking in the
scene from the edge of action; the description is minimal, and
the economy is absolute. The eye turns and the listener, or
the reader, is given only a vague sense of physical motion, a
whole body aware of itself with the precision of the eye in

the first three lines. You feel the slowing down, the endless, instantaneous decisions and hesitations involved in turning to face the gun again. It all moves in pieces, and you are in the song, in the riot, breathing its risk.

Sly saw a band as the means by which each member finds his or her own voice; while he is the source of vision, the emotion of every singer, his included, has been authentic because that vision is shared. I think this is so because Sly's vision, whether one of affirmation, as it was in the sixties, or negation, as it is on *Riot*, is always an attempt at liberation.

It is Sly's musical authority that gives his singers freedom, that builds a home where freedom seems worth acting out. The singing on the Family's records—complex, personal, and unpredictable—really was something new. As opposed to the Temptations or the Jackson 5, whose records were not inspired by Sly's sound so much as they formalized it (just as earlier Motown imposed order on the risky spontaneity of gospel music), what you hear in Sly's music are a number of individuals who have banded together because that is the way they can best express themselves *as* individuals. It's the freedom of the street, not the church.

This was made explicit in "Everybody Is a Star." That meant not that everyone lives in the spotlight, but that every man and woman finds moments of visibility appropriate to what he or she has to give. On *Riot* Sly took this aesthetic—of the group that sings like a band plays—away from the context of celebration, which had seemed not only appropriate but necessary, and made it the means to a dramatization of events and moods that are bitter, mocking, and scary. Voices stretch words until they are drained of their ordinary meanings, just as the guitars, drums, bass, horns, and organ reduce the sensational clichés of the earlier music to bone. The superstar clothes are removed, piece by piece, and what is left, in a weird and modern way, is the blues.

The equality is still there: no one is a star.

With "Family Affair," so direct in its musical impact and so elusive in its meanings, Sly comes close to a conventional lead vocal, but here he needs the isolation of the spot-

light because he is singing about the need to lean on other
people.

Both kids are good to mom
You see, it's in the blood
Blood's thicker than the mud

He sings from a distance, preaching, trying to explain
something that matters. Some people give up on you; some
don't, no matter what you do. Sometimes it's important to
find out who's who. Sly presented this to the Top 40 audience like a philosophy lesson, holding out knowledge he had
paid for.

> *You*
> *It's a family affair don't*
> *know*
> *who*
> *turned*
> *you*
> *in.*

With *Riot* Sly gave his audience—particularly his white
audience—exactly what they didn't want. What they wanted
was an upper, not a portrait of what lay behind the big
freaky black superstar grin that decorated the cover of the
album. One gets the feeling, listening, that the disastrous
concerts that preceded and followed this record were not so
much a matter of Sly insulting his audience as they were of
Sly attacking that audience because of what the demands of
the audience had forced him to produce. The concerts were
an attack on himself as well, for having gone along with those
demands and for having believed in them. All through *Riot*
Sly turned on himself: "Must be a rush for me/ To see a
lazy/ A brain he meant to be/ Cop out?" He removed the
question mark in the next verse, and ultimately covered the
question with poison: "Dyin' young is hard to take/ Sellin'
out is harder."

Those last words were shoved under the graveyard chorus, "Thank you, falettinme be mice elf Agin," and it is not hard to see why this record was so hard to listen to, which is to say, hard to take.

The bonds of a peculiar aesthetic democracy held, one last time, to reveal a world of terror and falsehood, that moment when Staggerlee runs into the limits his role was meant to smash, the same limits that turned Selma into Attica and "Satisfaction" into "You Can't Always Get What You Want." The endless fantasies piled onto the Staggerlee myth over the years were simple proof of the force of those limits, of the need to transcend them, but the fantasy, remade again and again, had its own force: it created new Staggerlees.

Staggerlee is a free man, because he takes chances and scoffs at the consequences. Others, especially whites, gather to fawn over him, until he shatters in a grimy celebration of needles, juice, and noise. Finally he is alone in a slow bacchanal, where his buddies, in a parody of friendship, devote themselves to a study of the precise moment of betrayal. Out of this disaster the man who lives it sometimes emerges whole: Malcolm did. Sometimes he dies young; sometimes he cops out.

On the way to this silent riot Sly shouldered the racial and sexual fantasies of a huge audience and staggered under them, as if he were Staggerlee himself back from the dead to live up to his myth. The images of mastery, style, and triumph set forth earlier in Sly's career reversed themselves; his old politics had turned into death, his exuberance into dope, and his old music into a soundtrack for a world that didn't exist. As an artist, Sly used those facts to reverse the great myth itself.

The role is all too real. It was forced on Chuck Berry, who never wanted it, and he paid for it in prison; Hendrix resisted, but in the public mind, the role enclosed him anyway. *Riot* is the secret contained in the whole blazing tradition. Something more than a definition of the risks involved in getting your hands on Staggerlee's kind of freedom, more than an illustration of the neat duality of any cultural archetype, *Riot* claims the story.

When new roles break down and there is nothing with which to replace them, old roles, ghosts, come rushing in to fill up the vacuum. Whether or not he thought in these terms, Sly lived out one side of Staggerlee's life until the other side caught up, and took over. Once the first role broke down in the face of social and personal limits it could not countenance and still survive, the rage of Staggerlee intensified as his mastery was defrauded. Instead of breaking the bartender's glass Stack found himself aiming at the mirror behind the bar, and thus discovered that his target was himself.

SLY VERSUS SUPERFLY

The best pop music does not reflect events so much as it absorbs them. If the spirit of Sly's early music combined the promises of Martin Luther King's speeches and the fire of a big city riot, *Riot* represented the end of those events and the attempt to create a new music appropriate to new realities. It was music that had as much to do with the Marin shootout and the death of George Jackson as the earlier sound had to do with the pride of the riot the title track of this album said was no longer going on.

"Frightened faces to the wall," Sly moans. "Can't you hear your mama call? The Brave and Strong—Survive! Survive!"

I think those faces up against the wall belonged to Black Panthers, forced to strip naked on the night streets of Philadelphia so Frank Rizzo and his cops could gawk and laugh and make jokes about big limp cocks while Panther women, lined up with the men, were psychologically raped.

A picture was widely published. Many have forgotten it; Sly probably had not. This again is why *Riot* was hard to take. If its spirit is that of the death of George Jackson it is not a celebration of Jackson, but music that traps what you

feel when you are shoved back into the corners of loneliness
where you really have to think about dead flesh and cannot
play around with the satisfactions of myth.

The pessimism of *Riot* is not the romantic sort we
usually get in rock 'n' roll. Optimistic almost by definition,
pop culture is always pointing toward the next thing and
sure it is worth going after; rock 'n' roll is linked to a youthful sense of time and a youthful disbelief in death. Pop culture pessimism is almost always self-indulgent; not without
the power to move an audience, but always leaving the audience (and the artist) a way out. In retrospect, records made
in this spirit often seem like reverse images of narcissism.
Riot is the real thing: scary and immobile. It wears down
other records, turning them into unintentional self-parodies.
The negative of *Riot* is tough enough to make solutions seem
trivial and alternatives false, in personal life, politics, or
music.

Rock 'n' roll may matter because it is fun, unpredictable, anarchic, a neatly packaged and amazingly intense plurality of good times and good ideas, but none save the very
youngest musicians and fans can still take their innocence for
granted. Most have simply seen and done too much; as the
Rolling Stones have been proving for ten years, you have to
work for innocence. You have to win it, or you end up with
nothing more than a strained naïveté.

Because this is so pop needs an anchor, a reality princi-
ple, especially when the old ideas—the joy of the Beatles, the
simple toughness of the Stones—have run their course and
the music has begun to repeat its messages without repeating
their impact. Rock 'n' roll may escape conventional reality on
a day-to-day level (or remake it, minute-to-minute), but it
has to have an intuitive sense of the reality it means to escape; the audience and the artists have to be up against the
wall before they can climb over it. When the Stones made
"Gimmie Shelter," they had power because their toughness
had taken on complexity: they admitted they had doubts
about finding even something as simple as shelter, and fought
for it anyway. But because the band connected with its audi-

ence when they got that across, and because the music that
did it was the best they ever made, the song brought more
than shelter; it brought life, provided a metaphor that allowed the Stones to survive when Altamont proved
toughness was not the point, and gave them the freedom to
go on to sing about other things—soul survivors, suffocation,
and a trip down a moonlight mile.

Riot matters because it doesn't just define the wall; it
makes the wall real. Its sensibility is hard enough to frame
the mass of pop music, shuffle its impact, jar the listener,
and put an edge on the easy way out that has not really been
won. It is not casual music and its demands are not casual; it
tended to force black musicians to reject it or live up to it.
Some months after Riot was released—from the middle of
1972 through early 1973—the impulses of its music emerged
on other records, and they took over the radio.

I don't know if I will be able to convey the impact of
punching buttons day after day and night after night to be
met by records as clear and strong as Curtis Mayfield's "Superfly" and "Freddie's Dead," the Staple Singers' "Respect
Yourself" and the utopian "I'll Take You There," the O'Jays'
"Back Stabbers," War's astonishing "Slipping into Darkness"
and "The World Is a Ghetto," the Temptations' "Papa Was
a Rolling Stone," Johnny Nash's "I Can See Clearly Now,"
Stevie Wonder's "Superstition," for that matter the Stones'
Exile on Main Street (the white Riot)—records that were surrounded, in memory and still on the air as recent hits, by
Marvin Gaye's deadly "Inner City Blues," by the Undisputed Truth's "Smiling Faces Sometimes (Tell Lies)," by
the Chi-Lites' falsetto melancholy, by Riot itself. Only a year
before such discs would have been curiosities; now, they
were all of a piece: one enormous answer record. Each song
added something to the others, and as in a pop explosion, the
country found itself listening to a new voice.

To me, the Temptations took the prize. Imagine—or
simply remember—the chill of driving easily through the
night, and then hearing, casually at first, then with interest,
and then with compulsion, the three bass patterns, repeated

endlessly, somewhere between the sound of the heart and a
judge's gavel, that open "Papa Was a Rolling Stone." The
toughest blues guitar you have heard in years cracks through
the building music like a curse; the singer starts in.

More than one person I knew pulled off the road and sat
waiting, shivering, as the song crept out of the box and filled
up the night.

Four children have gathered around their mother to ask
for the truth about their father, who has been buried that
very day. They don't know him; he was just another street-
corner Stagolee. So they ask. Was he one of those two-faced
preachers, mama—"Stealing in the name of the Lord?" * A
drunk? A hustler? A pimp? With another wife, more kids?
They slam the questions into their mother, and all she can
give them is one of the most withering epitaphs ever written,
for them, as well as for him: "When he died, all he left us
was alone."

Some thought "Back Stabbers" hit even harder. It
moved with a new urgency, heading into its chorus with an
unforgettable thump; it was like hearing the Drifters again,
but the Drifters robbed of pop optimism that let them find
romance even in the hard luck of "On Broadway." The
O'Jays sounded scared when they climaxed the song with an
image that was even stronger than the music: "I wish somebody'd take/ Some a' these *knives* outta my back!"

Stevie Wonder reached number one with "Superstition"—his first time on top in ten years. It was the most ominous hard rock in a long while, a warning against a belief in
myths that no one understood; Wonder made the old chicka-
chicka-boom beat so potent it sounded like a syncopated version of Judgment Day.

All these records were nervous, trusting little if anything, taking *Riot*'s spirit of black self-criticism as a new aesthetic, driven (unlike *Riot*) by great physical energy, determined to get across the idea of a world—downtown or

* A reference to Paul Kelly's single of the same name, which, along with Jerry
Butler's "Only the Strong Survive," had opened up the new territory the Tempts
were exploring.

uptown, it didn't matter—where nothing was as it seemed. These black musicians and singers were cutting loose from the white man's world to attend to their own business—and to do that, they had to tell the truth. And so they made music of worry and confinement that, in their very different way, the Chi-Lites took to even greater extremes.

The Chi-Lites—like all the artists discussed here—had been around for many years, but they broke into the Top 40 in the seventies, with a dark chant called "(For God's Sake) Give More Power to the People." Stylistically, this was an old kind of record, but it was a new kind of politics; instead of a demand, or an affirmation, it was a plea, and a desperate one at that. The Chi-Lites' persona was open and vulnerable, the antithesis of machismo (something they explicitly dismissed with the great "Oh, Girl"). Other hits—"A Lonely Man," "Have You Seen Her," and "The Coldest Day of My Life"—undercut the high-stepping burst of mastery on which Wilson Pickett and so many other black artists of the sixties had based their careers; the Chi-Lites made Pickett's old bragging music sound fake. Pickett had told his audience that ninety-nine and a half won't do and made them believe it, but the Chi-Lites seemed ready to settle for a lot less—or to beg for something else altogether. The key to any black singer is in that old catch phrase about the way you talk and the way you walk; the Chi-Lites spoke softly and moved with great care.

This new music was a step back for a new look at black America; it was a finger pointed at Staggerlee and an attempt to freeze his spirit out of black culture. On many levels—direct, symbolic, commercial, personal—this music was a vital, conservative reaction to the radical costs Sly had shown that Staggerlee must ultimately exact. And since Stack was roaming virtually unchallenged in the new black cinema, this musical stance amounted to a small-scale cultural war.

All the new black movies—from *Hit Man* to *Trouble Man* to *Detroit 9000* to *Cleopatra Jones*—were cued by the reality behind one very carefully thrown-away line from *The Godfather* (a movie, it is worth remembering, that attracted mil-

lions of black Americans, even though it had no black characters, let alone any black heroes).

"They're animals anyway," says an off-camera voice, as
the Dons make the crucial decision to dump all their heroin
into the ghettos. "Let them lose their souls."

The Mafia may have missed the contradiction in that
line, but Francis Coppola certainly did not; neither did the
black men and women in the theaters. They suffered it; in
Lady Sings the Blues, Diana Ross was stalking screens all over
the country showing just what it meant. That audience had a
right to revenge.

And so the fantasy went to work again. If that line had
opened up the abyss, the old black hero shot up from the
bottom and pushed in the white man instead. Stack slipped
through the hands of the white sheriff, won his fight, got his
girl, and got away.

Superfly summed up the genre; perhaps its first scene
did, more than it was meant to. The hero, cocaine dealer
Priest (played by Ron O'Neal, who looked uncomfortably
like a not-very-black Sean Connery) stirs in the bed of his
rich white mistress. Some black fool has made off with his
stash. Priest chases him through the alleys, up the side of a
building, and traps him in a tiny apartment. There, in full
view of the man's family, Priests beats him half to death.
This was John Hurt's Billy, but Lloyd Price's Staggerlee.

Still, Priest is nervous. Hustling's all the Man has left
us, he tells his partner, who thinks that's just fine; Priest
wants out of The Life, but the invisible whites who run the
show want him in—or dead. He bets everything on one last
big deal. He turns on the pressure; one of his runners, Freddie, can't take it, and he panics and gets himself killed. Another man, a sort of father figure (who started Priest out peddling reefers when just a lad) is talked into the game, and he
too loses his life to Priest's bid for freedom. Priest's partner
weighs the odds and sells him out.

Moving fast, Priest penetrates the white coke hierarchy,
takes out a first-class Mafia contract on Mr. Big to cover his

bet, unmasks Mr. Big as a queer, and, with his money and his strong black woman, gets away clean. He turned up one movie later as a crusader for social justice in Africa, where life was simpler.

It was a delusion; but like most of the Staggerlee movies, *Superfly* had a soundtrack by an established soul singer, and in this case Curtis Mayfield's songs were not background, but criticism. (Mayfield had appeared in the picture singing in a dealers' bar, grinding out an attempted parody of his audience—but they thought it was a celebration.) His music worked against the fantasy, because to him one incident in the movie counted for more than all its triumphs: Freddie's dead. "Pushin' dope for *the Man!*" he sang, incredulous and disgusted. The movie hadn't even slowed to give Freddie an epitaph, but Mayfield clearly aimed his song at the hero as well.*

Superfly had a black director, Gordon Parks, Jr.; there was a surface ghetto realism, and there were touches of ambiguity, but the movie had Hollywood in its heart, and that was enough to smother everything else. Most of the pictures that followed simply shuffled *Superfly* clichés, but they kept coming.

Young black men began to imitate the movies, and real life put on its own endings. In the tiny black town of Brooklyn, Illinois, the mayor deputized a hustler named Bollinger to run a militant out of town (Priest had only contempt for black politics—not violent enough, he said, he'd deal with the Man his own way). With the competition out of business, Bollinger took over; he ran the town the way Capone ran Cairo, until another black man named Skinner—lacking the hustler's long coat and broad-brimmed hat—faced him down. Anyone doubting they had been to the movies can read the dialogue.

---

* Interestingly, these lyrics were not in the movie, even though the backing track was. Mayfield held off until the film was in the theaters, then wrote the words, released the record, and so took on the picture on his own turf: the radio. You could say he chickened out, and you could also say he was very smart.

" 'I guess you're lookin' for me,' said Bollinger calmly.

" 'That's right,' replied Skinner. 'I'm lookin' for you, man. I know you've heard I'm the police chief now.'

" 'I'm not giving up a goddamn thing,' said Bollinger."

Skinner shot Bollinger dead; then the hustler's girl stood over him. She said: "He lived like a man. He died like one too." *

The story out of Detroit was worse. A group of three young men—determined, like the heroes of so many new black movies, to clean the smack out of their neighborhood—began to lean hard on dealers and junkies. They were armed and violent. A run-in with STRESS (Stop Robberies Enjoy Safe Streets), the killer squad of the Detroit police, which the three men suspected had ties with the heroin trade, seemed inevitable. When it was over two cops were dead and the vigilantes were on the run. The youngest was caught in Detroit, and survived; his two comrades were tailed to Atlanta, set up, and executed. And all the while, in uptown movie houses across the country, Staggerlee killed and fucked and killed and fucked and white sheriff near died of envy and Billy died to let Stack kill and fuck another day.

One movie was different, but it never found its audience, not among blacks, or whites either. *Across 110th Street* (directed by Barry Shear, who earlier made *Wild in the Streets*, the most paradoxical youth exploitation picture; written by Luther Davis) looked enough like all the others to make it easy for nearly all critics to dismiss it. The film was almost unbelievably violent, which gave reviewers license to attack it. It began with the same clichés everyone else used, but intensified them mercilessly. It pumped so much pressure into the world of the new black movies that it blew that world apart.

Three black men—Jamaica, Superflake, and Dry Clean—murder a pack of black and white Mafia bankers and make off with the week's take for all of Harlem. They don't steal because they hate the mob; they steal because they want

---

* Dialogue quoted from "High Noon after Nightfall," *Time*, December 17, 1973.

the money. A Mafia lieutenant—played by Tony Franciosa—is sent out to bring back the money and execute the thieves, knowing full well he can forget his future if he fails. Anthony Quinn plays a bought cop caught in the middle. He has to take the case straight to make his pension, and a new black cop is keeping an eye on him, but he has to do it without losing his payoff—or his life—to the Mafia hirelings who control his district: a black man who runs a taxi company and looks like Fats Domino risen from the swamp of evil, and his bodyguard, a Staggerlee who watches over the entire film with the cold eyes of someone who sold his soul to the devil the day he was old enough to know he had one.

You paid for every bit of violence, perhaps because the film refused its audience the pleasures of telling the good guys from the bad guys, and because the violence was so ugly it exploded the violence of the genre. It wasn't gratuitous, but it wasn't "poetic" either. Every character seemed alive, with motives worth reaching for, no matter how twisted they might turn out to be; every character (save for Taxi Man and his gunman) fled through the story scared half out of his wits, desperate for space, for a little more time, for one more chance.

The thieves speed away from the litter of corpses, divide up the money, and go into hiding. Superflake is too proud of himself to stay holed up; good times are what it was all for, right? His best hustler's clothes—tasteless Sly Stone, but gaudy—have been hanging for this moment. Down at the best whorehouse in Harlem Superflake has a dozen women and he's bragging.

Franciosa picks up the scent, and with Taxi Man's Staggerlee at his side, his eyes glazing over with a sadism that masks his own terror, he rips Superflake out of the whorehouse bar. When Quinn finds Superflake crucified, castrated, and skinned alive, you realize that along with no heroes, this movie may offer no way out. It was made to take your sleep.

Jamaica and Dry Clean pass the word and panic; they know that Superflake had to finger them. Dry Clean shoves

his money into a clothes bag from his shop and hails a cab for
Jersey. The driver spots the markings on the bag, radios back
to Taxi Man, and delivers Dry Clean straight to Franciosa at
110th Street—the border of Harlem and the one line the
movie never crosses. Dry Clean breaks away; Franciosa traps
him on a roof, ties a rope to his leg, and hangs him over a
beam, dangling him into space. Staggerlee holds the rope; his
eyes show nothing as he watches the white man torture the
black. If Dry Clean talks, they say, they won't kill him; he is
so scared he believes them. He talks, and the rope shoots
over the side.

Jamaica and his girl meet in his wretched apartment
(there is a little torn-out picture of Martin Luther King taped
to the wall, a gray reminder of some other time) to plan an
escape, or a better hideout. And in one of the most extraordinary scenes in any American movie, a death's-head reversal
of every warm close-up you have ever seen, Jamaica begins
to talk—about green hills and a blue sky; about quiet, rest,
peace of mind; about going home. He has only killed nine
men to get there. His face is scarred by smallpox; his eyes
try hard to explain. Jamaica goes on; you don't hear him; the
camera stays in tight. Every few seconds his whole face
shudders, seems almost to shred, as a ghastly, obscenely
complex twitch climbs from his jaw to his temple, breaks,
and starts up again.

It is the visual equivalent of that last song on *Riot*,
"Thank You for talkin' to me Africa," another reach for a
home that isn't there. Like Sly's music, the scene is unbearably long, it makes you want to run, but each frame like each
note deepens the impact, until everything else in the world
has been excluded and only one artistic fact remains. Jamaica's twitch traces the fear of every character in the movie;
it is a map of the ambiguities the other movies so easily shot
away; and in this film, it is most of all the other side of
Staggerlee's face, which never moves.

Finally, Franciosa, Quinn, and their troops converge on
the abandoned tenement where Jamaica and his girl are hiding. Taxi Man gets word of the showdown. "Wanna watch,"

says Staggerlee. "No," says Taxi Man. "I know how it's gonna turn out."

A bullet cuts through the girl's forehead and pins her to the wall behind Jamaica. She stays on camera, standing up dead, a blank ugliness on her face. When Jamaica turns to see her you can feel the life go out of him, but he keeps shooting. Franciosa is killed; the cops take over. Jamaica flees to the roof with his gun and his bag of money, still firing. He kills more. Staggerlee, sent to cover for Taxi Man, watches from another rooftop. Jamaica falls, and in the only false moment in the picture, flings his money down to children in a playground. Staggerlee sets up a rifle, takes aim on Quinn, who has proved himself too weak to be worth the mob's time, and kills him.

In one way, then, this movie was like all the others: Staggerlee wins. But this time, the audience was not given the benefit of any masks; they had to take him as he came, and they were not about to pay money to see that.

Almost always, there is a retreat once something like the truth is out. Audiences respond to that moment of clarity, but they only want so much of it; scared of their own vision or not trusting their audiences, artists grow timid and hedge their bets. Follow hard rock with a ballad, follow a threat with reassurance. The O'Jays and their producers, Kenny Gamble and Leon Huff, put as much distance between themselves and "Back Stabbers" as they could with "Love Train" (the tough "992 Arguments" had died); the Temptations, as usual, copied themselves with the horrendous "Ghetto" ("Hmmm, life sure is tough here in the ghetto") and turned art into schlock in record time. The perfectly named Brighter Side of Darkness got a hit with "Love Jones," and made dope romantic. The restraint of the Chi-Lites became so stylized they went off the deep end with "We Need [Law and] Order." The music seemed to lose its edge; it went bland, as if to prove that the only alternative to Stagolee was an imitation of white middle-class respectability.

At the core of the attempt to make artistic and commercial sense out of the world *Riot* revealed—and in terms of black music, almost invented—was a new triumph of black capitalism and controlled craftsmanship, a kind of poetic efficiency. Most of the records discussed here were created by producers, not groups, and while the producers would take virtually any risk to break onto the charts, their real ambition seemed to be to stay on the charts without taking any risks at all.

The team of Gamble and Huff, working out of Philadelphia, epitomized the style. Their records featured beautifully intricate hooks, a sophisticated blend of R&B force and mainstream strings, and irresistible internal riffs that stood up under hundreds of listenings, which meant that when the records got on the radio they stayed there. The Spinners' "I'll Be Around" (produced by Gamble-Huff disciple Thom Bell) featured an up-and-down guitar line that could have carried a French lesson without losing any of its commercial force. But cultural force was something else again.

The new black hit factories—Willie Mitchell in Memphis with Al Green (who found his voice in the gap between Pickett's arrogance and the Chi-Lites' weakness), Lambert and Potter in Los Angeles with the Four Tops (whose "Keeper of the Castle" affirmed the family over hustling—or politics), and Gamble-Huff—spoke of consistency and stability as the crucial values. After that one burst of unity and vitality (which, if we call it a fad, will tell us how good fads can be), black music drifted back into something like a parallel of the most conventional black reality (save for Stevie Wonder and Marvin Gaye, who produced their records with their own money, and kept moving). This was a limit not only on violence and excess, but on real cultural ambition: a black version of "benign neglect." Daniel Moynihan thought if you removed the promise you would remove the threat; here, the threat submerged, but so did the promise, because the paradox that gives *Riot* its tension is that Sly knows that Staggerlee holds the key to vitality as well as disaster.

What makes *Riot* truly bleak, after all, is not that Sly

ever resists the role Staggerlee has carved out, not that he shrinks from its momentum, but that he cannot survive it. And it was this truth that made *Riot* so different from all the other records, no matter how good they were. The producers' singers moved easily from music that could have made history to music that merely reflected it; many even lost the energy that in popular music can usually be substituted for vision. They drifted, like all cultural reflections, into accommodation, into music for a new normalcy.

"An insufferable deadness had invaded our lives," Frank Kermode has written of the thirties, though his words do well enough for our own time. "We needed . . . to be violently stirred into life . . . intolerable social constraints grew daily upon us."

Nixon's rule made those lines seem quite familiar; their meaning has seeped down into our bones, like a secret second nature. It is a debilitating secret to which those who keep it can barely admit, because, in spite of all the clichés about how nothing can ever imprison an idea or a dream, dreams can be imprisoned inside those who once held to them.

Those dreams are worn down and dissolved as the world mocks them by its versions of reality; they are dissolved because the one who once felt alive because of them must live in that world. He or she does not conform to it, necessarily, but adjusts to it in a hundred ways every day: with every thought he turns away from, with every word she does not speak, with every fantasy of violence, liberation, or death that fades into the nightly dreams one does not understand and does not much want to.

Too much war and too much public crime has poisoned the country to be easily put to rest by any kind of reform or vengeance. There is simply too much to forget. Our politics have robbed the good words of ethics of their meaning; an impenetrable official venality has robbed the good ideas of the last few years of theirs. What, in the sixties, looked like a chance to find new forms of political life, has been replaced by a flight to privacy and cynicism; the shared culture that grew out of a love affair with the Beatles has collapsed (not without their help) into nostalgia and crackpot religion. The revisionists have already gone to work on the last decade—which was, no matter how smug, self-righteous, or naïve, a time of greater cultural and political freedom than most of us will likely know again. Those who, in Leslie Fiedler's words, "lived the mythic life of their generation," those who made it and were remade by it, can now hardly remember it.

Throughout the years of Nixon's ascendancy the *New Yorker* opened most issues with a page of unsigned commentary that tried to see through each week's dose of lies—the obvious lies told by those in power, and the more subtle, pathetic lies told by those who twisted to escape the first. It was something better than comforting to read that commentary every week, and something worse. There was satisfaction in knowing that someone had the will and the talent to work to find the truth no matter how pointless the effort seemed; there was a queasy disgust in knowing that someone else had to do that work for me. Whether my own talents were not up to the job, or my will too weak, didn't much matter. It was too easy to lose touch with rage, with a sense of what is good and evil, to lose touch with the idea that it is worth something to make, and try to live out, such a distinction.

These are politics of the freeze-out. They turn into a culture of seamless melancholy with the willful avoidance of anything—a book, some photographs, a record, a movie, even a newspaper—that one suspects might produce really deep feeling. Raw emotions must be avoided when one knows they will take no shape but that of chaos.

Within such a culture there are many choices: cynicism, which is a smug, fraudulent kind of pessimism; the sort of camp sensibility that puts all feeling at a distance; or culture that reassures, counterfeits excitement and adventure, and is safe. A music as broad as rock 'n' roll will always come up with some of each, and probably that's just as it should be.

Sometimes, though, you want something more: work so intense and compelling you will risk chaos to get close to it,

music that smashes through a world that for all of its desolation may be taking on too many of the comforts of familiarity. Sly created a moment of lucidity in the midst of all the
obvious negatives and the false, faked hopes; he made his
despair mean something in the midst of a despair it is all too
easy to think may mean nothing at all. He was clearing away
the cultural and political debris that seemed piled up in
mounds on the streets, in the papers, in the record stores; for
all of the darkness of what he had to say and how he said it,
his music had the kind of strength and the naked honesty
that could make you want to start over.

A QUIET REBELLION

Sly clearly could not push *Riot* much farther, not without releasing a whole album of silence; and not, perhaps,
without losing the audience he had worked to win. *Fresh*, the
album that did follow, in 1973, showed Sly clicking his heels
for Richard Avedon's camera, and the songs did their best to
keep up with the title and the cover. "There's a mickie in the
tastin' of disaster," was the first line of *Fresh*—Sly's instinctive paraphrase of Nietzsche's belief that he who gazes into
the abyss will find the abyss looking back; that he who looks
too long at monsters may well become one.

The music was good, but it lacked the fire of *Riot*, the
tiny explosions of a bass riff or a horn part stuttering along
vocal lines, ambushing words and transforming emotions.
Save for "Que Sera, Sera," which Sly and Rosie Stone
turned into a blues (this following months of bizarre rumors
of a romance between Sly and Doris Day—"*Riot* or no *Riot*,"
said a friend, "he hasn't lost his sense of humor"), the music
and the singing lacked risk. Most critics applauded Sly's step
toward "a more positive" stance, but there was little on *Fresh*
to prove that it was more than a stance.

Worse, the complexity of Sly's music, from *New Thing*
to *Riot*—the tension between the individual and the group,
the tension of politics orchestrated in personal terms—was
overtaken by a straightforward presentation of Sly's role, and

the group now seemed little more than his servant. The album's hit, "If You Want Me to Stay," was a conventional comment on the ambiguities of stardom, and there were too many references to Sly's coke habit (switched to pep, he said), the time lag between LP's, and the like. Such subjects may have been meant to work outside the limited context of Sly's personal dilemma, but they did not connect. Still, there was "Que Sera"—and the album could be seen as an attempt to figure out how it would feel to live with honesty and energy in a country that had forced the recognitions of *Riot*, but that had more to show those who knew how to look.

A tour followed the release of *Fresh*—the first Sly and the Family Stone had made in two years (two original members had quit and been replaced)—and the show I saw in Berkeley in the summer of 1973 was both interesting and a fraud. It was Sly's homecoming concert, and he presented it as such; his last in the Bay Area had been a post-*Riot* shambles, with Sly walking off the stage after a few bitter minutes, shouting something about how the audience couldn't handle what he had to give them. He had played the Cow Palace then, which holds 16,000; the Berkeley Community Theatre was nearly full, but it seats only about 3,000.

Sly celebrated trumpet player Cynthia Robinson's birthday by bringing her mother out on stage; he talked quietly about his parents, smiling broadly, trying to get across how appropriate it seemed to him that his mother had given him the ideas for some of his best songs. That was interesting, and moving. It was the music that was a fraud.

The playing was mostly mechanical; as Dave Marsh, who walked out on a similar show on Long Island put it, the songs were "a rehash of older, more frivolous material . . . also a rehash of the part of [the past] which is most insidious, bypassing the strength of songs like 'Everybody Is a Star' and 'Everyday People' for the relatively empty 'Stand!' and 'M'Lady.' " There was not a single tune from *Riot*; the only performance that had conviction was a stunning "Que Sera," which for a moment almost saved the show; and the concert ended, as all Sly's concerts ended back in the Woodstock days, with "I Want to Take You Higher," which was always facile and is now a stupid lie. It wasn't even an effective one; the audience probably wanted to go farther more than they wanted to be taken higher, and the old piece of frenzy fizzled out in three or four minutes, as if neither the audience nor the band had much heart for the deception.

"It's one thing to change on record, in private," Dave Marsh said to me when we compared notes on the tour. "It's something else to look all those people in the face and tell them the good old days are gone." Maybe so. Perhaps, if Sly had woven a new show out of *Riot* and *Fresh*, the next tour would have had him playing to empty seats. Neither record includes much of an obvious crowd pleaser, and something had already brought Sly down from the big arena to the theater.

Most of all, though, Sly seemed eager to say that *Riot* had been a bad dream best forgotten. But if the weakness and failure of nerve of the concert I saw is what really grows out of *Riot*, that only means that the world Sly discovered and made real on that record is as debilitating as he said it was.

Whether the retreat is one of vision, as I think it is in Sly's case, or of craftsmanship and accounting, as with the black record producers, Sly's truest work has its own momentum ("Never trust the artist, trust the tale," D. H. Lawrence wrote, noting that American artists, because they cannot escape their audiences, are always desperate to cover up whatever they reveal); Sly's work penetrates into black politics just as it changed black music and haunts black movies. The turnaround of the Black Panther party— from the politics of violent rhetoric and armed self-defense to the politics of elections and alliance with the black church— parallels the retreat of the black producers and of *Fresh*. The Panther retreat may produce the same kind of guarded success; it may also tell us how necessary such retreats are. But it is worth remembering that Eldridge Cleaver and Huey Newton fought a war over this change in politics—a very strange war.

After a murderous shootout provoked by the Oakland police in 1968, Cleaver was to be returned to prison as a parole violator. He was willing to stand trial, but he was convinced he would be killed in jail; he would not go back. And there was more to it. He told Gene Marine:

When I went back to prison before, it didn't matter, you know? Nobody cared about me anyway, I was in the same prison, you know? The prison of being alone. Out or in, it didn't matter. But this time—this time I've found something, since I've been in the movement and working with all these cats. I've found people who really dig me, people I really dig. People care about me, people *like* me. I've never had that before, never at all. I can't go back in there now and leave that out here. I've got friends—I've got friends for the first time in my life, and man, I just don't think I can do without that anymore.*

Pushed into a corner, Cleaver jumped bail, escaped to Cuba, and eventually set up headquarters in Algeria. There, if the Panther newspaper is accurate, he terrorized his wife, took a new mistress, murdered a rival, and tumbled into fantasies of sweeping across America at the head of a guerilla gang. He denounced Newton, tried to seize the party from exile, and ordered his followers on the East Coast and in Los Angeles to put his vision into practice. The war for the party commenced; bodies began to turn up.

Newton and Seale had founded the Black Panthers (drawing up their statement of aims and demands while playing Dylan's "Ballad of a Thin Man" over and over) as a local self-defense organization, but the idea was irresistible and soon there were Panther chapters all over the country. As Bobby Seale says so well, Staggerlee was crucial to these new politics. A killer, a thief, setting himself up against his own people, plundering them to get what he wanted—they

---

* From Gene Marine, *The Black Panthers* (New York: Signet, 1969).

began there. They seized the fact of criminal violence, and tried to turn that fact into a political threat. Since no one doubted the fact was real, the threat was taken seriously.

Newton's idea came down to a new kind of power, growing out of the barrel of a gun that was good only as long as it didn't have to be fired, because once it was fired, the other side was going to win. The Panthers walked that fine edge, threatened by their own rhetoric, which called for actions they could not afford to take; their rhetoric won them some of the space necessary for action, but the police also forced them to live up to it. Police raids on chapter after chapter decimated the party; many of those who were left were junkies, hoods, and spies. Both Newton and Seale had been off the street while murder raps, ultimately tossed out, were hung over their heads; the party had lost its center. Either it changed drastically or it died, and once Newton got out of jail he moved to quiet it down and clean it out.

Cleaver, a confessed rapist who had spent nine years in California prisons, had been valuable to the Panthers not only because he was a superb recruiter and a good theorist, but because their politics were rooted in the streets. Newton's genius had been to bring Staggerlee into politics and there transform him; that also meant Newton had to risk him. Newton's careful arrogance and perfect nerve under the guns of San Francisco cops had inspired Cleaver to join the party, but Newton is a man of tremendous self-discipline; the demands his politics made on all party members were in some ways too much of a reflection of his own unquestionable ability to live up to them. Staggerlee was a mask Newton could put on at will; Cleaver was not always under control, and the myth held more traps for him. But he could take it farther, even as politics: he really was Staggerlee, and the explosive threat of his performance was vital to his role in the party.

Cleaver's worth lay in his ability to balance that role between his exploitation of it and it of him. In Algeria, cut off from the people who had changed his life, that balance shattered absolutely, and his old nemesis roared back with a vengeance. He had been a political man whose politics were rooted in a vitality and rage that had once come out in crime, but he emerged a criminal once again, out for blood.

There were no politics. The balance broke down because the political space necessary to it had been taken away, and what was left was murder, not for a five-dollar Stetson hat, but the old story all the same. Cleaver fell back to Staggerlee; he went all the way into his hands, and it may be that the only way he will ever get out will be with the epitaph John Hurt gave to his Stag-o-lee, the cruelest epitaph of all:

Standing at the gallows
Head way up high
At twelve o'clock they killed him
They was all glad to see him die.

And that is the context of *Riot*.

These events and Sly's understanding of his own career came together, as most likely they never will again, to form a music of extraordinary depth and power. Sly questioned his earlier music and our love for it; he implied that whatever the beauty of "Everybody Is a Star," that may have been only another way of saying that everybody is a mark. Sly's work was deeply personal and inescapably political; innovative and tough in its music; literate and direct in its words; a parody of the past and an unflinching statement about the present that its present has hardly contained.

Sly returned to the pop arena at a time when black music had remade itself on terms he had defined; he damned those terms and invented new ones. He recognized the expectations of his audience, and moved to subvert them.

If after a time he allowed his audience to subvert his work, or simply played on and followed where his music led, *There's a riot goin' on* stands as a quiet, bitter, open act of rebellion. It is a rebellion the resolution of which depends as much on the audience as it does on Sly Stone, and a rebellion which as music or politics is not likely to work itself out for a long time. And if that musical insurrection can be captured in a line, it is probably a remark Josef von Sternberg once made: "Obviously, it is easier to kill than to create."

RANDY NEWMAN
Every Man Is Free

I believe . . . that to be very poor and very beautiful is most probably a moral failure much more than an artistic success. Shakespeare would have done well in any generation because he would have refused to die in a corner; he would have taken the false gods and made them over; he would have taken the current formulae and forced them into something lesser men thought them incapable of. Alive today he would undoubtedly have written and directed motion pictures, plays, and God knows what. Instead of saying, "This medium is not good," he would have used it and made it good. If some people called some of his work cheap (which some of it is), he wouldn't have cared a rap, because he would know that without some vulgarity there is no complete man. He would have hated refinement, as such, because it is always a withdrawal, and he was much too tough to shrink from anything.

RAYMOND CHANDLER, 1949,
from *Raymond Chandler Speaking*

POP

Chandler's statement, written in the midst of his failed attempts to do good work in Hollywood, tells us how completely he understood what it means to be an American
artist. The momentum of democracy (of equality) (of
conformity) that powers American life does not, as Tocqueville thought it might, bleed all the life out of culture; it has
created a wholly new kind, with all sorts of new risks and
possibilities. At its worst it can do just what Tocqueville expected, and there is always a good example around: *The
Sound of Music* ("The audience," Pauline Kael wrote bitterly,
"becomes the lowest common denominator of feeling—
a sponge."); *Love Story;* the pop group "America" (Tocqueville smiling in his grave at the elegance of their conceit).
There is, though, Chandler also wrote, "a vast difference between writing down to the public (something which always
flops in the end) and doing what you want to do in a form
that the public has learned to accept."

There have been great American artists who have
worked beyond the public's ability to understand them easily, but none who have condescended to the public—none
who have not hoped, no matter how secretly, that their work
would lift America to heaven, or drive a stake through its
heart. This is a democratic desire (not completely unrelated
to the all-time number one democratic desire for endless
wealth and fame), and at its best it is an impulse to whole-
ness, an attempt not to deny diversity, or to hide from it, but
to discover what it is that diverse people can authentically
share. It is a desire of the artist to remake America on his or
her own terms.

This impulse powers the strongest popular artists as it
powers pop culture itself. It is an urge to novelty and necessity; it exhausts most talents with terrific speed and goes on
to something else.

The inability of the vital American artist to be satisfied
with a cult audience, no matter how attentive, goes right

back to the instinctive perception that whatever else America might be, it is basically *big;* that unless you are doing something big, you are not doing anything at all. The Beatles ("those imaginary Americans," Leslie Fiedler called them), madly in love with American popular culture and living out their own American dream, increased their ambitions as they got closer to their goals: first they wanted to be Eddie Cochran, then they decided they could be Elvis, and then they were on their own. They understood, finally, that they could affect the lives of kids all over the world. The fact that they succeeded tells us how much big pop ambitions are worth; everyone who might conceivably read this book has been changed for the better because of what the Beatles did.

When it is alive to its greatest possibilities—to disturb, provoke, and divide an entire society, thus exciting and changing a big part of society—pop says that the game of a limited audience is not really worth playing. It is as contradictory and as American as a politician who can't stand dissent, who gets and keeps his power by dividing the country and turning the country against itself, and then wants everyone to love him.

This is not simply a matter of the depth of the artist's idea, anymore than the contours of American history really turn on how well Andrew Jackson understood macroeconomics. What matters is the depth and breadth of response an artist can evoke in an audience, and whether or not that artist is really challenging the audience and not simply playing off its fears and weaknesses. In the case of someone extraordinary like Elvis Presley, or the Beatles, this process becomes its own idea—and a pretty deep one. But who knows if "Eight days a week is not enough to show I love you" is a deep idea, or a trivial one, or any kind of idea at all? And who cares? The joy of pop is that it can deliver you from such questions by its immediacy and provoke them by its impact.

Rock 'n' roll is a combination of good ideas dried up by fads, terrible junk, hideous failings in taste and judgment, gullibility and manipulation, moments of unbelievable clarity and invention, pleasure, fun, vulgarity, excess, novelty and utter enervation, all summed up nowhere so well as on Top 40 radio, that ultimate rock 'n' roll version of America. As one writer put it, presenting a classic segue of a pimple commercial right into Bob Dylan's "George Jackson": "Right on."

We fight our way through the massed and leveled collective safe taste of Top 40, just looking for a little something we can call our own. But when we find it and jam the radio to hear it again it isn't just ours—it is a link to thousands of others who are sharing it with us. As a matter of a single song this might mean very little; as culture, as a way of life, you can't beat it.

And what about Randy Newman, who is, unfortunately, somewhere else entirely (that is, buried on an occasional FM radio or in the back of someone's record collection)? "All combined," Newman is fond of saying, "my records have sold as many copies as James Taylor's last album sold in Des Moines. But I'm fantastically wealthy, so nothing matters." Spoken like a pop master: only money counts. But obviously if his public failure didn't matter Newman wouldn't bother to complain about it. To the degree that he knows his work is good he will want to use it to affect everyone in sight. And more than that, a singer whose songs contain an astonishing affection for every American from the middle-class couple wasting away in Florida to the rapist preying on their daughter cannot be satisfied with the attention of an elite, of critics and a few more, because a cult contradicts the best impulses of his work.

NEWMAN'S AMERICA, I

He is, all in all, one of the strangest performers to emerge in rock 'n' roll since the heady days of *Sgt. Pepper*. Born in New Orleans in 1944, and raised in Southern California, Newman was heir to both a family movie music dynasty (the most famous member is his Oscar-winning Uncle Alfred, whose credits are ubiquitous on late night TV), and along with everyone else his age, to rock 'n' roll. Fats Domino was his man.

Newman took up the piano, was classically trained at UCLA, and got a job with a music publishing company, hacking out songs for money. He made a lot, as he says, but since he didn't much like the way other people did his stuff, he began recording it himself.

Since the release of his first album, in 1968, Newman's singing has shifted from a style that could be called Jewish to one that can only be called black. He has become, as his producer Lenny Waronker likes to call him, "The King of the Suburban Blues Singers."

What Newman has taken from black singers is not what most rock 'n' roll singers have taken: assertiveness, aggression, melancholy, sexual power. His somnambulant personality determined his choice of a lazy, blurred sound, where words slide into each other, where syllables are not bitten off, but just wear out and dissolve. The blues practice of dropping a key word off the end of a line, to hint at ominous sexual mastery or knowledge too strong to put into words, becomes with Newman a wonderful throwaway, a surface lack of seriousness that at first hides, and after a few listenings intensifies, a sense of Newman's commitment to his material. It is as if Randy's real blues hero wasn't Howlin' Wolf, but Stepin Fetchit—and as if Randy had a pretty good idea of what secrets were hidden in the shuffle.

The movie music side of Newman's songs grows out of a tradition so well absorbed by generations of film fans that by now it seems completely American, regardless of its classy European antecedents. Listening to Newman, irrespective of the lyric of any particular song, you might see John Wayne in Monument Valley, Charles Boyer in a final clinch. Chances are it won't be anything so specific; you will hear a hundred movies whose titles you just cannot recall.

Newman's music is stronger than any to be found in those movies; his music is from a movie no one ever made, the score that was never quite written. It is everything that movie music aspired to, richer on his records because he is making records, not movies.

He uses the familiarity of the music to set us in the moods and situations the music automatically calls up; we respond in predictable ways to the music, and as we do, Newman's words and his singing pull us in other directions, or shift the story just enough to make it new. The music defines for us the way we want it to be, the way the movies have told us it is, and then Newman tells us how it looks to him. The tension that comes is almost never facile, because the movie dreams the music evokes are real to him too, and because he loves the music itself. It's not merely a device, but at the heart of the matter; not just half of his strategy, but half of his aesthetic.

When I saw Newman perform one night, I was startled by how many of his songs mattered to me. I was a casual fan, but after each number another came into my head that I had to hear. I hadn't been part of a rock 'n' roll audience that laughed so well since Dylan's tours in the mid-sixties (we forget how funny crowds found "Desolation Row," and how right they were).

Newman could put on the chill, too. He told an old man he ought to give it up and die; he made you feel, with "God's Song," that life is indeed a joke, and that all the laughs belong to its Author. Newman did his Southern California beach song—which must derive, somehow, from "Surf City"—about a girl who has fled from her graduation dance to offer herself to the gears of the beach-cleaning machine, which scoops her up along with the beer cans, candy wrappers, and condoms, like a California teenager hungry after a swim. He sang some of his easy-target tunes, like "Burn On," about the firetrap Cuyahoga River. Best of all was "Davy the Fat Boy," sung in the voice of "Davy's only friend," who has made a deathbed promise to the fat boy's parents to take care of the freak and keeps it by putting him into a sideshow. It reminded me of that unbearable climactic scene in Von Sternberg's *Blue Angel,* where Emil Jannings—

the fallen professor forced to stand before his ex-students imitating a chicken—holds his body like one enormous club-foot, his face in a frozen mask of terror and madness, and produces a squawk that can shrivel the soul. As Davy's friend orders him to begin "his famous fat boy dance," Newman leaned back from his piano for a little music, letting the audience see the scene as he did; and as the song ended, one of its lines echoed with a gruesome kind of love: *"You've got to let this fat boy in your life!"*

Newman had asked for requests, and I yelled out for "Davy" because I vaguely remembered being moved by it some years before. If I had remembered it better I probably would have kept my mouth shut.

Except in its weaker moments, this was not satire. It was a whole world, irresistibly funny and extremely uncomfortable, like W. C. Fields with the Hollywood varnish rubbed off. But the laughter was not smug, and the scariness of the songs was not smug on Newman's part, but simply presented as what he did for a living, what he did better than anyone else. When he sang his "Suzanne," the tale of a rapist picking a girl's number off a phone booth wall, you were caught up in the girl's terror and the rapist's lust. Both were real, both mattered.

The song was in the great rock 'n' roll tradition of answer records; in this case, an answer to Leonard Cohen's "Suzanne," the tender ballad of a river nymph, as erotic as a $500 book of pornographic etchings. Cohen's song screamed Poetry and Art; it virtually raped the listener with its mastery of the Higher Schlock. "This is not Leonard Cohen's 'Suzanne,' " Newman said. "It's on a somewhat lower moral plane, actually."

He said that with such modesty, fading his comment as if he were throwing away one of his best lines, that you had to think that sometimes, late at night when he couldn't make a song work, he might even believe it.

Newman is afraid of his sensibility, to the degree that he has to get it over to an audience. On one album he sang a version of that old Cotton Club favorite, all about the colored singing and dancing, summed up in the classic line: "That's why darkies were born." He sang it straight—beautifully in fact—and you just couldn't tell. Where was he? Or more to the point, where did he put you? Here he was, a struggling singer whose only possible audience would be urbane, liberal rock 'n' roll fans, and he was unveiling . . . the charms of racism. He would not perform the song in front of an audience: "I was afraid someone might beat me up," he said. The night I saw him he sang his own "Yellow Man"; apparently no one had told him he was singing in a Chinese movie theater in the middle of the biggest Chinese community in the U.S.A. Or maybe he thought his height would save him. His distance from his material is always a bit uncertain.

If Newman's songs are the result of Southern R&B and an after-the-ball cul-de-sac of Hollywood movie music, they also grow out of a cul-de-sac pure and simple: Los Angeles, the Edge of America, the City of the Future. As an Angeleno, Randy Newman is something like Nathanael West on the verge of having a good time in spite of himself.

West thought Southern California was where America came to make its last stand, to reach for the last chance; inevitably betraying those hopes, Los Angeles became, to West and to Chandler and others, the place where those now resentful Americans would turn to fantasies of revenge, violence, and death. Looking for rebirth, dreamers found only that they felt older than they had seemed at home. These discrepancies—presented over and over again, in Chandler's *Big Sleep* and *Farewell, My Lovely*, in *Sunset Boulevard*, from a Holy Roller church in downtown LA to the Kirke Order of Dog Blood roaming the desert—created, against the backdrop of an industry based on the inexhaustibility of banal fantasy, a curious sort of moral ambivalence, a state of mind equally capable of producing commonplace boredom and uncommon crime. This ambivalence, I think, grows out of an attempt to come to terms with that sense of discrepancy: an aggressive and in many ways positive denial of the need for roots, a perception that everything that is old must be covered in neon and sandstone before anyone can be really free.

Once this is accomplished, of course, there is little left
on which to base an idea of what that freedom could be for.
People improvise; nothing seems completely out of the question. Some can endure, and use, this kind of freedom. Some
can't; they lust after authority, and there are always too
many to provide it: pimps, the Children of God, organized
crime, weird figures of extraordinary charisma walking the
street devouring souls.

Such a story is familiar enough. The same scared and
lustful Americans who changed their names and killed for
new lives in Chandler's books crawl through Ross Mac-
Donald's; the rubber horse clumped at the bottom of a
swimming pool in *Day of the Locust* was dumped into a bed in
The Godfather. But because such a vision of Los Angeles
pushed West and Chandler into a queer sort of Puritanism,
they never noticed something else that matters about Southern California: its incredible exuberance, the talent of Southern Californians for enjoying themselves. It's a little too easy
to look at the movement of the place and call it hysterical,
too easy to quote Thoreau and pronounce that "the mass of
men lead lives of quiet desperation," and think that you have
told the whole truth. Put the Beach Boys of the early sixties
up against West, and *he* sounds hysterical; there isn't a hint
of their warmth and friendliness in his "definitive" book, but
no one can tell me that "Fun, Fun, Fun" is a lie. The Beach
Boys don't wipe out Chandler's world, but they enlarge it;
and if finally the Beach Boys held hands with Charlie Manson as the sixties ended, that only meant that they were
as vulnerable to the LA of West and Chandler as they
might have been to the Beach Boys'. You can say that the
energy and pride the Beach Boys found cruising the strip in
"I Get Around" was never meant to last, that it hardened
and cracked like cheap Santa Monica stucco when they found
out it was not enough and embraced the authority of the
dread Maharishi. You can write their delight off to sun and
money, but its value is still strong, still full of life. They felt
free to enjoy themselves in every way imaginable, and that

RANDY NEWMAN: EVERY MAN IS FREE 121

freedom from tradition, the freedom to invent, cuts deeply
and all across the board. There's no way to separate the
Beach Boys' smiling freedom from Manson's knife. Because
this new world is a rich one, Randy Newman, as an artist,
can work in it—he can laugh well and realize his fantasies of
violence and death. "Suzanne" really is the other side of
"Surf City"—or part of it.

Nathanael West was an Easterner; in spite of the fact
that "West" was a name he chose, he was never at home in
California—he was unable to imagine that anyone could be.
But many Southern Californians, were they to be told that
murder was the price of a way of life based on fun and fantasy, might still pay it. Newman accepts the deal because LA
provides the indolence that suits his personality, and the risk
that suits his art.

As an American artist, Newman represents some kind
of opening up of the classic archetype of the keeper of the
American imagination; and this too has a lot to do with the
peculiar freedoms of Los Angeles. Most American critics—
Nathaniel Hawthorne, say—throw up all sorts of horror and
pretend they do so only to condemn it. If West, through his
transplanted Easterner hero Todd Hackett, admitted com-
plicity in the LA nightmare, he had to satisfy the guilt such a
confession produced by destroying the city in a private apocalypse. Since Newman takes the moral shapelessness of his
hometown as a given, such fantasies would be ridiculously
melodramatic for him (they're more than a little ridiculous in
West, too). Like the Beach Boys, Newman builds freedom
out of what he's got; his humor is his version of the Beach
Boys' open naïveté; Newman laughs all around his world,
never at it. He is too at home in the place to feel guilty about
it, and anyway, he is a rock 'n' roll singer, and such attitudes
are not in the rock 'n' roll style. As with almost any popular
art, the moment rock 'n' roll tries to criticize something, it
becomes hopelessly self-righteous and stupid. It effectively
criticizes by rendering a situation with such immediacy, or
by affirming it to the point of such absurdity, that you can

no longer take it straight. That is why there is no tougher an-
tidrug song than the Velvet Underground's "Heroin," which
also risks creating new addicts.

Perhaps because of the ambivalence of Southern California, Newman can sing with the same insulated force. He
always writes, and what is harder, sings, in the voices of his
characters (except when they are women, but he will manage
that someday); no matter what grotesquerie is involved, he
does not sing about, he sings *as*. He feels this is dangerous,
which it is.

The imagination has fallen upon sorry days in post-
Beatles rock 'n' roll. Audiences are no longer used to the idea
that someone might make something up, create a persona and
effectively act it out, the way Chuck Berry and Bob Dylan
used to do. Audiences take everything literally, partly because sensitive personal confession, "honesty," and one-to-
one communication between the singer and whoever is listening is so attractive and reassuring in times when pop culture
and politics have lost their grander mythic dimensions, when
there are no artists and no politics to create community, and
every fan is thrown back on himself. Let me quote from a
typical ad for a troubled troubador, supposedly appropriate to
such times, presumably addressed to a troubled audience:

A few rare performers immediately become your friend the first
time you listen to them. Jonathan Edwards is about to become
your friend.

His songs are sensitive and warm, containing feelings and recollections which are sure to remind you of things in your life as well.

Jonathan Edwards. A new friend.

Courtesy Atlantic Records and Tapes, a Division of
Warner Communications, the friendly giant conglomerate.

Note the style of the ad. The cadence is wonderfully
smooth, caressing. The grammar is perfect, proper. The
voice is fatherly. The whole thing is absolutely unbearable.

But it's always fun to fill in the blanks. Let's say:

A few rare performers immediately become your friend the first time you listen to them. Mick Jagger is about to become your friend.

His songs are loud, brutal, and mean, containing feelings you like to pretend you do not have, recollections you would like to forget, and temptations that up until now you have wisely avoided.

Mick Jagger. A new friend.

Courtesy Rolling Stones Records and Tapes, distributed by Atlantic Records and Tapes, a Division of Warner Communications . . . rock 'n' roll may have no center, but it is nothing if not pluralistic. Newman records for the same company, naturally.

Rock 'n' roll is suffering from that old progressive school fallacy that says if what you write is about your own feelings, no one can criticize it. Truth telling is beginning to settle into a slough where it is nothing more than a pedestrian autobiography set to placid music framed by a sad smile on the album cover. This is about as liberating as thinking typecast movie stars are "really like" the roles they play. In many cases, though, this *has* come to be true in rock 'n' roll: singers have dispensed with imagination and songs are just pages out of a diary, with nothing in them that could give them a life of their own. A good part of the audience has lost its taste for songs that are about something out there in the world that the singer is trying to make real—usually by convincingly assuming the burden of that reality; replacing such songs are tunes that desperately deny the world by affirming the joys of solipsism. The success of this genre, represented by no one so well as James Taylor (along with the Rowan Brothers, Shawn Phillips, "America," and many others who will no doubt be forgotten by the time this book is published), only reminds me of an old philosophy student joke: "Solipsism is great, everyone should try it." That was, actually, the cornerstone of Nixon's Second Inaugural: "What can I do for myself?"

As the members of an audience grow older, they lead

less public lives. Their deepest affections shift from a multiplicity of friends—from the idea of friendship itself—to hus-
bands, wives, children; they exchange the noisy heteroge-
neity of school for the quiet homogeneity of a job. They
travel less freely, act less impulsively. If politics once meant
the fellowship of the street or the political community of a
campus for those who were lucky enough to have known
such things, more and more politics comes to mean voting—
the most solitary political act there is—or, at best, talk with a
few friends. A life that was fluid with possibility can solidify
into loneliness. One looks harder for the comforts of similar-
ity, and shies from the risks of diversity. It becomes easy to
think that nothing is new under the sun, or that if there is,
that one can no longer be a part of what is new. Too much
is settled.

   If at its best rock 'n' roll *is* a kind of public life
(" 'School's Out' is my favorite song and I've been out of
school for ten years!" my friend Simon Frith wrote. "What
does that mean?"), the cults that have fragmented an audience potentially as big and broad as America itself speak for a
less open life, as do the names of some successful post-
Beatles record companies: Island, Shelter, Haven, Chrysalis,
Asylum. Newman works against the limits of privacy, do-
mesticity, and solipsism with his fantasies and the role playing of his songs, and yet he lacks the obsessive pop ambition
to do more than that. Against the ideal community of music
he feels the emotional and imaginative poverty of an America
where men and women live estranged. But to drive the aesthetic of his fantasies into our heads would require him to
value his music more than anything else, to be on the road
constantly, to risk the collapse of his own family life, the
shelter of his own privacy, and even—after the rock 'n' roll
deaths of the last years I don't feel very romantic saying
this—his sanity and his life.

   "If I couldn't perform I'd give up," said Rod Stewart.
"It's not a question of the money side of it. I don't have to
work for the rest of my life. I don't want to. But not having
that ninety minutes up there anymore. Phew. I don't like to

think about it. It frightens me." And he went on: "I'm not willing to get married, because I think there are some people who just shouldn't get married. Elvis Presley should never have been married." He's not talking about the fall-off in a movie star's mail when he takes the sacred vows, but about the freedom to act in the midst of an audience. To be the kind of rock 'n' roll star Stewart is is to be like a politician who campaigns every moment of his life.

"In America," Newman sings, "every man is free/ To take care of his home, and his family." But no more than that, is the bitter, unsung line. And that may not be enough, even if it is all most of us see.

The constriction of vision produced by that kind of life points to why Newman is right when he feels it is risky to get up on stage and sing from inside the soul of a rapist. It's not just a matter of what people will think of Newman; what if someone heard the song and went looking for a girl to rape? Oh, ridiculous, we might say. That's like pretending someone could listen to the Beatles sing a good old rock 'n' roll fuck song like "Helter Skelter" and take it as a sign to go out and murder seven people.

Good art is always dangerous, always open-ended. Once you put it out in the world you lose control of it; people will fit it into their lives in all sorts of different ways. If so much of the rock 'n' roll of the post-Beatles era is closed off and one-dimensional, like the politics it serenades and reinforces, if the aesthetic of solipsism is freezing the imagination and our ability to respond openly, it is Newman's risk taking that makes him so valuable. As a rather lazy Southern Californian who just wants a good life with his wife and his kids, his sense of risk makes him shrink from his audience; but as an artist, that sense makes him reach for bigger risks.

NEWMAN'S AMERICA, II

To introduce his greatest song, Randy will tell a little story about a movie he almost made, with all the big stars: " 'Van,' that's Van Morrison, Elton, you know Elton. . . ."

The joke of this small-time rock 'n' roller up there with the big guns is more than obvious, but still funny. It would be even better if Newman made the whole thing up; it would somehow add to the charm of a song he will do later, "Lonely at the Top." It was written for Frank Sinatra, who, most likely thinking it was a slur on his need for a toupee, turned it down.

Up on stage Newman is still entranced by his tale of the silver screen stardom he might have had. Each singer will be given fifteen minutes to prepare and perform any kind of scenario he wants—do it all. And Newman has a wonderful idea. He will dress himself in a pure white planter's suit, white shoes, white hat—perhaps a red string tie, for color. As the camera zooms in for its opening shot, Newman is poised on the quarterdeck of a great clipper ship, testing his profile against the wind. What's he doing there? He's a recruiter for the slave trade, naturally.

His profile suitably established, Newman steps ashore. He is met by a hushed crowd of Africans, who hang on his every word. (Finally, Newman is a star.) He begins to sing, in a voice that combines the lazy drawl of the black man (something his audience will invent in their new land) with the gentle assurance of the holiest rabbi. The music, as Newman ultimately recorded it, comes in on the soundtrack (in the theater, Newman begins the song on his piano), and it is awesomely beautiful. And the slaver sings:

In America
You'll get food to eat
Won't have to run through the jungle
And scuff up your feet
You'll just sing about Jesus and drink wine all day
It's great to be an American

We are back in Harmonica Frank's medicine show, and it is the softest sell of all. "By the second verse," Randy confides, "they're already running for the boat."

Climb aboard little wog
Sail away with me

And if they are caught up in Newman's vision, the pure feel of it, so am I. "Sail away," he sings, "Sail away," and the grace of his singing conquers the last resistance. It is majestic. You can see the glassy waters, the birds hovering over the ship as the last glimpse of Africa drops over the horizon.

We will cross the mighty ocean into Charleston Bay *

You can dredge through all the antebellum fantasies kicked up to defend the peculiar institution and you will never find an image of slavery as lovely as this one.

This peaceful, quiet song is more outrageous than anything the Rolling Stones have ever done—or would be, if the nation heard Newman do it on the radio every day. Scary, astonishing, Newman has presented an American temptation—tempting not only the Africans, who became Negroes, and went on to create the music that finally tossed up Elvis Presley, rock 'n' roll, Newman, and his audience, but tempting America to believe that this image of itself just might be true.

"Sail Away" moves on one of the most seductive melodies ever to grace a popular song. It is just out of reach, with a fabulous edge of déjà vu, calling up the classic Ray Charles records of the early sixties—"Born to Lose," "You Don't Know Me," "That Lucky Old Sun"—calling up a thousand songs and a thousand happy endings.

The power of the song is in the simple, perfectly accomplished idea that something as horrible and charged with guilt as slavery could take on such real beauty. The focus is not on those who are to be enslaved, but on the singer, the confidence man. Of course he is lying. He has seen babies thrown into the sea, smelled the death and excrement in the

* Words and Music by Randy Newman. © 1972 WB Music Corp. & Randy Newman. All rights reserved. Used by permission of Warner Bros. Music.

hold, watched the brand burn into the flesh. He has looked
without flinching into the bewildered eyes that are perhaps
the most terrible of all. But for the moment, he believes himself. A secret ambivalence of four hundred years of American
life finds a voice in this song. It is not particularly liberating;
too strange for that, it is like a vision of heaven superimposed
on hell.

Y'all gonna be an American

Rock 'n' roll has always specialized in racial paradoxes,
but none as queer as this. It has virtually nothing to do with
"rock 'n' roll" as a musical form (save that Newman's singing
owes so much to the blues) and everything to do with the
rock 'n' roll audience. Newman offers it a vision its members
have spent years driving from their minds, bringing them
back to a home that was never there.

The song transcends its irony. It is, in the end, what
America would like to believe about itself, and what ten
years of a war across the ocean and ten years of bitter black
faces will never let it believe, even in secret: that everything
America did was for the good. Better than good: that God's
work really was our own and meant to be. That we brought
something new and precious into the world, a land even the
most miserable slaves would recognize as Eden.

For if they did not, how could we believe it?

Sailing across the ocean, the slaver and his slaves are in
love.

NEWMAN'S FAILURE

"Every great artist must create for a great audience,"
Bob Christgau pronounced one night when we were delving
into The Great Randy Newman Mystery (Why isn't this genius as big as he deserves to be?). Christgau meant an aggressive, critical audience, with a conscious sense of itself *as* an
audience, but he also meant a big, broad audience, one

whose complexity and diverse needs can push an artist beyond comfortable limits.

When a single like the O'Jays' "Back Stabbers" rams home the result of years of shifting black consciousness and takes over the charts, it creates a cultural moment shared by a good part of the country, shoving a particular sensibility through all sorts of ordinary barriers that grow up between audiences. The passion and clarity of the song can connect a black pimp, whose life it was virtually meant to define, to a middle-class white kid, who just digs the beat and will find his or her place in the lyrics soon enough. When a movie like *The Godfather* becomes the national pastime, you can feel, as you sit for perhaps the first time in a theater half black and half white, that for better or for worse America's fantasies are at last becoming common property; that artists and audiences have come to a verge, that the stakes of American life have been raised.

If *The Godfather* had succeeded as merely a genre classic, it would have been a very different movie—the response it provokes changes how we see and understand it. Like "Back Stabbers," it matters, has its particular meanings, partly *because* it is a hit. Without massive public response, we would not even get close to two crucial democratic questions, questions worth asking about any interesting work of popular culture: How far can this work take its audience? How far can its audience go with it? Only works that can't be ignored— liking them is hardly the point—raise such questions and bring them to life. In one way or another we are all affected by hits, and are forced to define ourselves in terms of our response to them, just as we are all, for good or ill, affected by the romantic heroism of the Westerns, and not necessarily by, say, the chaotic heroism that is the subject of Orson Welles' movies. Certainly we are caught up in these things that impelled Welles, but his version of them, the shape of his vision, has not inevitably become part of us; we don't have to live in the world as he tried to define it, as we help- lessly live out and respond to the nostalgia of John Ford or

Howard Hawks. The life of a whole generation is authentically quickened and brightened by the Beatles, but it is not disturbed and sharpened by Randy Newman. The point is not that it would be "good for people" if the radio was playing "Sail Away" all day long, but that such exposure might be the only way to find out how strong the song really is. But Newman is quite different from Orson Welles, who lost a great fight with Hollywood in his attempt to get his movies made, because Newman is barely on the battlefield.

His quandary is not unlike the one the Kinks fell into in the late sixties. After a string of post-Beatles Invasion hits based on a chopped and channeled version of "Louie, Louie," the sensibility of Ray Davies, their resident ex-art-student genius (every British band had one in those days), began to take over the group. The Kinks became less of a band, less a bundle of ambition and lust for money, fame and fun, and more of a means to Davies's fantasies. He became a social critic, or more appropriate for rock 'n' roll, a social complainer. He squeezed a few hits out of this stance, but the last chart success he got in the sixties crystallized his new view of the world and dropped the commercial bottom out of the group. "Sunny Afternoon" (1966) could have been another put-down of the English middle class, but instead the hunter was captured by the game. This was an ode to upper-class boredom. The Kinks became a classy little outfit, neurotic, long on intelligence and short on raunch, and their album sales dropped into the low thousands. They were idolized by the critics and ignored by everybody else.

You couldn't call Davies's world dark, exactly; it was dimmed. Like Newman's, it was completely idiosyncratic, if generally a lot less compelling. An anthem Davies wrote to himself defined it best: a fearsome, ferocious piece of hard rock he slipped onto the flip side of "Sunny Afternoon," and which didn't surface on an American album until seven years later—"I'm Not Like Everybody Else."

Davies opened the song as a sickly kid pushed up against the wall by a gang of thugs (that is, everybody else), and then broke wide open with a rage that negated the whole world he wouldn't serve, that he wouldn't and couldn't change into. By the last fiery choruses he was free, as free to ignore his listeners as they had always been to ignore him. It was a great record.*

Davies commenced to delineate the subtleties of nostalgia, the quirks of inadequacy, the aesthetics of oddball. For a time his insulation produced appropriate fantasies, and also his best songs (such as "Waterloo Sunset," an unbearably lovely tune about an old man who watches lovers from his window). Artistic privacy also produced terrible self-indulgence and embarrassing cuteness. The critics cheered the good and the bad, as they do with Newman, but finally even they began to weary in their proselytizing. Paul Williams, an original Kinks booster, reviewed their last bomb "for those who love the Kinks," formally ending the great struggle to spread the word.

But not quite. Davies had written *Arthur*, an "opera" about a post-Victorian lost in a twentieth-century world; some of it was brilliant and some of it was crap, as with all Kinks albums, which shouldn't have made any difference one way or the other. But an extraordinary push by two *Rolling Stone* reviewers (one of whom, I confess, was me), and its release at the same time as the Who's *Tommy* (suddenly nothing was as salable as the concept of Opera, which is to say, Art), made *Arthur* a decent success. The Kinks stumbled back to America for their first tour in years, and eventually got another hit, a big one, with "Lola," the tender tale of a shy country boy meeting up with a big-city transvestite— superb rock 'n' roll and a pop masterpiece.

The Top 40 audience, which had grabbed for the record, not "the Kinks," settled back, but as happens whenever a group gets a hit, the band picked up enough new fans to make them successful, seventies-style. Instead of a little cult, they had a big cult. Davies's insulation was gone, and the sharp edge of his feel for being different collapsed into

---

* And I swear I hear a hint of the closet Davies later came out of; doesn't he scream, "I won't go to bed like everybody else?"

gross parody of the big bad world. His songs became either hysterically unfunny (the next album was called *Lola v. the Power-Mad Money Men*, or something like that) or merely dull. An uncritical audience—a cult—was even worse for the band than uncritical critics. Davies's outsider stance, which had given his work what strength and vitality it had, was vitiated by the presence of an automatic audience.

And yet the echo of that wonderful statement, "I'm Not Like Everybody Else," is still there—not in Davies's work, but in Newman's: the idea that communication is failure, because if you get what you have to say across to a mass audience, that means what you have to say is not deep enough, or strong enough, to really matter. Newman has said he feels his songs are disturbing; that his lack of success is due to the weight of his material and the discomfort of his version of the truth. He is not surprised by his small audience, just frustrated by it, because if he cannot get his work across he is failing his work. That is, he can't win.

Newman's most accessible songs (as he performs them, which is all that concerns me, and all I think really concerns Newman) are generally his sledge-hammer ironies like "Political Science" (Let's drop the bomb on all our snotty so-called allies) or "Burn On." The genre only parodies the depth of Newman's talent, and it is impossible that he doesn't know it. If his thinnest, weakest work gets the most applause, what's he to think? That his audience isn't good enough for him? That he panders to his audience? This genre may expand anyway, because one part of Newman wants the great audience because he knows his work deserves it. And what often happens to the American popular artist, who feels he must grab the country itself and fails to even scratch it, is that he tries so desperately and honestly to alter his work in order to make it matter (not even compromising to make it palatable, though the line is hard to draw, especially for the artist), that he loses all sense of what impelled him in the first place. Either his career declines, and he is forgotten, or he hits, and decides that he has betrayed himself—and his audience. Someday this may happen to Newman; his music will

lose its subtleties, even his humor will fall flat. Then he will
be easier to accept, and useless as an artist.

Well, he knows all this, puttering around the house
watching *Secret Storm* and vaginal deodorant commercials just
like I do when I'm trying to avoid doing some *serious work*
like writing this book, but in one sense none of it matters—in
his case—because the deepest thing keeping Randy Newman
from the American audience is his own sensibility.

There is something to Newman's idea that his marginal
status in the rock 'n' roll world is a matter of the darkness
and perversity of his vision, but I think it has more to do
with the ambivalence that underlies that vision. Pop careers
are not gifts of the muse, they are won, and Newman, finally, is all doubt as to whether or not the fight is worth it.
There is one song he has written that captures his ambivalence so perfectly I can hardly believe he ever cranked
himself up to write another one; it's called "My Old Kentucky Home." Imagine one of those automatic LA country
backing tracks, straw on the studio floor, anything that helps
set the scene, and then Randy (not Jewish or black this time,
just drunk), warbling a timeless tribute to nothingness,
negating the ambition rock 'n' roll demands just as Davies
wiped out his audience:

> *Turpentine and dandelion wine*
> *I've turned the corner and I'm doin fine*
> *Shooting at the birds on the telephone line*
> *Pickin' em off with this gun a mine*
>
> *Brother Gene he's big and mean*
> *And he don't have much to say*
> *He had a little woman who he whupped each day*
> *But now she's gone away*
> *He got drunk last night*
> *Kicked mama down the stair*
> *But I'm alright so I don't care*

You can't get any farther into ambivalence than that.
The connection between Newman's sense of himself, and the

way the world looks to him, could hardly be more exact. He might turn into a homosexual someday, he told Susan Lydon, get religion, find a God. Maybe his entire generation would. Maybe the whole world will turn upside down and Newman will say Yes to all of it. Or something.

He's not particularly ambiguous; his meanings, though they expand if you keep his songs in your head, are clear enough—even if some singers have willfully deluded themselves into recording "Sail Away" as if it were a rewrite of "Born Free" (changing that disagreeable line about "Climb aboard, little wog" to "little child," which I suppose means they know quite well what the song is about after all).

But if his meanings are clear, their value is something else. We know what the slavemaster has in mind and what will happen to his audience as soon as he gets it on the ship, but who knows how to take it? You can't get out from under, that music just washes over you and makes you feel clean. When beauty and evil are so perfectly intertwined, what choices are really possible?

There are no cheap thrills in "Davy the Fat Boy," because Newman's performance is strong enough to force the listener into all its roles: purveyor, victim, and drooling carny audience. His best songs implicate the listener. He goes far enough to wonder if everything might not be worth doing, which means he is far enough gone to wonder if anything *is* worth doing—such as pursuing an audience. If God, as Newman likes to see Him, is something worse than ambivalent in His heaven, how could *man* be any better? Since man is cursed anyway ("I recoil in horror," says Newman's God, "from the foulness of thee . . . / How we laugh up here in heaven at the prayer you offer Me/ That's why I love mankind"), wouldn't any act of will lead straight to that realm of folly and sin that is Newman's garden—so far limited to his art, not yet taking over his life? Isn't it almost true by Newman's definition of how the world works that desire and action produce disaster at worst and failure at best? If Newman is necessarily ambivalent about the ambitions of his

characters, how could he regard his own ambitions any differently?

The answer is that he could be filled with such rage at
the world for being the way it is that nothing could stop him
from conniving against it. Herman Melville's view of the
world was not so different, and when he finally understood
the trap God had set for man (and he was no older than
Newman), he had the time of his life trying to write his way
out of it. Even though he saw clearly enough to know he
would never make it, he was caught up in a vision of what a
remarkable fight it would be.

But if such a perception of the nature of things was
enough to set an American's teeth on edge more than a
hundred years ago, it may not be anymore. America is tired;
Newman is not a driven artist like Melville, or for that matter a sixties Bob Dylan (hero of another young America, itself grown weary by the time Newman arrived to stake a
claim to it)—perhaps he cannot afford to be. Newman is ambivalent even about his own talent; as a factual matter of
daily life, he cannot decide if it is worth writing a song, let
alone recording it once it is written. He lacks what Chandler
called "the hard core of selfishness necessary to exploit talent
to the full"—the aggression and insanity that lie beneath the
pop version of the Alger dream. Newman is very distant
from that, and close enough to see it for what it is; he is a
Bartleby, the man who would prefer not to.

Newman skirts the rock 'n' roll audience, but he and a
few others keep the margins of possibility open. Aesthetically a figure of real genius and culturally a born cult hero,
his America does not come across quite as readily as that of
Chuck Berry, the Rolling Stones, or the Band. In his own
peculiar way, Randy Newman is much closer to the Sly
Stone of *Riot*.

Newman's rock 'n' roll is short on musical force, vocal
exuberance, and the promise of good times no matter what
(everything Sly willfully removed from *Riot*); his work lacks

the undeniable satisfaction we get from Mick Jagger roaring
he can't get none. *That* kind of satisfaction is what we ask
from rock 'n' roll; but if Norman Mailer is right when he
says that the worst American promise is the promise of an
unearned freedom from dread, Randy Newman's songs may
give us some of what we need. I doubt if Mick Jagger would
be very surprised that sometimes it is even harder to get
what you need than it is to get what you want.

Laconic, funny, grim, and solitary, Randy Newman is a
typical figure in the American imagination: the man who
does not like what he sees but is wildly attracted to it anyway, a man who keeps his sanity by rendering contradictions
other people struggle to avoid. For the moment, he carries
the weight of one version of America on his shoulders—not
that anyone has asked him to, as audiences have asked Bob
Dylan, Elvis Presley, and Sly Stone—but his real task is to
make his burden ours.

ELVIS
Presliad

FANFARE

Elvis Presley is a supreme figure in American life, one whose presence, no matter how banal or predictable, brooks no real comparisons. He is honored equally by long-haired rock critics, middle-aged women, the City of Memphis (they finally found something to name after him: a highway), and even a president.* Beside Elvis, the other heroes of this book

---

* Richard Nixon had Elvis over to the White House once, and made him an honorary narcotics agent. Nixon got his picture taken with the King. An odd story, though, from rock critic Stu Werbin: "It seems that the good German who arranges the White House concerts for the President and his guests managed to travel the many channels that lead only in rare instances to Col. Tom Parker's phone line. Once connected, he delivered what he considered the most privileged invitation. The President requests Mr. Presley to perform. The Colonel did a little quick figuring and then told the man that Elvis would consider it an honor. For the President, Elvis's fee, beyond traveling expenses and accommodations for his back-up group, would be $25,000. The good German gasped.

seem a little small-time. If they define different versions of America, Presley's career almost has the scope to take America in. The cultural range of his music has expanded to the point where it includes not only the hits of the day, but also patriotic recitals, pure country gospel, and really dirty blues; reviews of his concerts, by usually credible writers, sometimes resemble biblical accounts of heavenly miracles. Elvis has emerged as a great *artist*, a great *rocker*, a great *purveyor of schlock*, a great *heart throb*, a great *bore*, a great *symbol of potency*, a great *ham*, a great *nice person*, and, yes, a great American.

Twenty years ago Elvis made his first records with Sam Phillips, on the little Sun label in Memphis, Tennessee; then a pact was signed with Col. Tom Parker, shrewd country hustler. Elvis took off for RCA Victor, New York, and Hollywood. America has not been the same since. Elvis disappeared into an oblivion of respectability and security in the sixties, lost in interchangeable movies and dull music; he staged a remarkable comeback as that decade ended, and now performs as the transcendental Sun King that Ralph Waldo Emerson only dreamed about—and as a giant contradiction. His audience expands every year, but Elvis transcends his talent to the point of dispensing with it altogether. Performing a kind of enormous victory rather than winning it, Elvis strides the boards with such glamour, such magnetism, that he allows his audience to transcend their desire for his talent. Action is irrelevant when one can simply delight in the presence of a man who has made history, and who has triumphed over it.

Mark now, the supreme Elvis gesture. He takes the stage with a retinue of bodyguards, servants, singers, a band, an orchestra; he applies himself vaguely to the hits of his past, prostrates himself before songs of awesome ickiness; he acknowledges the applause and the gasps that greet his every

---

'Col. Parker, nobody gets paid for playing for the President!'

'Well, I don't know about that, son,' the Colonel responded abruptly, 'but there's one thing I do know. Nobody asks Elvis Presley to play for nothing.' " (*Creem*, March, 1972).

movement (applause that comes thundering with such force you might think the audience merely suffers the music as an excuse for its ovations); he closes with an act of show-biz love that still warms the heart; but above all, he throws away the entire performance.

How could he take it seriously? How could anyone create when all one has to do is appear? "He *looks* like Elvis Presley!" cried a friend, when the Big E stormed forth in an explosion of flashbulbs and cheers, "What a burden to live up to!" It is as if there is nothing Elvis could do to overshadow a performance of his myth. And so he performs from a distance, laughing at his myth, throwing it away only to see it roar back and trap him once again.

He will sing, as if suffering to his very soul, a song called "This Time, You [God, that is] Gave Me a Mountain," which sums up his divorce and his separation from his little girl. Having confessed his sins, he will stand aside, head bowed, as the Special Elvis Presley Gospel Group sings "Sweet, Sweet Feeling (in This Place)." Apparently cleansed of his sins, he will rock straight into the rhythm and blues of "Lawdy, Miss Clawdy" and celebrate his new-found freedom with a lazy grin. But this little melodrama of casual triumph will itself be a throwaway. As with the well-planned sets, the first-class musicians, the brilliant costumes, there will be little life behind the orchestration; the whole performance will be flaccid, the timing careless, all emotions finally shallow, the distance from his myth necessitating an even greater distance from the musical power on which that myth is based.

Elvis gives us a massive road-show musical of opulent American mastery; his version of the winner-take-all fantasies that have kept the world lined up outside the theaters that show American movies ever since the movies began. And of course we respond: a self-made man is rather boring, but a self-made king is something else. Dressed in blue, red, white, ultimately gold, with a superman cape and covered with jewels no one can be sure are fake, Elvis might epitomize the worst of our culture—he is bragging, selfish, narcissistic, condescending, materialistic to the point of insanity.

But there is no need to take that seriously, no need to take anything seriously. "Aw, shucks," says the country boy; it is all a joke to him; his distance is in his humor, and he can exit from this America unmarked, unimpressed, and uninteresting.

"From the moment he comes out of the wings," writes Nik Cohn, "all the pop that has followed him is made to seem as nothing, to be blown away like chaff." That is *exactly* what that first moment feels like, but from that point on, Elvis will go with the rest of it, singing as if there are no dangers or delights in the world grand enough to challenge him. There is great satisfaction in his performance, and great emptiness.

It is an ending. It is a sure sign that a culture has reached a dead end when it is no longer intrigued by its myths (when they lose their power to excite, amuse, and renew all who are a part of those myths—when those myths just bore the hell out of everyone); but Elvis has dissolved into a presentation of his myth, and so has his music. The emotion of the best music is open, liberating in its commitment and intangibility; Elvis's presentation is fixed. The glorious oppression of that presentation parallels the all-but-complete assimilation of a revolutionary musical style into the mainstream of American culture, where no one is challenged and no one is threatened.

History without myth is surely a wasteland; but myths are compelling only when they are at odds with history. When they replace the need to make history, they too are a dead end, and merely smug. Elvis's performance of his myth is so satisfying to his audience that he is left with no musical identity whatsoever, and thus he has no way to define himself, or his audience—except to expand himself, and his audience. Elvis is a man whose task it is to dramatize the fact of his existence; he does not have to create something new (or try, and fail), and thus test the worth of his existence, or the worth of his audience.

Complete assimilation really means complete acceptance. The immigrant who is completely assimilated into

America has lost the faculty of adding whatever is special about himself to his country; for any artist, complete assimilation means the adoption of an aesthetic where no lines are drawn and no choices are made. That quality of selection, which is what is at stake when an artist comes across with his version of anything, is missing. When an artist gives an all-encompassing Yes to his audience (and Elvis's Yes implicitly includes everyone, not just those who say Yes to *him*), there is nothing more he can tell his audience, nothing he can really do for them, except maybe throw them a kiss.

Only the man who says No is free, Melville once wrote. We don't expect such a stance in popular culture, and anyone who does might best be advised to take his trade somewhere else. But the refusal that lurks on the margins of the affirmation of American popular culture—the margins where Sly Stone and Randy Newman have done their best work—is what gives the Yes of our culture its vitality and its kick. Elvis's Yes is the grandest of all, his presentation of mastery the grandest fantasy of freedom, but it is finally a counterfeit of freedom: it takes place in a world that for all its openness (Everybody Welcome!) is aesthetically closed, where nothing is left to be mastered, where there is only more to accept. For all its irresistible excitement and enthusiasm, this freedom is complacent, and so the music that it produces is empty of real emotion—there is nothing this freedom could be for, nothing to be won or lost.

At best, when the fans gather around—old men and women who might see their own struggles and failures ennobled in the splendor of one who came from the bottom; middle-aged couples attending to the most glamorous nightclub act there is; those in their twenties and thirties who have grown with Elvis ever since he and they created each other years ago (and who might have a feeling he and they will make their trip through history together, reading their history in each other)—at best, Elvis will confirm all who are there *as* an audience. Such an event, repeated over and over all across the land, implies an America that is as nearly complete as any can be. But what is it worth?

When Elvis sings "American Trilogy" (a combination of "Dixie," "The Battle Hymn of the Republic," and "All My Trials," a slave song), he signifies that his persona, and the culture he has made out of blues, Las Vegas, gospel music, Hollywood, schmaltz, Mississippi, and rock 'n' roll, can contain any America you might want to conjure up. It is rather Lincolnesque; Elvis recognizes that the Civil War has never ended, and so he will perform The Union.

Well, for a moment, staring at that man on the stage, you can almost believe it. For if Elvis were to bring it off— and it is easy to think that only he could—one would leave the hall with a new feeling for the country; whatever that feeling might be, one's sense of place would be broadened, and enriched.

But it is an illusion. A man or woman equal to the song's pretension would have to present each part of the song as if it were the whole story, setting one against each other, proving that one American really could make the South live, the Union hold, and slavery real. But on the surface and beneath it, Elvis transcends any real America by evading it. There is no John Brown in his "Battle Hymn," no romance in his "Dixie," no blood in his slave song. He sings with such a complete absence of musical personality that none of the old songs matter at all, because he has not committed himself to them; it could be anyone singing, or no one. It is in this sense, finally, that an audience is confirmed, that an America comes into being; lacking any real fear or joy, it is a throwaway America where nothing is at stake. The divisions America shares are simply smoothed away.

But there is no chance anyone who wants to join will be excluded. Elvis's fantasy of freedom, the audience's fantasy, takes on such reality that there is nothing left in the real world that can inspire the fantasy, or threaten it. What *is* left is for the fantasy to replace the world; and that, night after night, is what Elvis and his audience make happen. The version of the American dream that is Elvis's performance is blown up again and again, to contain more history, more people, more music, more hopes; the air gets thin but the bubble does not burst, nor will it ever. This is America when it has outstripped itself, in all of its extravagance, and its emptiness is Elvis's ultimate throwaway.

There is a sense in which virtually his whole career has been a throwaway, straight from that time when he knew he had it made and that the future was his. You can hear that distance, that refusal to really commit himself, in his best music and his worst; if the throwaway is the source of most of what is pointless about Elvis, it is also at the heart of much of what is exciting and charismatic. It may be that he never took *any* of it seriously, just did his job and did it well, trying to enjoy himself and stay sane—save for those first Tennessee records, and that night, late in 1968, when his comeback was uncertain and he put a searing, desperate kind of life into a few songs that cannot be found in any of his other music.

It was a staggering moment. A Christmas TV special had been decided on; a final dispute between Colonel Parker (he wanted twenty Christmas songs and a tuxedo) and producer Steve Binder (he wanted a tough, fast, sexy show) had been settled; with Elvis's help, Binder won. So there Elvis was, standing in an auditorium, facing television cameras and a live audience for the first time in nearly a decade, finally stepping out from behind the wall of retainers and sycophants he had paid to hide him. And everyone was watching.

In the months preceding Elvis had begun to turn away from the seamless boredom of the movies and the hackneyed music of the soundtrack albums, staking out a style on a few half-successful singles, presenting the new persona of a man whose natural toughness was tempered by experience. The records—"Big Boss Man," "Guitar Man," "U.S. Male"—had been careful, respectable efforts, but now he was putting everything on the line, risking his comforts and his ease for the chance to start over. He had been a bad joke for a long time; if this show died, little more would be heard from Elvis Presley. Did he still have an audience? Did he still have anything to offer them? He had raised the stakes himself, but he probably had no idea.

Sitting on the stage in black leather, surrounded by friends and a rough little combo, the crowd buzzing, he sang and talked and joked, and all the resentments he had hidden over the years began to pour out. He had always said yes, but this time, he was saying no—not without humor, but almost with a wry bit of guilt, as if he had betrayed his talent and himself. "Been a long time, baby." He told the audience about a time back in 1955, when cops in Florida had forced him to sing without moving; the story was hilarious, but there was something in his voice that made very clear how much it had hurt. He jibed at the Beatles, denying that the heroes who had replaced him had produced anything he could not match, and then he proved it. After all this time he wanted more than safety; he and the men around him were nervous, full of adventure.

"I'd like to do my favorite Christmas song," Elvis drawls—squeals of familiarity from the crowd, the girls in the front rows doing their job, imitating themselves or their images of the past, fading into an undertone of giggles as the music begins. Elvis sings "Blue Christmas," a classically styled rhythm and blues, very even, all its tension implied: a good choice. He sings it low and throaty, snapping the strings on his guitar until one of his pals cries, "Play it dirty! Play it dirty!"—on a Christmas song! All right! But this is re-creation, the past in the present, an attempt to see if Elvis can go as far as he once did. Within those limits it works, it is beautiful. The song ends with appropriate, and calculated, screams.

"Ah think Ah'll put a strap around this and stand up," Presley says. AHAHAHAHAHAHAHAAHAHA! God, what's that? Nervous laughter from a friend. Slow and steady, still looking around for the strap no one has bothered to hook onto the guitar, Elvis rocks into "One Night." In Smiley Lewis's original, it was about an orgy, called "One Night of Sin" (with the great line, "The things I did and I saw/ Would make the earth stand still"); Elvis cleaned it up into a love story in 1958. But he has forgotten—or remembered. He is singing Lewis's version, as he must have always

wanted to. He has slipped his role, and laughing, grinning,
something is happening.

> . . . *The things I did and I saw, could make* . . .
> these dreams—*Where's the strap?*

Where's the strap, indeed. He falls in and out of the two
songs, and suddenly the band rams hard at the music and
Elvis lunges and eats it alive. No one has ever heard him sing
like this; not even his best records suggest the depth of passion in this music. One line from Howlin' Wolf tells the tale:
"When you see me runnin', you know my life is at stake."
That's what it sounds like.

Shouting, crying, growling, lusting, Elvis takes his
stand and the crowd takes theirs with him, no longer reaching for the past they had been brought to the studio to reen-
act, but responding to something completely new. The
crowd is cheering for what they had only hoped for: Elvis
has gone beyond all their expectations, and his, and they
don't believe it. The guitar cuts in high and slams down and
Elvis is roaring. Every line is a thunderbolt. *AW, YEAH!*,
screams a pal—he has waited years for this moment.

> *UNNNNNNH! WHEW! When* . . . I ain't nevah did no
> wrong!

And Elvis floats like the master he is back into "One
night, with you," even allowing himself a little "Hot dog!",
singing softly to himself.

It was the finest music of his life. If ever there was
music that bleeds, this was it. Nothing came easy that night,
and he gave everything he had—more than anyone knew was
there.

Something of that passion spilled over into the first
comeback album, from *Elvis in Memphis;* into "Suspicious
Minds," the single that put him back on top of the charts;
into his first live shows in Las Vegas; and then his nerves

steadied, and Elvis brought it all back home again. You can still hear the intensity, the echo of those moments of doubt, in the first notes of most songs Elvis sings on stage—just before he realizes again that the crowd cares only that he is before them, and that anyway, the music would be his if he wanted it, that his talent is so vast it would be demeaning to apply it. So he will revel in his glory, acting the part of the King it has always been said he is; and if that is a throw-away, it is at least thrown at those who want it. A real glow passes back and forth between Elvis and his audience, as he shares a bit of what it means to transcend the world of weak-ness, failure, worry, age and fear, shows what it means for a boy who sprung from the poor to be godly, and shares that too.

I suppose it is the finality this performance carries with it that draws me back to Elvis's first records, made when there was nothing to take for granted, let alone throw away. Those sides, like "One Night," catch a world of risk, will, passion, and natural nobility; something worth searching out within the America of mastery and easy splendor that may well be Elvis's last word. The first thing Elvis had to learn to transcend, after all, was the failure and obscurity he was born to; he had to find some way to set himself apart, to es-cape the limits that could well have given his story a very dif-ferent ending. The ambition and genius that took him out and brought him back is there in that first music—that, and much more.

HILLBILLY MUSIC

"This is the mystery of democracy," intoned Woodrow Wilson (dedicating the log cabin where Abraham Lincoln was born, in words ponderous enough to suit the mayor of Tupelo, Mississippi, when he dedicated the birthplace of Elvis Presley), "that its richest fruits spring up out of soils which no man has prepared and in circumstances where they are least expected. . . ."

I like those words. The question of history may have

been settled on the side of process, not personality, but it is not a settlement I much appreciate. Historical forces might explain the Civil War, but they don't account for Lincoln; they might tell us why rock 'n' roll emerged when it did, but they don't explain Elvis any more than they explain Little Peggy March. What a sense of context does give us, when we are looking for someone in particular, is an idea of what that person had to work with; but for myself, it always seems inexplicable in the end anyway. There are always blank spots, and that is where the myths take over. Elvis's story is so classically American (poor country boy makes good in the city) that his press agents never bothered to improve on it. But it is finally elusive too, just like all the good stories. It surrounds its subject, without quite revealing it. But it resonates; it evokes like crazy.

Now, the critical (and least tangible) point in the biography of any great man or woman is just that place where their story begins to detach itself from those of countless others like them. Take Lincoln again; was it that famous hike when he brought the borrowed book back? The moment on the stand facing Douglas when he knew he had him licked and loved it?

ELVIS ECHOES: Introducing a series of interruptions of Presley-Presence that, occuring while this chapter was written, are an essential part of its context, but that do not fit anywhere else.

EE #1. Elvis is to perform at the Oakland Coliseum in 1972. Back in the Dark Ages, two San Francisco high school girls win a "Why I Love Elvis" contest and are flown to Hollywood to be kissed. *Their principal expels them:* "We don't need that kind of publicity," he explains. Now, some babies and divorces later (for Elvis, too), the winners return. The word is passed; they are ushered backstage; they are kissed once more. It is a link to the past, but I am willing to bet that most of those in the hall (16,000) are meeting Elvis in the flesh for the first time, as am I. I have a bad seat, and the fortyish woman next to me passes her binoculars. I trade off with her preteen daughter. I notice that the best seats are occupied by couples who look old enough to substitute for El's grandparents. A thought from my friend Mary Clemmey comes to mind: In his present-day audience, Elvis sees the ghost of his mother, and the family life he has had to give up in order to be what he is. Behind me, a hippie pulls furiously on a joint. Is he performing an act of rebellion? Against Elvis? Or affirming that, in a bouffant utopia, he alone keeps the true Presley spirit alive?

The day he was born? You can't answer such questions, not computer-style, but you have no claim on the story unless you risk a guess.

They called Elvis the Hillbilly Cat in the beginning; he came out of a stepchild culture (in the South, white trash; to the rest of America, a caricature of Bilbo and moonshine) that for all it shared with the rest of America had its own shape and integrity. As a poor white Southern boy, Elvis created a personal culture out of the hillbilly world that was his as a given. Ultimately, he made that personal culture public in such an explosive way that he transformed not only his own culture, but America's. I want to look at that hillbilly landscape for a bit—to get a sense of how Elvis drew on his context.

It was, as Southern chambers of commerce have never tired of saying, A Land of Contrasts. The fundamental contrast, of course, could not have been more obvious: black and white. Always at the root of Southern fantasy, Southern music, and Southern politics, the black man was poised in the early fifties for an overdue invasion of American life, in fantasy, music, and politics. As the North scurried to deal with him, the South would be pushed farther and farther into the weirdness and madness its best artists had been trying to exorcise from the time of Poe on down. Its politics would dissolve into night-riding and hysteria; its fantasies would be dull for all their gaudy paranoia. Only the music got away clean.

The North, powered by the Protestant ethic, had set men free by making them strangers; the poor man's South that Elvis knew took strength from community.

The community was based on a marginal economy that demanded cooperation, loyalty, and obedience for the achievement of anything resembling a good life; it was organized by religion, morals, and music. Music helped hold the community together, and carried the traditions and shared values that dramatized a sense of place. Music gave pleasure, wisdom, and shelter.

"It's the only place in the country I've ever been where

you can actually drive down the highway at night, and if you listen, you hear music," Robbie Robertson once said. "I don't know if it's coming from the people or if it's coming from the air. It lives, and it's rooted there." Elegant enough, but I prefer another commend Robbie made. "The South," he said, "is the only place we play where everybody can clap on the off-beat."

Music was also an escape from the community, and music revealed its underside. There were always people who could not join, no matter how they might want to: tramps, whores, rounders, idiots, criminals. The most vital were singers: not the neighbors who brought out their fiddles and guitars for country picnics, as Elvis used to do, or those who sang in church, as he did also, but the professionals. They were men who bridged the gap between the community's sentimentalized idea of itself, and the outside world and the forbidden; artists who could take the community beyond itself because they had the talent and the nerve to transcend it. Often doomed, traveling throughout the South enjoying sins and freedoms the community had surrendered out of necessity or never known at all, they were too ambitious, ornery, or simply different to fit in.

The Carter Family, in the twenties, were the first to record the old songs everyone knew, to make the shared musical culture concrete, and their music drew a circle around the community. They celebrated the landscape (especially the Clinch Mountains that ringed their home), found strength in a feel for death because it was the only certainty, laughed a bit, and promised to leave the hillbilly home they helped build only on a gospel ship. Jimmie Rodgers, their contemporary, simply hopped a train. He was every boy who ever ran away from home, hanging out in the railroad yards, bumming around with black minstrels, pushing out the limits of his life. *He* celebrated long tall mamas that rubbed his back and licked his neck just to cure the cough that killed him; he bragged about gunplay on Beale Street; he sang real blues, played jazz with Louis Armstrong, and though there was melancholy in his soul, his smile was a good one. He sounded like a man who could make a home for himself anywhere. There's so much *room* in this country, he seemed to be saying, so many things to do—how could an honest man be satisfied to live within the frontiers he was born to?

Outside of the community because of the way they lived, the singers were tied to it as symbols of its secret hopes, of its fantasies of escape and union with the black man, of its fears of transgressing the moral and social limits that promised peace of mind. Singers could present the extremes of emotion, risk, pleasure, sex, and violence that the community was meant to control; they were often alcoholic or worse, lacking a real family, drifters in a world where roots were life. Sometimes the singer tantalized the community with his outlaw liberty; dying young, he finally justified the community by his inability to survive outside of it. More often than not, the singer's resistance dissolved into sentiment. Reconversion is the central country music comeback strategy, and many have returned to the fold after a brief fling with the devil, singing songs of virtue, fidelity, and God, as if to prove that sin only hid a deeper piety—or that there was no way out.

By the late forties and early fifties, Hank Williams had inherited Jimmie Rodgers' role as the central figure in the music, but he added an enormous reservation: that margin of loneliness in Rodgers' America had grown into a world of utter tragedy. Williams sang for a community to which he could not belong; he sang to a God in whom he could not quite believe; even his many songs of good times and good lovin' seemed to lose their reality. There were plenty of jokes in his repertoire, novelties like "Kawliga" (the tale of unrequited love between two cigar store Indians); he traveled Rodgers' road, but for Williams, that road was a lost highway. Beneath the surface of his forced smiles and his light, easy sound, Hank Williams was kin to Robert Johnson in a way that the new black singers of his day were not. Their music, coming out of New Orleans, out of Sam Phillips' Memphis studio and washing down from Chicago, was loud, fiercely electric, raucous, bleeding with lust and menace and loss. The rhythmic force that was the practical legacy of Robert Johnson had evolved into a music that overwhelmed *his* reservations; the rough spirit of the new blues, city R&B, rolled right over his nihilism. Its message was clear: What life doesn't give me, I'll take.

Hank Williams was a poet of limits, fear, and failure; he went as deeply into one dimension of the country world as anyone could, gave it beauty, gave it dignity. What was missing was that part of the hillbilly soul Rodgers had celebrated, something Williams' music obscured, but which his realism could not express and the community's moralism could not contain: excitement, rage, fantasy,, delight—the feeling, summed up in a sentence by W. J. Cash from *The Mind of the South*, that "even the Southern physical world was a kind of cosmic conspiracy against reality in favor of romance"; that even if Elvis's South was filled with Puritans, it was also filled with natural-born hedonists, and the same people were both.

To lie on his back for days and weeks [Cash writes of the hillbilly], storing power as the air he breathed stores power under the hot sun of August, and then to explode, as that air explodes in a thunderstorm, in a violent outburst of emotion—in such a fashion would he make life not only tolerable, but infinitely sweet.

In the fifties we can hardly find that moment in white music, before Elvis. Hank Williams was not all there was to fifties country, but his style was so pervasive, so effective, carrying so much weight, that it closed off the possibilities of breaking loose just as the new black music helped open them up. Not his gayest tunes, not "Move It on Over," "Honky Tonkin'," or "Hey Good Lookin'," can match this blazing passage from Cash, even if those songs share its subject:

To go into the town on Saturday afternoon and night, to stroll with the throng, to gape at the well-dressed and the big automobiles, to bathe in the holiday cacophony . . . maybe to have a drink, maybe to get drunk, to laugh with the passing girls, to pick them up if you had a car, or to go swaggering or hesitating into the hotels with the corridors saturated with the smell of bicloride of mercury, or the secret, steamy bawdy houses; maybe to have a fight, maybe against the cops, maybe to end, whooping and god-damning, in the jailhouse. . . .

The momentum is missing; that will to throw yourself all the way after something better with no real worry about how you are going to make it home. And it was this spirit, full-blown and bragging, that was to find its voice in Elvis's new blues and the rockabilly fever he kicked off all over the young white South. Once Elvis broke down the door, dozens more would be fighting their way through. Out of nowhere there would be Carl Perkins, looking modest enough and sounding for all the world as if he was having fun for the first time in his life, chopping his guitar with a new kind of urgency and yelling: "Now Dan got happy and he started ravin'—He jerked out his razor but he wasn't shavin' "—

> He hollered R-R-RAVE ON *chillen, I'm with ya!*
> RAVE ON CATS *he cried*
> *It's almost dawn and the cops're gone*
> *Let's* <u>alllllllll</u> *get dixie fried!*

Country music (like the blues, which was more damned and more honestly hedonistic than country had ever been) was music for a whole community, cutting across lines of age, if not class. This could have meant an openly expressed sense of diversity for each child, man, and woman, as it did with the blues. But country spoke to a community fearful of anything of the sort, withdrawing into itself, using music as a bond that linked all together for better or for worse, with a sense that what was shared was less important than the crucial fact of sharing. How could parents hope to keep their children if their kids' whole sense of what it meant to live—which is what we get from music when we are closest to it—held promises the parents could never keep?

The songs of country music, and most deeply, its even, narrow sound, had to subject the children to the heartbreak of their parents: the father who couldn't feed his family, the wife who lost her husband to a honky-tonk angel or a bottle, the family that lost everything to a suicide or a farm spinning off into one more bad year, the horror of loneliness in a world that was meant to banish that if nothing else. Behind that uneasy grin, this is Hank Williams' America; the romance is only a night call.

Such a musical community is beautiful, but it is not hard to see how it could be intolerable. All that hedonism was dragged down in country music; a deep sense of fear and resignation confined it, as perhaps it almost had to, in a land overshadowed·by fundamentalist religion, where original sin was just another name for the facts of life.

RAISED UP

Now, that Saturday night caught by Cash and Perkins would get you through a lot of weekdays. Cash might close it off—"Emptied of their irritations and repressions, left to return to their daily tasks, stolid, unlonely, and tame again"— and he's right, up to a point. This wasn't any revolution, no matter how many cops got hurt keeping the peace on Saturday night. Regardless of what a passport to that Southern energy (detached from the economics and religion that churned it up) might do for generations of restless Northern and British kids, there is no way that energy can be organized. But the fact that Elvis and the rest could trap its spirit and send it out over a thousand radio transmitters is a central fact of more lives than mine; the beginning of most of the stories in this book, if nothing near the end of them.

For we are treading on the key dividing line that made Elvis *King of Western Bop* (they went through a lot of trouble finding a name for this music) instead of just another country crooner or a footnote in someone's history of the blues: the idea (and it was just barely an "idea") that Saturday night could be the whole show. You had to be young and a bit insulated to pull it off, but why not? Why not trade pain and boredom for kicks and style? Why not make an escape from a way of life—the question trails off the last page of *Huckleberry Finn*—into a way of life?

You might not get revered for all time by everyone from baby to grandma, like the Carter Family, but you'd have more fun. Reality would catch up sooner or later—a pregnant girlfriend and a fast marriage, the farm you had to take over when your daddy died, a dull and pointless job that drained your desires until you could barely remember them—but why deal with reality before you had to? And what if there was a chance, just a chance, that you *didn't* have to deal with it? "When I was a boy," said Elvis not so long ago, "I was the hero in comic books and movies. I grew up believing in a dream. Now I've lived it out. That's all a man can ask for."

Elvis is telling us something quite specific: how special he was; how completely he captured and understood what for most of us is only a tired phrase glossing the surfaces of our own failed hopes. It is one thing, after all, to dream of a new job, and quite another to dream of a new world. The risks are greater. Elvis took chances dreaming his dreams; he gambled against the likelihood that their failure would betray him, and make him wish he had never dreamed at all. There are a hundred songs to tell that story, but perhaps Mott the

EE # 2. May 1972. I read in *Modern Screen* that top GOP politicos are giving *serious consideration* to placing Elvis's name in nomination for the vice-presidency (a plot to get around that $25,000 fee?). The article is illustrated by fifteen-year-old shots of girls waving ELVIS-FOR-PRESIDENT banners. Elvis, the story says, thinks this is a good idea, and has recently addressed a group of Black Panthers in order to test his forensic skills. He told them, and I quote: "Violence is not where it's at. It's a real turn-off, man." I do not know how to take this, especially as I recall it a year later when a TV trailer announces, "Tonight, immediately following the President's speech on Watergate, see Elvis further the cause of rock 'n' roll in *Roustabout*." I am more disoriented by the idea that Elvis could further the cause of *anything* in a movie like *Roustabout* than I am by the missed chance of his involvement in the Watergate scandal. But then, he would have known how to handle it. To Elvis, Watergate would have been something like a cosmic paternity suit.

Hoople, chasing the rock 'n' roll fantasy Elvis made of the American dream, said it best: "I wish I'd never wanted then/ What I want now twice as much."

Always, Elvis felt he was different, if not better, than those around him. He grew his sideburns long, acting out that sense of differentness, and was treated differently: in this case, he got himself kicked off the football team. Hear him recall those days in the midst of a near-hysterical autobiography, delivered at the height of his comeback from the stage at the International Hotel in Las Vegas: ". . . Had pretty long hair for that time and I tell you it got pretty weird. They used to see me comin down the street and they'd say, 'Hot dang, let's get him, he's a squirrel, he's a squirrel, get him, he just come down outta the trees.'"

High school classmates remember his determination to break through as a country singer; with a little luck, they figured, he might even make it.

Out on the road for the first time with small-change country package tours, though, Elvis would plot for something much bigger—for everything Hollywood had ever shown him in its movies.

On North Main in Memphis, as Harmonica Frank recalls Elvis, this was nothing to put into words. Talking trash and flicking ash, marking time and trying to hold it off, what did Elvis really have to look forward to? A year or so of Saturday nights, a little local notoriety, then a family he didn't quite decide to have and couldn't support? It would be all over.

Elvis fancied himself a trucker (if there weren't any Memphis boys in the movies, there were plenty on the road), pushing tons of machinery through the endless American night; just his version of the train whistle that called out to Johnny B. Goode and kept Richard Nixon awake as a boy. If it is more than a little odd that what to Elvis served as a symbol of escape and mastery now works—as part of his legend—as a symbol of everything grimy and poor he left behind when he did escape, maybe that only tells us how much his success shuffled the facts of his life, or how much he raised the stakes.

You don't make it in America—Emerson's mousetrap to the contrary—waiting for someone to come along and sign you up. You might be sitting on the corner like a Philly rock 'n' roller and get snatched up for your good looks, but you'll be back a year later and you'll never know what happened. Worst of all, you may not even care. What links the greatest rock 'n' roll careers is a volcanic ambition, a lust for more than anyone has a right to expect; in some cases, a refusal to know when to quit or even rest. It is that bit of Ahab burning beneath the Huck Finn rags of "Freewheelin' " Bob Dylan, the arrogance of a country boy like Elvis sailing into Hollywood, ready for whatever kind of success America had to offer.

So if we treat Elvis's words with as much respect as we can muster—which is how he meant them to be taken—we can see the first point at which his story begins to be his own. He took his dreams far more seriously than most ever dare, and he had the nerve to chase them down.

Cash's wonderful line—"a cosmic conspiracy against reality in favor of romance"—now might have more resonance. Still, if the kind of spirit that romance could produce seems ephemeral within the context of daily life, you would not expect the music it produced to last very long either. Not even Elvis, as a successful young rocker, could have expected his new music to last; he told interviewers rock 'n' roll was here to stay, but he was taking out plenty of insurance, making movies and singing schmaltz. You couldn't blame him; anyway, he liked schmaltz.

Within the realm of country music, the new spirit dried up just like Saturday fades into Monday, but since rock 'n' roll found its own audience and created its own world, that hardly mattered. Rock 'n' roll caught that romantic conspiracy on records and gave it a form. Instead of a possibility within a music, it became the essence; it became, of all things, a tradition. And when that form itself had to deal with reality—which is to say, when its young audience began to grow up—when the compromise between fantasy and reality that fills most of this book was necessary to preserve the possibility of fantasy, the fantasy had become part of the reality that had to be dealt with; the rules of the game had changed a bit, and it was a better game. "Blue Suede Shoes" had grown directly into something as serious and complex, and yet still offhand, still take-it-or-leave-it-and-pass-the-wine, as the Rolling Stones' "You Can't Always Get What You Want," which asks the musical question, "Why *are you* stepping on my blue suede shoes?"

EE#3. Elvis's 1973 TV special, *Aloha From Elvis in Hawaii*, was beamed by satellite to one-third of the world's population. Or so his publicity men announced. Perhaps it was that if the one-third of the world—principally the heathen part—had TV sets, they could have watched. It doesn't matter; the conceit of the concept is what matters.

You can see him now, Col. Thomas Andrew Parker, ex-carny barker, the great medical menagerist, tossing helplessly on his bed, scheming—after all these years, still peddling Elvis pens at press conferences, hustling glossies in the aisles at concerts, Colonel Parker does not rest—and what keeps him awake is that *even now there are people who do not know about Elvis Presley!* There are worlds to be conquered! There is work to be done!

Finally, he drops off to sleep. Yes, there are poor beggars somewhere in the Amazon jungle who have yet to get the word (perhaps the King would succeed where dozens of casseroled missionaries have failed—make a note of that), but the Colonel will deal with that tomorrow . . . wait for tomorrow.

Parker dreams.

It is perhaps 1990. Elvis is in his middle fifties now, still young, still beautiful. His latest single—"Baby Let Me Bang Your Box," backed with "My Yiddishe Mama"—has topped all charts. Parker has had his third heart transplant. The world has received the long-awaited actual communication from intelligent beings beyond the solar system. Earth's greatest scientists have assembled in Japan to decipher the message, and after years of error they have succeeded. It consists of only one word, one question on which the fate of ten billion people may rest:

"ELWIS?"

So Colonel Parker rests easy. Age has mellowed him, and his expectations do not go beyond the Milky Way.

Echoing through all of rock 'n' roll is the simple demand for peace of mind and a good time. While the demand is easy to make, nothing is more complex than to try to make it real and live it out. It all sounds simple, obvious; but that one young man like Elvis could break through a world as hard as Hank Williams', and invent a new one to replace it, seems obvious only because we have inherited Elvis's world, and live in it.

Satisfaction is not all there is to it, but it is where it all begins. Finally, the music must provoke as well as delight, disturb as well as comfort, create as well as sustain. If it doesn't, it lies, and there is only so much comfort you can take in a lie before it all falls apart.

The central facts of life in Elvis's South pulled as strongly against the impulses of hedonism and romance as the facts of our own lives do against the fast pleasures of rock 'n' roll. When the poor white was thrown back on himself, as he was in the daytime, when he worked his plot or looked for a job in the city, or at night, when he brooded and Hank Williams' whippoorwill told the truth all too plainly, those facts stood out clearly: powerlessness and vulnerability on all fronts. The humiliation of a class system that gave him his identity and then trivialized it; a community that for all its tradition and warmth was in some indefinable way not enough; economic chaos; the violence of the weather; bad food and maybe not enough of that; diseases that attached themselves to the body like new organs—they all mastered him. And that vulnerability produced—along with that urge to cut loose, along with that lively Southern romance— uncertainty, fatalism, resentment, acceptance, and nostalgia: limits that cut deep as the oldest cotton patch in Dixie.

Vernon Presley was a failed Mississippi sharecropper who moved his family out of the country with the idea of making a go in the city; it's not so far from Tupelo to Memphis, but in some ways, the journey must have been a long one—scores of country songs about boys and girls who lost their souls to the big town attest to that. Listen to Dolly Parton's downtown hooker yearning for her Blue Ridge mountain boy; listen to the loss of an America you may never have known.

They don't make country music better than that anymore, but it's unsatisfying, finally; too classical. This country myth is just one more echo of Jefferson pronouncing that, in America, virtue must be found in the land. I like myths, but this one is too facile, either for the people who still live on the land or for those of us who are merely looking for a way out of our own world, for an Annie Green Springs utopia. The myth is unsatisfying because the truth is richer than the myth.

"King Harvest (Has Surely Come)," the Band's song of blasted country hopes, gives us the South in all of its earthly delight and then snuffs it out. All at once, the song catches the grace and the limbo of the life that must be left behind.

The tune evokes a man's intimacy with the land and the refusal of the land to respond in kind. The music makes real, for the coolest city listener, a sense of place that is not quite a sense of being at home; the land is too full of violence for that. One hears the farmer's fear of separating from the land (and from his own history, which adhering to the land, is not wholly his own); one hears the cold economic necessities that have forced him out. The melody—too beautiful and out of reach for any words I have—spins the chorus into the pastoral with a feel for nature that is *really* hedonistic—

Corn in the field
Listen to the rice as the wind blows cross the water
KING HARVEST HAS SURELY COME *

—and a desperate, ominous rhythm slams the verses back to the slum streets that harbor the refugees of the pastoral disaster: "Just don't judge me by my shoes!" Garth Hudson's organ traces the circle of the song, over and over again.

The earliest picture of Elvis shows a farmer, his wife, and their baby; the faces of the parents are vacant, they are

---

* Copyright © 1969 by Canaan Music, Inc. All rights reserved. Used by permission of Warner Bros. Music.

set, as if they cannot afford an unearned smile. Somehow, their faces say, they will be made to pay even for that.

You don't hear this in Elvis's music; but what he left out of his story is as vital to an understanding of his art as what he kept, and made over. If we have no idea of what he left behind, how much he escaped, we will have no idea what his success was worth, or how intensely he must have wanted it.

Elvis was thirteen when the family left Tupelo for Memphis in 1948, a pampered only child; ordinary in all respects, they say, except that he liked to sing. True to Chuck Berry's legend of the Southern rocker, Elvis's mother bought him his first guitar, and for the same reason Johnny B. Goode's mama had in mind: keep the boy out of trouble. Elvis sang tearful country ballads, spirituals, community music. On the radio, he listened with his family to the old music of the Carter Family and Jimmie Rodgers, to current stars like Roy Acuff, Ernest Tubb, Bob Wills, Hank Williams, and to white gospel groups like the Blackwood Brothers. Elvis touched the soft center of American music when he heard and imitated Dean Martin and the operatics of Mario Lanza; he picked up Mississippi blues singers like Big Bill Broonzy, Big Boy Crudup, Lonnie Johnson, and the new Memphis music of Rufus Thomas and Johnny Ace, mostly when no one else was around, because that music was naturally frowned upon. His parents called it "sinful music," and they had a point—it was dirty, and there were plenty of blacks who would have agreed with Mr. and Mrs. Presley— but Elvis was really too young to worry. In this he was no different from hundreds of other white country kids who wanted more excitement in their lives than they could get from twangs and laments—wanted a beat, sex, celebration, the stunning nuances of the blues and the roar of horns and electric guitars. Still, Elvis's interest was far more casual than that of Jerry Lee Lewis, a bad boy who was sneaking off to black dives in his spare time, or Carl Perkins, a musician who was consciously working out a synthesis of blues and country.

The Presleys stumbled onto welfare, into public hous-
ing. Vernon Presley found a job. It almost led to the family's
eviction, because if they still didn't have enough to live on,
they were judged to have too much to burden the county
with their troubles. Elvis was a loner, but he had an eye for
flash. He sold his blood for money, ushered at the movies,
drove his famous truck, and divided the proceeds between
his mother and his outrageous wardrobe. Looking for space,
for a way to set himself apart.

Like many parents with no earthly future, the Presleys,
especially Gladys Presley, lived for their son. Her ambition
must have been that Elvis would take all that was good in the
family and free himself from the life she and her husband endured; she was, Memphian Stanley Booth wrote a few years
ago, "the one, perhaps the only one, who had told him
throughout his life that even though he came from poor
country people, he was just as good as anybody."

On Sundays (Wednesdays too, sometimes) the Presleys
went to their Assembly of God to hear the Pentecostal minis-
ters hand down a similar message: the last shall be first. This
was democratic religion with a vengeance, lower class and
gritty. For all those who have traced Elvis's music and his
hipshake to his religion (accurately enough—Elvis was the
first to say so), it has escaped his chroniclers that hillbilly
Calvinism was also at the root of his self-respect and his
pride: the anchor of his ambition.

His church (and the dozens of other Pentecostal sects
scattered throughout the South and small-town America) was
one part of what was left of the old American religion after
the Great Awakening. Calvinism had been a religion of authority in the beginning; in the middle-class North, filtered
through the popular culture of Ben Franklin, it became a system of tight money, tight-mindedness, and gentility; in the
hillbilly South, powered by traveling preachers and their
endless revivals, the old holiness cult produced a faith of
grace, apocalypse, and emotion, where people heaved their
deepest feelings into a circle and danced around them. Momentum scattered that old authority; all were sinners, all

were saints. Self-consciously outcast, the true faith in a land
of Philistines and Pharisees, it was shoved into storefronts
and tents and even open fields, and no less sure of itself for
that.

Church music caught moments of unearthly peace and
desire, and the strength of the religion was in its intensity.
The preacher rolled fire down the pulpit and chased it into
the aisle, signifying; men and women rocked in their seats,
sometimes onto the floor, bloodying their fingernails scratch-
ing and clawing in a lust for absolute sanctification. No battle
against oppression, this was a leap right through it, with
tongues babbling toward real visions, negating stale red
earth, warped privvies, men and women staring from their
sway-backed porches into nothingness. It was a faith meant
to transcend the grimy world that called it up. Like Saturday
night, the impulse to dream, the need to escape, the romance
and the contradictions of the land, this was a source of energy, tension, and power.

Elvis inherited these tensions, but more than that, gave
them his own shape. It is often said that if Elvis had not
come along to set off the changes in American music and
American life that followed his triumph, someone very much
like him would have done the job as well. But there is no
reason to think this is true, either in strictly musical terms,
or in any broader cultural sense. It is vital to remember that
Elvis was the first young Southern white to sing rock 'n' roll,
something he copied from no one but made up on the spot;
and to know that even though other singers would have come
up with a white version of the new black music acceptable to
teenage America, of all that did emerge in Elvis's wake, none
sang as powerfully, or with more than a touch of his magic.

Even more important is the fact that no singer emerged
with anything like Elvis's combination of great talent and
conscious ambition, and there is no way a new American
hero could have gotten out of the South and to the top—
creating a whole new sense of how big the top was, as Elvis

did—without that combination. The others—Perkins, Lewis, Charlie Rich—were bewildered by even a taste of fame and unable to handle a success much more limited than Presley's.

If Elvis had the imagination to come up with the dreams that kept him going, he had the music to bring them to life and make them real to huge numbers of other people. It was the genius of his singing, an ease and an intensity that has no parallel in American music, that along with his dreams separated him from his context; and for the rest of this chapter, we can try to discover what that singing was all about.

THE ROCKABILLY MOMENT

There are four of them in the little studio: Bill Black, the bass player; Scotty Moore, the guitarist; in the back, Sam Phillips, the producer; and the sexy young kid thumping his guitar as he sings, Elvis Presley, just nineteen. 1954.

Sam Phillips is doing all right for himself. He has been among the first to record men who will be giants in the world of postwar blues: B. B. King, Junior Parker, and the Howlin' Wolf himself. The names on Phillips's roster show his willingness to try anything: wonderful names like Big Memphis Ma Rainey, the Ripley Cotton Choppers, Dr. Ross, Hardrock Gunter, Rufus "Bear Cat" Thomas, Billy the Kid Emerson, the Prisonaires (a vocal group from the state pen), the immortal Hot Shot Love. There are plenty more knocking on the door, and with no more than this, Phillips's place in the history of American music would be assured—not that a place in history is quite what he is looking for.

In the records Phillips makes you can discern something more than taste, something like vision. He has cooked up a sound all his own: hot, fierce, overbearing, full of energy and desire, a sound to jump right out of the jukebox. But Phillips wants money, a lot of it, and he wants something new. Deep down in a place not even he sees clearly, he wants to set the world on its ear.

The kid with the guitar is . . . unusual; but they've

been trying to put something on the tape Sam keeps running back—a ballad, a hillbilly song, anything—and so far, well, it just doesn't get it.

The four men cool it for a moment, frustrated. They share a feeling they could pull something off if they hit it right, but it's been a while, and that feeling is slipping away, as it always does. They talk music, blues, Crudup, ever hear that, who you kiddin', man, dig this. The kid pulls his guitar up, clowns a bit. He throws himself at a song. *That's all right, mama, that's all right* . . . eat shit. He doesn't say that, naturally, but that's what he's found in the tune; his voice slides over the lines as the two musicians come in behind him, Scotty picking up the melody and the bassman slapping away at his axe with a drumstick. Phillips hears it, likes it, and makes up his mind.

All right, you got something. Do it again, I'll get it down. Just like that, don't mess with it. Keep it simple.

They cut the song fast, put down their instruments, vaguely embarrassed at how far they went into the music. Sam plays back the tape. Man, they'll run us outta town when they hear it, Scotty says; Elvis sings along with himself, joshing his performance. They all wonder, but not too much.

Get on home, now, Sam says. I gotta figure what to do with this.

They leave, but Sam Phillips is perplexed. Who is gonna play this crazy record? White jocks won't touch it 'cause it's nigger music and colored will pass 'cause it's hillbilly. It sounds good, it sounds sweet, but maybe it's just . . . too weird? The hell with it.

Sam Phillips released the record; what followed was the heyday of Sun Records and rockabilly music, a moment when boys were men and men were boys, when full-blown legends emerged that still walk the land and the lesser folk simply went along for the ride.

Rockabilly was a fast, aggressive music: simple, snappy drumming, sharp guitar licks, wild country boogie piano, the music of kids who came from all over the South to make records for Sam Phillips and his imitators. Rockabilly came and it went; there was never that much of it, and even including Elvis's first Sun singles, all the rockabilly hits put together sold less than Fats Domino's. But rockabilly fixed the crucial image of rock 'n' roll: the sexy, half-crazed fool standing on stage singing his guts out.

Most important, the image was white. Rockabilly was the only style of early rock 'n' roll that proved white boys could do it all—that they could be as strange, as exciting, as scary, and as free as the black men who were suddenly walking America's airwaves as if they owned them. There were two kinds of white counterattack on the black invasion of white popular culture that was rock 'n' roll: the attempt to soften black music or freeze it out, and the rockabilly lust to beat the black man at his own game.

Sam Phillips had the imagination to take in a country folksinger like Johnny Cash and a Stan Kenton fan like Charlie Rich; he was commercial enough to get rock 'n' roll out of both of them. Phillips gave a funny-looking kid named Roy Orbison the chance to growl that no girl had the style to match him, and the music to prove it. Sun tossed up Warren Smith, who claimed he had a girl who looked like a frog; Sonny Burgess, who dyed his hair red to match his red suit and his red Cadillac and told anyone who would listen he wanted to boogie with a red-headed woman; Sun offered us Billy Lee Riley, who blithely argued that rock 'n' roll was so strange it had to come from Mars. The little green men taught him how to do the bop, was the way he put it.

Carl Perkins found greatness here, and nowhere else; Jerry Lee Lewis simply took greatness as his due. ("*I* played on 'em," Jerry Lee told an interviewer who had asked the names of the musicians who had played on his records, "what else do you need to know?") Jerry Lee stormed his way through the whorehouse rock of "Deep Elem Blues" like Elmer Gantry moonlighting from the revival tent (celebrating the Dallas red light district that crawled with sin and blues piano); he tumbled into "Big Legged Woman," leering at an

imaginary audience with the arrogance that would bring him
down.

> *Let me tell ya, tell ya, tell ya something*
> <u>What I'm talkin' about</u>
> *I bet my bottom dollar there ain't a cherry in this house* *

While it lasted, Sun was a space of freedom, a place to
take chances. The music Sun produced was ominous, funny,
kicking up rhythm and bursting with exuberance, determination, and urgency, full of self-conscious novelty and experi-
ment. Most of the first rock 'n' roll styles were variations on
black forms that had taken shape before the white audience
moved in and forced those forms to turn its way; rockabilly
was almost self-contained, a world of its own, and as authentically new as any music can be.

Back in those days I knew some country kids who captured the spirit of the music as well as any 45: farm boys,
long, lean, tough, and good-humored. They flashed me my
first picture of Little Richard, kicked raccoons to death with
their bare feet, rustled sheep, chased Indian girls into the
bushes, and made it into town on Saturday night to watch
the razor fights. They were easy to idolize; one night they
got drunk, drove their car to the railroad tracks, and got
themselves blown to pieces.

Rockabilly was squeaky Charlie Feathers, a country
singer of no special talent or even much drive, trekking up to
Cincinnati, after failures at Sun, for the chance to yell, "Aw,
turn it *loose!*" and then disappear. He reached once, and he
missed, but these lines have stayed with me ever since a
scratchy tape of his one great song arrived in the mail:

> *Well, I'm a tip-top daddy an' I'm gonna have my way*
> *Dontcha worry 'bout me baby, dont worry what they say*
> *I got one hand, baby, let it swing by my side*
> *Just gimme one hand loose, and I'll be satisfied*
> *Satisfied!* †

---

* Copyright © P. Donald White. Used by permission.
† Copyright © 1956 by Fort Knox Music Company.

"Maybe someday your name will be in lights," Chuck
Berry promised the young rockers, and most of them never
got past the "maybe." There was a price for all that unex-
pected vitality and flash. Carl Perkins, still billing himself
"The King of Rock 'n' Roll" on the thin line of one hit and a
score of failures, sunk into alcohol; Johnny Cash nearly killed
himself on pills; Gene Vincent found himself exiled to England, where some still remembered, and died of a bleeding
ulcer before he was forty. Johnny Burnette, Eddie Cochran,
Buddy Holly, chasing after Elvis's pot of gold, died in ac-
cidents, in fast cars and chartered planes. Most simply vanished and were forgotten—if they were lucky enough to have
been known at all. They fell back into the predictability of
country music or the day-to-day sameness they had meant to
escape. All they left behind was rock 'n' roll, and an audience
that twenty years later was still acting out their fantasies and
seeking novelty and amusement in their ghosts.

It was an explosion, and standing over it all was Elvis.
In the single year he recorded for Sam Phillips—August
1954 through August 1955—ten sides were released (four
more were used by RCA to fill up Elvis's first album); about
half derived from country songs, the rest took off from blues.
His music stands to the rest of rockabilly as genius does to
talent.

The blues especially have not dated at all. Not a note is
false; their excitement comes through the years intact, unburdened by cuteness, mannerism, or posturing.* Nothing is
stylized. The music is clean, straight, open, and free.

That's what these sides are about: finding space in the

* For most of us, the songs are unburdened by any sort of nostalgia as well. In their
time, they were little heard outside of the South, and they turned up on albums
only when Elvis was off in the army and RCA had to scrape its vaults for something
to release. None ever made the national pop charts. Today they are rarely played on
the radio (though spinning the dial on Elvis's thirty-eighth birthday, I picked up
"That's All Right"—on a country station). Colonel Parker, or Elvis himself,
deems it vital that the King be protected from his past, so the songs have not, as
with most classic rock, been reissued in a package that might attract an audience.
Given the publicity that has come with Elvis, these sides are almost invisible, the
result of a prepop moment; but *their* result is as public as rock 'n' roll. From one
point of view they are the basis of the whole show. So there is a lot of power
packed into these records, and not all of it is musical.

crunch of the worn-out and overfamiliar; finding a way to feel free in that space and finding the voice to put that feeling across.

The best evidence of Sam Phillips' spirit is in the sound of the records. Each song is clear, direct, uncluttered, and blended into something coherent. There is that famous echo, slapping back at the listener, and a bubbling tension that is never quite resolved; no comforts of vocal accompaniment, but the risk of one young man on his own. The sound is all presence, as if Black and Moore each took a step straight off the record and Elvis was somehow squeezed right into the mike. "I went into the studio," Sam Phillips recalled years later, "to draw out a person's innate, possibly unknown talents, present them to the public, and let the public be the judge. I had to be a psychologist and know how to handle each artist and how to enable him to be at his best. I went with the idea that an artist should have something not just good, but totally unique. When I found someone like that, I did everything in my power to bring it out." *

The sides Phillips cut with Elvis might have worked in the twenties, and they might do for the eighties; not simply as listenable music—there is no doubt about that—but as music that still sounds new, that still breaks things open.†

* From an interview with John Pugh, *Country Music*, November 1973.
† Even the lyrics evade any possibility of camp—unlike so much of fifties rock 'n' roll, including Elvis's RCA material, which was made with a trendy commercial ear. The blues and country motifs of the Sun sides are as lively today as they were old in 1954; if it takes little effort to trace "That's All Right" and "Milkcow Blues Boogie" back to Son House's epic "My Black Mama," cut in 1930, it takes even less to follow the trail forward to the Rolling Stones or the Allman Brothers.

Not surprisingly, on the album that today features House's masterpiece (*Really! The Country Blues*), there is an ancient, quiet statement of the theme Elvis brought home with such force. Made in 1928, it comes deadpan, spoken over a pretty little guitar line by one William Moore—an old, old mood, there too in Harmonica Frank or the Allmans' "Pony Boy," but to modern ears, *about* what Elvis *was*. This is "Old Country Rock": "Come on, Bill, let's take them for an old country rock. Let's go back down the Rappahanock, down Tappahanock way. Look at Bill while everybody rocks. Get that old rock, Bill. Everybody rock. Old folks rock. Young folks rock. Boys rock. Girls rock. Trot back, man, and let me rock. Rock me, sis, rock me. Rock me till I sweat. Trot back, folks, let your pappy rock. Pappy knows how. Children rock. Sister Ernestine, show your pappy how you rock. Mighty fine, boys,

Elvis can tell us what was new and distinctive about his time without being trapped by it, and without trapping us. He can do it because to a great degree ELVIS PRESLEY was the distinctive item. For all the writers who have found a neat logic to the development of the music Elvis made, and have lost his genius in a process, that is not what I hear; I hear a whole world of music that by no means had to crystallize as it did. "I heard the news," Elvis would sing in "Good Rockin' Tonight"—but he was the news.

Elvis's Memphis records—"Milkcow Blues Boogie," "You're a Heartbreaker," "Good Rockin' Tonight," "Baby Let's Play House"—might be his best; a choice between the Sun sides and "Hound Dog," "Don't Be Cruel," "All Shook Up," "Reconsider Baby," "Suspicious Minds" and "Long Black Limousine" is not one I ever want to make. Elvis's first music deserves a close and loving attention not simply because it represents all that Elvis and those he has sung for have lost—youthful exuberance, innocence, haven't we tired of that story?—but because this is unquestionably great music, fun to think about, and because this music foreshadows, and contains, the entire aesthetic Elvis has worked out over the twenty years of his career. This is emotionally complex music that can return something new each time you listen to it. What I hear, most of the time, is the affection and respect Elvis felt for the limits and conventions of his family life, of his community, and ultimately of American life, captured in his country sides; and his refusal of those limits, of any limits, played out in his blues. This is a rhythm of acceptance and rebellion, lust and quietude, triviality and distinction. It can dramatize the rhythm of our own lives well enough.

---

rock it, rock it till the cows come home. Whip that box, Bill, whip it. Too sad, I mean too sad for the public. Now up the country, back down the country again on that old rock. Rappahanock. Tappahanock. Cross the river, boys, cross the river. Man, it's sporty. Play it, Bill, play it till the sergeant comes." No one could ask for a better statement than that.

ELVIS MOVES OUT

Elvis first went into Sam Phillips's studio in early 1954, and though it took him months of work to get to the point where he could make his first record, it is impossible to imagine a more natural sound. There's more here than anyone could have guessed, he seems to be saying: more soul, more guts, and more life.

The tune was one of three Arthur Crudup songs Elvis recorded. Crudup had cut many sides for RCA's Bluebird outlet in the forties and early fifties; he wrote good songs, pointed little messages of loss fitted to bright blues melodies, but he was a minimal guitarist and an erratic singer, a bit one-dimensional. Only on numbers that verged on country or pop styles (as with his lovely "So Glad You're Mine," which Elvis recorded in a disinterested manner soon after reaching RCA) does Crudup seem to hit his stride.

Elvis reduces the bluesman's original to a footnote. He takes over the music, changing words and tightening verses to suit himself, hanging onto the ends of lines as Scotty Moore chimes in with pretty high-note riffs. Elvis sounds very young, sure of himself, ready to win; he turns Crudup's lament for a lost love into a satisfied declaration of independence, the personal statement of a boy claiming his manhood. His girl may have left him, but nothing she can do can dent the pleasure that radiates from his heart. It's the blues, but free of all worry, all sin; a simple joy with no price to pay.

Phillips put out the record on August 6, 1954, and it soon earned its place on the Memphis R&B charts, along with new hits by Muddy Waters and Johnny Ace. *Cashbox*, oblivious to Presley's color, reviewed the side as a blues; *Billboard*, prophetically, saw potential in all markets. It was an event, to some a scary one, but if "That's All Right" brought home the racial fears of a lot of people, it touched the secret dreams of others; if it was a threat, it was also another ride on the raft. "It was like a giant wedding ceremony," said Marion Keisker, Sam Phillips's secretary, and the one who first heard in Elvis's voice everything Phillips was after. "It was like two feuding clans who had been brought together by marriage."

"That's All Right" was a tremendous hit with teenagers, and in Memphis, where the record broke first, the current greeting among the teenagers is still a rhythmical line from the song: "Ta dee dah dee dee dah."

The Memphis *Press Scimitar*, 1954

You can't get that kind of success in *Billboard;* "Sun's Newest Star," as the *Press-Scimitar* called Elvis, wasted no time taking advantage of it. He tried out his material in the local clubs, drew three thousand people to the opening of a shopping center, and busted up a big country review when he sang a song called "Good Rockin' Tonight." Phillips, for his part, wasted no time getting Elvis back into the studio and a new record into the stores.

"That's All Right" was an easy ride. "Good Rockin' " is a cataclysm; it reflects the new confidence of a young man who knows what it means to satisfy an audience, to take them beyond their expectations. The record is charged with an authority that no other country rocker ever approached.

Roy Brown, the most influential blues singer of the forties, wrote the tune, and Wynonie Harris made it a hit in 1949. Harris was a sophisticated uptown R&B vocalist; his "Good Rockin' " is a conventional jump blues, lacking real tension or drama. He seems unable to exploit the stomping promise of the lyrics in rhythm or phrasing; he bumps words into each other and sometimes trips on them. He's too removed from the country revel the song is all about, and too cool.

Elvis opens with a high, wild "WELLLLLLLLL . . ." and pulls fast and hard into the first verse before the echo of his shout has had a chance to fade. His voice is raw, pleading and pushing, full of indescribably sexy asides, the throaty nuances that would flare up into "All Shook Up" and "Burning Love." Elvis slows for a second in the middle of a line, drawling softly, over his shoulder, as if he can't quite bring himself to say out loud how good the party's going to be; and then suddenly he is out of breath, as if he's run for miles to tell his story, but there's good rockin' tonight and everybody *has* to know—how could they live if they miss it? Tonight his girl will get everything *she's* been missing. "We're gonna rock—ALL OUR BLUES AWAY!" He can't tell it fast enough, he can barely keep up with himself. Near to bursting, the song slams home.

"Milkcow Blues Boogie" came out in January 1955, with writer's credit on the label going to Kokomo Arnold, a Georgia-born blues singer who recorded "Milk Cow Blues" in Chicago in 1934. One always reads that Elvis re-created Arnold's song, though apparently no one has bothered to listen to both men—Elvis takes all of one verse from the bluesman. Presley's style might well owe something to Arnold; they share a fast, nervous delivery, full of unpredictable swoops and moans, a flair for crazy-quilt tempo changes of tremendous excitement, and the ability to come down with a great force on a key line. But "Milkcow" was a song held in common long before Elvis was born, recorded by more blues and country singers than anyone has bothered to count. What Elvis did, in fact, was to throw a bit of Arnold—who perhaps Phillips played for him—into Bob Wills's western swing hit, "Brain Cloudy Blues," which was cut in 1946. "Brain Cloudy," highlighted by Wills's fiddle and a tough guitar solo, featured the straight, insulated vocal of Tommy Duncan up against Wills's patented cornball asides, which worked very effectively to bleed the punch out of every line. Elvis started with Wills's second verse, dropping the "brain cloudy" motif; faded to Arnold; and then finished off with Wills's words, changing lyrics when Duncan's crisp, almost effete diction threw him off.

I go into the musicology of this song in some detail because of what it can tell us about how these first records came about. The book on Elvis's early music is that it was "spontaneous," "without any evident forethought," "unselfconscious." In other words, Elvis was the natural (and, the implicit assumption is, likely unthinking) expression of a folk culture. I've tried to present some hints of the culture Elvis came out of as a set of forces that could have held him back and worn him down as easily as they gave him life; to build a context that puts us in touch with will and desire, not just smug sociology. Researching his biography of Elvis, Jerry Hopkins dug back into the world Elvis left behind in Memphis, and he found that nearly every record Elvis made with Sam Phillips was carefully and laboriously constructed out of hits and misses, riffs and bits of phrasing held through dozens of bad takes. The songs grew slowly, over hours and hours, into a music that paradoxically sounded much fresher than all the poor tries that had come before; until Presley, Bill Black and Scotty Moore had the attack in their blood, and yes, didn't have to think about it. That's not exactly my idea of "spontaneity" or "unself-consciousness."

Elvis had the nuance of cool down pat—the pink pants-and-shirt outfit he wore to his audition, the carelessness of his swagger, or the sneer around the edges of his smile— because the will to create himself, to matter, was so intense and so clear. He strolled into the studio and didn't leave until every note was perfect. Even later at RCA, still on the way up and wavering between complete self-confidence and a lingering doubt, he would demand thirty takes on "Hound Dog," pleading for one more try long after everyone else was satisfied.

Try to wash the images of success from your mind and picture a twenty year old in a tacky studio on perhaps his fifteenth take of a song that is coming together out of fragments of memory, old 78's, and pure instinct. Everything was riding on each new release: whether Elvis could really take his career beyond the commonplace expectations of those around him; whether he could top that last record; whether he could find a sound that would give him room to breathe and yet hold the fans he had won and spread the word. The little success he had achieved was fragile; each new record risked it. He had to take that energy of desire and distance himself from it, throw it into the song so that it would be coherent and powerful *as* a song; so that when he sang, "Tonight she'll know I'm a mighty mighty man," it would sound like an obvious, thrilling statement of the facts. Whatever strain there might have been in his voice or his hopes—that unpleasant hint of the small time that you can hear so plainly in Bill Haley and so many of Elvis's imitators—it had to go. The talent was there, and it was extraordinary, but it was complex, and it needed a form. They were in the studio a long, tiresome time to catch the spirit of a boy who, on record, sounded as if he flew in, stopped long enough to blow the walls back, and exited through the unhinged back door with a grin.

With "Milkcow Blues Boogie" we are back to the image Cash chose as the essence of the soul of the back country South: hot heavy air bursting all over the sky in lightning and rain. No music of any kind captures it better than this record.

Wills and Arnold move right into the song; Elvis lingers over the first lines, and his voice drips an erotic tension that must have melted the mike. "Oh well, Ah woke up . . . this moanin'—An' Ah looked out . . . the doah—." He has you;

EE #4. At a DJ convention early in 1973, I sit drinking with Bobby Vee and Brian Hyland, veterans of the Now-That-Elvis-Is-in-the-Army-We-Can-Cash-in-on-the-Vacuum-Era. I am interviewing Bob (he has changed his name back to Veline and is a folksinger now) in order to pen six thousand words of liner notes to a greatest hits package, an essay that will no doubt be the only extended critical discussion of his *oeuvre*. Bob tells me that, yes, for him it all began with Elvis—and suddenly the whole tone of the conversation is different. Professional cool drops away and we are shameless fans, awed by our subject. Vee and Hyland have met Elvis: he got drunk with Hyland (so Brian says) and was surly to Vee (I believe that). Well, they are outcasts in the rock 'n' roll world now, two very ordinary looking men; for all their triviality as rock singers, they once did their best to live up to Elvis and keep the faith. You can almost feel them gazing at Elvis as he is today, as if in his comeback they still see a glimmer of a future for themselves, just as they did when he started out years ago.

you're hungering for whatever comes next, but he cuts you
off. "Hold it fellas!" he shouts. "That don't *move* me!" Soft
and sultry again: "Let's get real . . . *real* gone, for a change."
It's too perfect; you think he must be reading lines, as if this
is a scene from one of his movies; and it is, I guess, even if at
this point the dreams were only in his head.

Elvis charges the song, shooting that boundless
Wellllllllll out ahead of himself, and the three of them are
off. Elvis spurs the changes with his guitar, flying all over
the story he is telling—his woman is gone and he wants her
back but she's got about five minutes to make up her mind—
singing with the crazy shifts from high to low that with
Buddy Holly sounded funny and with Elvis sound frightening. In two and a half minutes he carries his listener through
anger, loss, bemusement, melancholy, violence, defiance, fatalism, menace, delight, freedom, and regret. The song is as
sure and tough a tale of breaking loose as any there is.

Yodeling, roaring his anger, yelling out to Scotty
Moore—"Let's *milk* it!"—he comes off the guitar solo in a
new mood, almost reflective now, meditating, this is all moving very fast but his guitar has somehow settled the music,
and if his girl is gone, if that milkcow is never coming home,
he still has time to step back and bring us into the song with
a little blues philosophy:

> *Wellll, good evenin'*
> *Don' that sun look good goin' down*
> *Wee-eee-ell, good evenin'*
> *Don' that sun look good goin' down*
> *Well, dont that old moon look lonesome*
> *When your bay-ay-ayby's not around?*

And then rage pours back over his acceptance. He calls
back his woman and faces her down, the song picking up
momentum, his voice shimmering and shaking through night
air:

> *Well I tried everything*
> *To git along with you*

Now I'm gonna tell you what I'm gonna do
I'm gonna quit my crying
I'm gonna leave you alone

and suddenly driving even harder, cursing with two of the most perfect lines in blues:

If you dont believe I'm leavin'
YOU CAN COUNT THE DAYS I'M GONE

Again, it is his authority that is so astounding. Scores of singers, black and white, have sung those lines, but few if any have ever made them seem so real, so *final*. The fatalism that is written right into the song, in that lovely image of the setting sun and the rising moon, will not do for Elvis, and he sings those last hard lines with an intensity that wipes out everything that has come before. A blues singer would use this verse as balance, to dramatize the rise and fall of his spirit, translating the circle the natural world draws around him into a metaphor for his inability to master his life. For Elvis, young and on his way, feeling his growing power over audiences, the growing space between himself and everything he should have taken for granted, there comes a point where he cannot settle for what others have made of this song, and the balance tips to fury. Our boy will get what he deserves; everyone else can get out of the way.

THE BOY WHO STOLE THE BLUES

I slicked myself up,
Till I looked like a guinea!
          CARL PERKINS, "Put Your Cat Clothes On"

For Carl Perkins and the rest of the rockabilly heroes, the liberation of the new music must have been a bit like a white foray into darktown, a combination of a blackface minstrel show and night riding—romantic as hell, a little dangerous, a little ridiculous. At the start, Elvis sounded black to

those who heard him; when they called him the Hillbilly
Cat, they meant the white Negro. Or as Elvis put it, years
later: ". . . made a record and when the record came out a
lot of people liked it and you could hear folks around town
saying, 'Is he, is he?' and I'm going, 'Am I, am I?' "

Well, I can't hear that anymore. I hear a young man,
white as the whale, who was special because in his best
music he was so much his *own* man, one who took the musical and emotional strengths of the blues as a natural and necessary part of the world he was building for himself—one
part of that world, no more, but clearly the finest stuff
around at the time.

True as it is in an historical or commercial sense, too
much has been made of Elvis as "a white man who sang
black music credibly," as a singer who made black music acceptable to whites. This and too many whites trying to do
the same thing have corrupted any sense of what Elvis *did*
do, of what was at stake in his personal culture. Most white
blues singing is singing *at* the blues; what comes out is either
entirely fake, or has behind it the white impulse to become
black: to ask for too much without offering anything in return.

Real white blues singers make something new out of the
blues, as Jimmie Rodgers, Dock Boggs, Elvis, and Bob
Dylan have; or, they sing out of a deep feeling for the blues,
but in a musical style that is not blues—not formally, anyway. But we can trace their strength to the blues; what links
their music to the blues is an absolute commitment to the
material, an expressive force open to some whites because
they have been attracted to another man's culture in a way
that could not be denied. This is the music of whites not so
much singing the blues as living up to them.

Van Morrison's "Listen to the Lion" would have to be
my best example, but Rod Stewart and Charlie Rich have
done their work here too, singing as if the fate of the whole
world rested on their ability to reach deeply enough into
their souls to get all the way into ours. I saw Rich do it not
so long ago, in a setting so anachronistic he came near to

leaving his audience behind him, because they were in a mood to be confirmed, not moved.

It was in August 1973, at a country music affair sponsored by Columbia Records, attended mostly by record industry heavies and hangers-on. Singer after singer took the stage, offering songs that made pain trivial and good times bland; music as sterile as it was predictable as it was (within a tight, well-regulated country market) commercially effective. The producers and song publishers and publicists sat near the stage, waiting for the singers to humble themselves before them, and as each did, I thought the humility might be worth a lot more if it were cynical than if it were real. It was that kind of day; I yearned for some rock 'n' roll arrogance, no matter how fake *that* might be.

Charlie Rich, who has always had too much of the blues in his style to fit easily into the country music market, was riding a number one country single that had, because it was more than country, crossed over into the upper reaches of the pop charts. He closed the show. Forty years old, a big man with white hair and lines deep in his face, he took his seat behind the piano and sang a harmless tune from his current album. After almost twenty years in the music business he had only three hits to show for it; even as "Behind Closed Doors" was climbing, the clerk in the record store marked up my Charlie Rich album under "nostalgia." A song Rich's wife Margaret Ann wrote about him, a haunting ballad of failure called "Life's Little Ups and Downs," tells the truth of Rich's career, but that day at the convention the crowd's truth was that Rich was on top and would stay there. Right as they may have been, I could not believe it was more than a public moment in an invisible career, and that made each song more precious and each missed chance that much more depressing.

Rich sang his hit, and it had grown for him. It meant more now than it had when it was just another throw of the dice, and it was a triumph. Because Rich was the star of the day, the men running the show gave him an encore. Staring into the keys, trying to balance the moment, Rich introduced his song. "I wrote this for Peter Guralnick," he said, "who wrote the book *Feel Like Going Home.*" Named for the most terrifyingly lonely of all Muddy Waters' songs, it is probably the most loving book ever written about American music; Charlie Rich is the subject of its finest chapter.

"Today," Rich said, "I would like to dedicate this song to the President of the United States." And so for Nixon, just then slipping over the line to the point where his whole existence would become a national joke, Rich sang,

> *I tried and I failed*
> *And I feel like going home.*

The words stayed in my mind throughout the strange, difficult song; they didn't change the president, or the country, or the world, but they changed how a few of us who were there to listen understood those things. They cut through everything I believe to uncover a compassion that I never, never wanted to feel.

We won't find Elvis here. The idea that the blues is a feeling and not a form can bring us closer to what Rich did that afternoon—but for Elvis, the blues was a style of freedom, something he couldn't get in his own home, full of roles to play and rules to break. In the beginning the blues was more than anything else a fantasy, an epic of struggle and pleasure, that he lived out as he sang. Not a fantasy that went beneath the surface of his life, but one that soared right over it.

Singing in the fifties, before blacks began to guard their culture with the jealousy it deserved, Elvis had no guilty dues to pay. Arthur Crudup complained his songs made a white man famous, and he had a right to complain, but mostly because he never got his royalties. Elvis sang "That's All Right" and "My Baby Left Me" (one of his first sides for RCA, and the only one in the Sun rockabilly style) with more power, verve, and skill than Crudup did; his early records were more than popular with blacks; but still the implication, always there when Crudup or Willie Mae

Thornton (who made the first version of "Hound Dog")
looked out at the white world that gave them only obscurity
in exchange for their music and penned them off from getting anything for themselves, is that Elvis would have been
nothing without them, that he climbed to fame on their
backs. It is probably time to say that this is nonsense; the
mysteries of black and white in American music are just not
that simple. Consider the tale of "Hound Dog."

Jerry Leiber and Mike Stoller were Jewish boys from
the East Coast who fell in love with black music. Hustling in
Los Angeles in the early fifties, they wrote "Hound Dog,"
and promoted the song to Johnny Otis, a ruling R&B band-
leader who was actually a dark-skinned white man from Berkeley who many thought was black. Otis gave the song to
Thornton, who recorded it in a slow bluesy style, and Otis
also took the composer's credit, which Leiber and Stoller had
to fight to get back. Elvis heard the record, changed the song
completely, from the tempo to the words, and cut Thornton's version to shreds.

Whites wrote it; a white made it a hit. And yet there is
no denying that "Hound Dog" is a "black" song, unthinkable
outside the impulses of black music, and probably a rewrite
of an old piece of juke joint fury that dated back far beyond
the birth of any of these people. Can you pull justice out of
that maze? What *does* Huck owe Jim, especially when Jim is
really Huck in blackface and everyone smells loot? All you
can say is this was Elvis's music because he made it his own.

Here's a better story. In 1955 the Robins (a black vocal
group that had passed through seven labels with no real success) and Richard Berry (a black singer with two duds to his
name) were brought together by Leiber and Stoller.
Together they made the classic "Riot in Cell Block #9,"
which helped change the Robins into the Coasters and
brought Berry his first notoriety. Leiber and Stoller went on
to fame and fortune and the Coasters at least to fame; Berry,
after losing out with "The Big Break," an outrageous follow-
up to "Riot," made "Louie, Louie" in 1957, but though it
was his biggest hit, it never made the pop charts.

In 1962 a white group called the Kingsmen unearthed "Louie, Louie," and their version was number two in the country. Paul Revere and the Raiders, then a local Seattle band, rode the tune into a gold mine on the West Coast. As rock records, these discs were virtually definitive: hard rhythm, harder lead guitar, and a vocal that made no sense whatsoever. Within months every high school band in the country was playing "Louie, Louie," and every other person you met had a copy of the *real* lyrics, which were reputedly obscene. Some highlights I recall from locker room days: "Gonna make her again," "Gotta rag on," "Fuck that girl across the sea." (Not much, I admit, but those were thin years for rock 'n' roll.) Soon even Congress got into the act; they investigated the tune, duly played it (at 45, 33, 78, and 16 rpm), and charmingly pronounced the song "indecipherable at any speed." By this time, everyone but the man who owned the copyright—and likely him too—had forgotten all about Richard Berry, whose original lyrics would have been beside the point anyway.

Ten years later a white New York group called Stories released a single called "Brother Louie," and the record went to number one. "Louie, Louie, Loo-aye," went the chorus—familiar, to say the least. Obviously, the chorus was what caught your attention; it always had been. Since rock 'n' roll had been around long enough for its fans to develop a sense of history, a few people remembered Richard Berry. And what was this new "Louie, Louie" about? A black girl and her white boyfriend—Louie—and his mean racist parents. "Ain't no difference if you're black or white," Stories sang. "Brothers, you know what I mean." But this time, the "brother" was white; and finally the old song contained the racial contradictions that had sustained it.

If Elvis drew power from black culture, he was not really imitating blacks; when he told Sam Phillips he didn't sing like nobody, he told the truth. No white man had so deeply absorbed black music, and transformed it, since Jimmie Rodgers; instead of following Rodgers's musical style, as

so many good white singers had—Lefty Frizzel, Ernest
Tubb, Tommy Duncan, and, in his more personal way,
Hank Williams, following that style until it simply wore
out—Elvis followed Rodgers' musical strategy and began the
story all over again.

Elvis didn't have to exile himself from his own community in order to justify and make real his use of an outsider's
culture (like the Jewish jazzman Mezz Mezzrow, who would
claim that his years on the streets of Harlem had actually
darkened his skin and thickened his lips; like Johnny Otis
and so many real white Negroes); as a Southerner and white
trash to boot, Elvis was already outside. In 1955 he had at
least as much in common with Bobby Bland as he did with
Perry Como. Which is to say that Elvis was also hellbent on
the mainstream, and sure enough of himself to ignore the
irony that it would be his version of the backdoor freedoms
of black music that would attract the mainstream to him, giving him the chance to exchange his hillbilly strangeness for
acceptability.

Elvis's blues were a set of sexual adventures, and as a
blues-singing swashbuckler, his style owed as much to Errol
Flynn as it did to Arthur Crudup. It made sense to make
movies out of it.

THE PINK CADILLAC

By the time "Baby, Let's Play House" came out in May
1955, the rockabilly singers were coming out of the swamps.
Phillips was shifting his company from black to white, setting up an outbreak of rock 'n' roll that would follow hard on
Presley's already discussed and taken-for-granted move up to
a national label. Phillips had Malcolm Yelvington (a Memphis country singer endowed with false teeth and the best
rockabilly name outside of Elvis's) cut the first of many
country rock versions of Stick McGhee's 1949 R&B classic,
"Drinkin' Wine Spo-Dee-O-Dee," and its message summed
up the new mood: drinkin' and fightin' are what life is all

about, and if anybody argues, give 'em a drink or lay 'em out.

Elvis had finished his early tours, ranging from Texas to Florida; he was set for San Francisco—alien territory, crucial to proving himself outside the South—and he was booked into the Cow Palace, the biggest arena in Northern California. The Colonel had made his initial connections. In Lubbock, Texas, a kid named Charles "Buddy" Holley bowed to the East every night and began getting a band together. There was, to put it mildly, excitement in the air.

Elvis's dive into "Baby, Let's Play House"—a wild crash of hiccups, gulps, and baby-baby-babys—measured perfectly the distance he had traveled since he broke into tears at the sight of his first record. There is a new spirit here, a lightness and a sense of fun, as if his whole little career has suddenly hit him as a wonderful joke. The dreams are coming true; that drive and secret ambition can afford to open up. He knows now that his mother was right, and he is safe. That throwaway superiority for which he has worked so hard can blossom out into arrogance, humor, and pure good times.

What was it his mother told him? That he was just as good as anybody? Or did she whisper, late at night when no one else was there to hear, that her boy could never lose?

Arthur Gunter, a black singer working for the Excello label in Nashville, wrote and recorded "Baby, Let's Play House," and got a hit with the black market in early 1955. He used a tight acoustic band and walked right through, vaguely interested in telling his girl that she might think she's hot stuff, but she'd better come on back and get down to it, or there'd be, you know, trouble. It was all very low-key (that splendid intro was all Elvis); Gunter's lack of concern was his charm. Still, he didn't sound very convincing.

Elvis wailed. He turned the song into a correspondence course in rock 'n' roll, and it was by far the most imitated of his first records. For pure excitement, he may never have matched it.

The rhythm was heavy, the syncopation astonishing—a fast, ominous bass tromping over a cottonmouth guitar—the band drove hard into every chorus and cut out for all the best lines. "Aw, let's play house," Elvis shouted, and Scotty punched out a few riffs; "HIT IT!" Elvis cried, and Moore and Black rammed home music so tough it wasn't touched until Elvis pushed them into the earthquake that was "Hound Dog."

Elvis made one crucial change in the lyrics. The girl he's after in this song is high-class stuff: she might go to college, he sings, she might go to school, but she'll never really get away, never be so sure of herself she can get along without the loving only he can give her. She might even get religion, Gunter had added, which won't help her either; but Elvis threw in a faster, flashier image that was more to his own point: "You may have a pink Cadillac/ But dontcha be nobody's fool!" Elvis had just bought one for himself.

Now, the obvious thing to say here is that The Pink Cadillac and All That It Implied proved Elvis's undoing: out there in mass culture America, Elvis would lose his talent in its reward. Dontcha be nobody's fool? The poor boy should have taken his own advice.

Well, we should be careful about this sort of thing. There is a deep need to believe that Elvis (or any part of American culture one cares about) began in a context of purity, unsullied by greed or ambition or vulgarity, somehow outside of and in opposition to American life as most of us know it and live it. Even RCA first presented Elvis as "a folksinger" (claiming, in the notes to his second album, that the simple-country-boy-with-guitar stance pictured on the cover was "most appropriate" for him). A writer as tough and sensitive as Stanley Booth can write (in a piece that seems to miss the point of its own title, "A Hound Dog, to the Manor Born"): "All that was really necessary was that [Elvis] stop doing his thing and start doing theirs. His thing was 'Mystery Train,' 'Milkcow Blues Boogie.' Theirs was 'Love Me Tender,' 'Loving You,' 'Jailhouse Rock,' 'King Creole.' " Charlie Gillett, author of *The Sound of the City*, as definitive a history of rock 'n' roll as we are likely to get, complains that Elvis sold out his true culture when he let RCA put *drums* on his records. It is virtually a critical canon that Elvis's folk purity, and therefore his talent, was ruined by (a) his transmogrification from naïve country boy into corrupt pop star (he sold his soul to Colonel Tom, or Parker just stole it), (b) Hollywood, (c) the army, (d) money and soft living, (e) all of the above.*

This approach may contain some figures, but not Elvis. "Milkcow Blues" was not "his thing"—it was one of many—so much as it was Sam Phillips's. Phillips loved money and he loved the blues, the basic pop combination; pairing a blues and a country tune on Elvis's first record gave him a successful commercial formula, and he stuck to it on every subsequent Presley release and on most of the records he cut by other rockabilly singers. But when Elvis left Memphis to confront a national audience as mysterious to him as he was to it, he had to define himself fully, and he did so by presenting his authentic multiplicity in music. I am, he announced, a house rocker, a boy steeped in mother-love, a true son of the church, a matinee idol who's only kidding, a man with too many rough edges for anyone ever to smooth away. Something in me yearns for a settling of affairs, he said with his pale music and his tired movies; on the other hand, he answered with his rock 'n' roll and an occasional blues, I may break away at any time. You never know. At RCA, where the commercial horizons were much broader than they were down at Sun, Elvis worked with far more "artistic freedom" than he ever did with Sam Phillips.

Two things did happen that led to the collapse of Elvis's music. His multiplicity opened up the possibility that he could be all things to all people, but his eagerness to prove it, with records like *Something For Everybody*, destroyed his abil-

---

* This Faustian scenario is an absolutely vital part of Elvis's legend, especially for all those who took part in Elvis's event and felt bewildered and betrayed by his stagnation and decline. We could hardly believe that a figure of such natural strength could dissolve into such a harmless nonentity; it had to be some kind of trick. Even now, Phil Spector is convinced that Colonel Parker hypnotizes Elvis.

ity to focus his talent. He wound up without a commitment
to any musical style; his music lost that dramatic shape Sam
Phillips helped give it. And his ambition, the source of so
much of the intensity and emotion he put into his early
music, plainly outstripped itself. Two years after making his
first record he had won more than anyone knew was there;
he had achieved a status that trivialized struggle and made
will obsolescent. His success turned his life upside down;
from this point on, he would have in his hands what he set
out to get, but he would have to reach for the energy and
desire that had made his triumph possible.

The Pink Cadillac was at the heart of the contradiction
that powered Elvis's early music; a perfect symbol of the
glamor of his ambition and the resentments that drove it on.
When he faced his girl in "Baby, Let's Play House" (like
Dylan railing at the heroine of "Like a Rolling Stone," or
Jagger surveying the upper-class women that star in "The
19th Nervous Breakdown," "Play With Fire," and "You
Can't Always Get What You Want"), Elvis sang with contempt for a world that had always excluded him; he sang
with a wish for its pleasures and status. Most of all he sang
with delight at the power that fame and musical force gave
him: power to escape the humiliating obscurity of the life he
knew, and power to sneer at the classy world that was now
ready to flatter him. Not the real upper class, of course; it
would be years before socialites set out in pursuit of the
Rolling Stones and academics began to fawn over the Beatles. Still, the jump Elvis made from the woods and welfare
to simple respectability was far more epic. Girls who had
turned up their noses in high school were now waiting in
line, just as today men and women who are barely hanging
on to the edge of the middle class wait in line to see a man
who has achieved an eminence class can never bring.

Elvis sang out his song with a monumental disdain for
all those folk who moved easily through a world that had
never been easy for him (anyone who had ever shown the
Presleys *exactly who they were*); he grinned at the big car he

had dreamed about, because finally it was within reach, and he could take it, on his terms.

A bit farther into the image of the Pink Cadillac, something more interesting was going on. If Elvis was looking down on his smart girl's Caddy from the vantage point of his own, he was implicitly presenting his new successful self as a target for his own resentments, and singing with more than enough emotion to hit the bullseye. He was The Star; not asserting, in the conventional Uriah Heep country style, that all his wealth don't buy him happiness (it does, it does), but burlesquing and damning the complacency of the rich and powerful by flaunting *his* power and riches, and getting away with it. Somehow taking both sides, Elvis could show his listeners just how much, and how little, that Pink Cadillac was worth: more and less than anyone would have guessed.*

This is a kind of rock 'n' roll drive—the vitality that endows the artifacts of materialism with life—that is captured perfectly in *The Harder They Come,* a movie about the Jamaican version of the American pop dream, when Jimmy Cliff steals a white Cadillac and spins it over a golf course with an unbeatable smile on his face. He's a refugee from the most terrifying poverty, a reggae-singing people's outlaw with reflexes instead of politics. "You can get it if you really want," he sings. "The harder they come, the harder they fall, one and all." He wants that car and the whole world it stands for; he doesn't want it, he wants to smash it all up. He hasn't made the connections; he hasn't worked it all out any

---

* In America, after all, the final proof of grace is *economic* sanctification; which is to say, Elvis can have the piety of the poor along with the ease of the rich and know that since he never lost the first, he deserves the last. Still full of the energy of his comeback in early 1969, Elvis went back to Memphis and sang a song called "Long Black Limousine"—the tale of a hometown girl punished for her sins and her fancy city ways, mourned and damned by the poor country boy who has waited all these years for a better ending than the car crash that did his sweetheart in. The tension as the song opens is almost unbearable, and Elvis never lets go of the song. He is completely convincing. And yet of course he is the country boy captured by the city if there ever was one; he's that girl, riding in her long black limousine on her way to the graveyard, as surely as he is King Elvis, speeding away from the studio in his own black limousine. When he smashes through the contradictions of his career with such music, we have Elvis at his greatest.

more than a twenty-year-old Elvis did. But he knows that car belongs to him because he can take more pleasure from it than anyone else.

What is most remarkable is that Elvis was able to laugh at the persona he drew from "Baby, Let's Play House" as convincingly as he acted it out—as if a combination of the freedom to realize his desires and a freedom to ignore them was what freedom really meant. He was less into the music than on top of it, feigning toughness, feigning anger, finding it, for the famous lines

> *I'd rather see you dead little girl*
> *Than to be with another man*

and then all fun again, as if the venom he'd put into those words struck him at once as ludicrous, and maybe a little frightening. He put even more of himself into the song, and still parodied his menace, lowering his voice to a rumble, getting out of the tune with a chuckle that gave it all away: deep down he was just a good boy, out for a real good time.

Put it together and you may have the quintessential performance of Elvis's career: an overwhelming outburst of real emotion and power, combined with a fine refusal to take himself with any seriousness at all. Finding that power within himself, and making it real, was part of the liberation he was working out in this music; standing off from that power, with a broad sense of humor and amusement, was another.

This was the saving grace of Elvis's ambition, and a necessary counter to it. It allowed him to transcend his success and his public image just as his ambition allowed him to achieve and enjoy his success; that casual élan would let him see at least part of the way through the unprecedented adulation he received, just as his ambition would ultimately make it impossible for him to be satisfied with anything less. And if that lack of seriousness today distances Elvis not only from the absurdity of his reward but from his talent too, gives us a throwaway and a man virtually unable to take anything seriously, this side of Elvis has also brought a marvelous warmth to his best music, no matter if it's in the records he made back in Memphis, or the live show he's sure to be putting on tonight.

ELVIS AT HOME: THE COUNTRY SIDES

Elvis's blues are music of drama, humor, and risk; the country tunes are very different. At their most vital, they capture the kind of beauty and peace of mind that can be found only within limits, when a lot has been given up, and you know exactly how far you can go.

Elvis gives us respect—for the musical form, for the established country music audience these songs were aimed at, for his mother, who was sure to be listening to *this* music—in place of resentment and personal authority. The music flows with the kind of grace the Allman Brothers found in their incandescent "Blue Sky": a sense of value that seems to come not from a feel for the open possibilities of life, but from a pretty deep understanding of its fragility.

There is a modesty of spirit. In this world you will hope for what you deserve, but not demand it; you may celebrate your life, but not with the kind of liberation that might threaten the life of someone else. The public impulse of the music is not to break things open, but to confirm what is already there, to add to its reality and its value.

This is the kind of freedom D. H. Lawrence had in mind when he wrote about America in an essay called "The Spirit of Place."

Men are free when they are in a living homeland, not when they are straying and breaking away. Men are free when they are obeying some deep, inward voice of religious belief. Obeying from within. Men are free when they belong to a living, organic, *believing* community, active in fulfilling some unfulfilled, perhaps unrealized purpose. Not when they are escaping to some wild west. The most unfree souls go west, and shout of freedom. Men are freest when they are most unconscious of freedom. The shout is a rattling of chains, always was.

Men are not free when they are doing just what they like. The moment you can do just what you like, there is nothing you care about doing.*

So speaks the stern English father to his rowdy American children; it's not a message America has ever had much time for. We much prefer Elvis's shout of freedom, sure that what chains there are in our world must be applied by other men. Something close to Lawrence's idea, though, that sense of staying at home in a place where one belongs, is part of what Elvis has always offered America—on the flipside, as it were.

Elvis's country sides, like his later gospel records for RCA, reveal how deeply he felt a pull at odds with the explosions of his new rock 'n' roll and the frenzy of his first stage shows. They let us in on the secret that his little drama of breaking loose could take on the extremes that gave it power because he knew he had a home to which he could always return; even as he set out to win his independence, he prepared his accommodation. The America that Elvis brings to life in this music grew out of his willingness to accept the limits of a community, and his desire for the pleasures of familiarity. It's a place of gentleness, and restraint.

In the least of this music, though—"I Forgot to Remember to Forget Her," "I Don't Care If the Sun Don't Shine," "Just Because," "I Love You Because," "I'll Never Let You Go (Little Darlin')"—it is the sound of a young man *confined* by his community that is most striking. Elvis is faceless, indistinguishable from a hundred others; he sounds less like a man who has been defeated than like one who has never wondered what it might mean to try to win. There's no real warmth in the music, only an imitation of it; if on the blues sides he took on the originals and outclassed them, here he defers. The emotional tone seems contrived, almost secondhand; this is the music of someone doing what he has always been told to do.

"I Don't Care If the Sun Don't Shine" has energy, but

* From *Studies in Classic American Literature* (New York: Viking, 1964).

not soul; "Just Because" has a little bounce, but no passion.
"I Love You Because" (actually the very first song Elvis recorded professionally) is truly painful to hear; he's so polite
to the material he can't even sing it. There is certainly nothing that could give that "believing community" any strength.

Here Elvis embodies exactly that world his blues fantasy
let him escape. If murder—the face of Richard Starkweather
imposed on Elvis's, the edge of sadism in Presley's music that
made one producer tag him as just right for *In Cold Blood*—
was the dark side of rockabilly flash and the flight from limits, then a death of possibility and a stupefying ordinariness
was the dark side of this music, the first version of Elvis's
empty Yes.

You can't have a community that grows and renews all
who are a part of it without the tension that comes from the
need to break away, without the resentment produced by the
tendency of any community to grow in on itself and shut out
the rest of the world. Tom Sawyer's fooling around won't
give us that tension; you need Huck's nerve and his suffering, perhaps an edge of Ahab's obsessions, and, in America,
you probably need Nigger Jim too.

Elvis was a rebel in the music that made him famous.
But he knew, and has always told anyone willing to listen,
how hard it is to break away, and how much you have to
give up to make it—more than he has been willing to part
with. So Elvis lives out his story by contradicting himself,
and we join in when we take sides, or when we respond to
the tension that contradiction creates. The liveliness of that
tension is as evident in the best of Elvis's country sides as it
is in his blues.

When Elvis sings Bill Monroe's "Blue Moon of Kentucky" as if he's going to jump right over it, he isn't, as has
always been said, singing the blues on a country song, any
more than he was really singing hillbilly on a blues with
"That's All Right." What Elvis is doing is both more complex and more coherent.

When I listened to an early take of "Blue Moon of Kentucky" (on a rockabilly bootleg that includes studio dialogue

as well as music *), I heard Elvis lost in the song, touching
each line gently, playfully, bringing every word to life. The
singing is rough, even though Elvis is clearly a long way past
the first tries; Scotty Moore has trouble following the vocal.
Scotty drops back, and then there is just Elvis, drawing out
an unbelievably sensual portrait of his Southern landscape.

It sounds so primitive to me; music out of the Mississippi woods, a hundred years gone. Sam Phillips hears something else.

PHILLIPS: Fine, *fine*, man, hell, that's different! That's a *pop song*
now, little guy! That's good!
SCOTTY MOORE: Too much vaseline!
Elvis laughs, nervously, proudly.
MOORE: I had it too!
ELVIS: Y'ain't just a-*woofin'!*
MOORE (imitating an eye-rolling black falsetto): Please, *please,*
please—
ELVIS: What?
MOORE: *Damn,* nigger!

By the time Elvis reached the fast, confident version that
appeared on the flip of his first record, most of the primitive
feeling had disappeared, but not the vaseline; Elvis was celebrating a classic piece of white country music, but more than
that he was celebrating himself. He was keeping the old song
alive by bringing something new to it, putting some life back
into his community by telling an old story in a way that no
one had heard before—and he was reaching beyond his community, with the "pop song" Sam Phillips knew he had to
make.

There is a delight in adventure and novelty here that we
can't touch with pure musicology: Elvis's affection for a song
he's heard for years, combined with the exuberance and satisfaction of a kid who's worked for months to make a record,
and who is now actually pulling it off. And there are the new
rhythms of "That's All Right," cut a few nights before—not

* *Good Rocking Tonight;* see Discography for details.

"blues" now, but Elvis's music, Scotty Moore's music—
Southern energy that blacks had trapped and put into the air
where anyone could get it.

EE #5. I know a woman, black and about sixty, who loves old
country blues. The albums I have given her are mostly unplayed, though,
because she lives with her mother, a devout woman in her eighties, who
forbids her to play them. The mother, who is blind, spends much of her
time listening to the TV set, and once I found her attending to a kind of
blues she apparently considered innocuous enough to tolerate: Elvis's
G.I. Blues.

I didn't know what to make of that. It seemed to represent a double
dead end of American cross-culture, but there was something I liked about
it. Partly, it was the movie itself. Elvis, as usual, plays a good-natured stud
who breaks into song about every ten minutes and makes all the women
snap their fingers (though curiously, none of them can keep time). The
Sergeant Bilko-reject plot has to do with El's attempt to raise a stake for the
nightclub he and his two army accompanists want to open when they get back
in mufti. It comes down to rival platoons placing bets on which can field a man
to seduce Juliet Prowse, the biggst glacier in Germany. Elvis, naturally . . .

He walks through the flick with the same air of What-Am-I-Doing-
Here bemusement he employs in most of his other movies. When he
strums his acoustic guitar, an electric solo comes out. When bass and guitar back him, you hear horns and electric piano. When he sings, the
soundtrack is at least half a verse out of sync. These films are the throw-
aways of a man—perhaps I ought to say an industry—who doesn't even
need to title his product as long as he can put his name on it, much like Elvis's post-comeback albums (randomly constructed out of leftover recordings, unmixed live tapes, plastered with shoddy composite promo photos
and ads for old LP's), all of which seem to be called simply "E L V I S," in
fact. The movies are so tacky no one else could possibly get away with
them—and still make money.

Someday, French film critics will discover these pictures and hail
them as a unique example of *cinema discrepant;* there will be retrospectives
at the *Cinemateque,* and five years after that Harvard students will cultivate
a lopsided grin and Elvis movies will be shown on U.S. educational TV,
complete with learned commentary deferring to the French discovery and
bemoaning America's inability to appreciate its own culture. Elvis will be
touring the People's Republic of China and during an audience with Chairman Mao will be drawn into a discussion of the conflicting aesthetics
of "Milkcow Blues Boogie" and "No Room to Rhumba in a Sportscar."
The Chairman, being a staunch advocate of "The Folk," will cite James
Agee's famous essay on the corruption of folk art by the nature of reality;

Elvis could not have sung "Blue Moon of Kentucky" as he did without the discoveries of "That's All Right"—but what he discovered was not his ability to imitate a black blues singer, but the nerve to cross the borders he had been raised to respect. Once that was done, musically those borders dissolved as if they had never existed—for Elvis. He moved back and forth in a phrase. But Scotty Moore might well have been speaking for the audience waiting outside the studio when he called Elvis a nigger—for many, it was the *fact* of a white boy singing a black man's song without clothing it in fiddles and steel guitar that they heard, not the strange ambiguities of the music. Perhaps if Phillips had put out the "country" side without the "blues," it would have warmed the community; the combination thrilled some and threatened others. There were country stations that refused to play any Elvis records, no matter how white they seemed to be. He was too complicated, this Presley boy; you couldn't tell what he might be slipping over, could you?

Yet "You're a Heartbreaker," another country side, is a

Elvis will reply that while he has never read the piece, he once saw some pictures from *Let Us Now Praise Famous Men* in a copy of *Life* he picked up on an airplane, and thought they were all right. "My 'folk' can be summed up very easily," he will tell Mao with a knowing smile. " 'The short and simple annals of the poor.' "

All right, then—where does all this fit in with an old woman hardening her heart against Skip James and passing her time with Elvis? Only in that at its blandest, the American mainstream has no limits at all; even Mao could get his hand caught in this tar-baby. It contains everyone from moment to moment, covering over and melting down and seducing the best along with the worst, until the toughest, wisest pessimist is defeated by his secret yearning for a happy ending and the cheap tears it brings to his eyes. And that mainstream—which could turn "Bartleby" into a musical as easily as it allowed Elvis to turn himself into *Tickle Me*—provides such a perfect antithesis to the realities of American life that inevitable discrepancies come out of the woodwork, come with enormous force—a surprise, again—and with them come the resentment and the humor that keep the soul of the place hanging onto life.

Big words? Heavy stakes? Too much to drop on a vitiated country boy and an old lady who in all probability was just too bored to change the channel? Well, if that's not America, I'll never recognize it.

masterpiece of reassurance. It is one of the most affecting
records Elvis ever made; it gives us a young man who takes
comfort, and pleasure, from a sure sense of all that he has to
fall back on when something goes wrong: his self-respect (the
rounded edge of the new superiority of the blues-boy); the
steady, ongoing patterns of life that never range too far in
one direction or the other. If the impulses of community
were at odds with the extremes of Southern life, here Elvis
captures the soul of the one just as he acted out the other
side. It is a tribute to his range and his honesty that he can
do this without making one feel he is offering less than the
whole story.

How would you act if you lived in a community that *did*
enclose extremes without making life banal and dull? You
might act as Elvis sounds on this song, with a delicate grace
and a modest affection. Flip the record over to "Milkcow
Blues Boogie," and the same story—Elvis's girl has left
him—is a matter of life and death. And yet, despite the ap-
parent lack of struggle, of intensity, a certain truth is being
told here; a balance is being worked out; and the song is satisfying, leaving any listener richer than before.

With "Trying to Get to You," the boy who always
seemed bent on escape in the blues now has his eyes turned
toward home. I got your letter and I came a-runnin' is the
plot—"I've been traveling over mountains," Elvis sings, and
you believe him. The passion is there (also humility—Elvis
remembers to thank the Lord for helping him along), but
what is interesting is how controlled the feeling is. This is an
elegant record. The arrangement is very professional, very
strict; Elvis sings beautifully, but he submits to the music.
He never really takes it over. Some emotions, he might be
saying, are authentic only when they are restrained—just as
some emotions are authentic only when they are utterly free.

"I'm Left, You're Right, She's Gone" is cut from the
same mold. It brings together a superb vocal, an unforgetta-
bly clean guitar solo, and a good rhythm—no rave-up, but
just over the line into rock 'n' roll. There is a happy ending—
Elvis finds a new girl—and maybe that's the real clue to these

sides. Everything works out, in the lyrics, in the music (even
the guitar parts are neatly resolved, while those in the blues
tempt chaos), in the commercial and cultural context the
singer can take as close to a given. What is missing is the sus-
pense of a man creating himself, by the pure force of his will
and desire, that one can hear in Elvis's blues.

There is an alternate version of "I'm Left," usually
called "My Baby Is Gone," that shows how naturally Elvis's
flair for this kind of material evolved into his later—and present-day—ballad style. All the mannerisms are there.* The
performance is stunning: every line is measured out as if it
costs the singer his soul to confess his loss. Elvis drops down
so low on the scale he can barely get the words out; he blows
up the subtleties of his phrasing into shameless melodrama,
and it works. The song tells us what Elvis was after and
where he was going as well as anything. The tune was written as a conventional country tear-jerker, but in this version
Elvis stepped gently away from his community even as he
gave that community something it could accept: a Hollywood movie, a Valentino love scene complete with heavy
breathing. "Blue Moon" takes this blending of cultures even
farther; it's more like "pre-Elvis" pop music than any of these
sides, and queerer, too. "Blue Moon" comes with clippity-
clop hoofbeats worthy of Gene Autry, and with a bit of Elvis's acoustic guitar; he sings like a swamp-spirit, making his
way through the fog to that lamp post Frank Sinatra used to
cart out for all his album covers. Whining and wailing between the lyrics—which, as Elvis sings them, sound quite
surreal—he turns this old standard into a combination of a
supper club ballad and an Appalachian moan.

This music is good enough, committed enough, to make
you almost forget Elvis's Wild West. He played both ends
against the middle; in the good moments, he escaped the
deadening artistic compromise the middle demands. This

---

* The mannerisms of his great ballads, like "I Was the One," "Is It So Strange,"
"Don't," "Fame and Fortune," "Anyway You Want Me," "If I Can Dream," or
"Suspicious Minds," and the awful ones, like "Tonight's Alright For Love," "Fool,"
"It's Impossible," and a couple of hundred others.

seems to have worked because both sides of his character, at
this point in his career, were pulling so hard.

Jerry Lee Lewis, second in the hierarchy of white
Southern rockers, had talent and drive that stopped just
short of Presley's, but he gained only a fraction of Presley's
success, perhaps because he lacked the broad scope of Elvis's
ambition and Elvis's sure sense of where he meant to go—not
to mention Elvis's understanding of how to act once he got
there. If Elvis had a bit of grace to him, Jerry Lee seemed
possessed; and Jerry Lee, far more than Elvis, came to represent all the mythical strangeness of the redneck South: lynch-
mob blood lust, populist frenzies, even incest. When Jerry
Lee made it onto national TV, Steve Allen didn't bother
squeezing him into white tie or chaining him to the floor: in a

EE #6. One night in 1973 we went out to catch El's latest movie;
the theater was almost empty. There were a few couples in their late twenties, an elderly pair who left almost immediately, an old black man sitting
alone, maybe just looking for a roof in the rain. The film was *Elvis on
Tour*, a documentary of his post-comeback apotheosis—with gestures toward History.

There are kinescopes of the first triumph: Elvis rocking out on the Ed
Sullivan Show with "Reddy Teddy." The performance is astounding,
otherworldly, and it is hard to believe anyone now living was really
around to see such a sight (though, of course, *we* were). "That's All Right"
plays under a shot of a train running on down the line, as Elvis talks about
his childhood. "Never saw a git-tar player was worth a damn," he remembers his Daddy telling him. "I was born about ten thousand years
ago," Elvis sings in one of his recent songs, and that seems to say it all, to
sum up the jumbled sense of time that governs the movie, and us; the
beginning of it all seems at least that distant, and brings home just how
long Elvis and we have been caught up with each other.

Somewhere near the end of the flick is a wonderful sequence of Elvis-
movie kisses, a perfect critical attack on the aggressive meaninglessness of
the movie years: like dominoes, one starlet after another falls into Elvis-
arms. Ah, Elvis says to us here, this is what I *became*, but this is not the
real me. Well, what is? That pudgy flyer up on the screen, filmed live in
concert after concert, mechanically grinding out the same songs and
choreographed karate chops (the seventies equivalent of swiveling hips?) as
if his life were a tape loop? The kiss sequence is meant to parody the past,
but it only parallels the present.

vain attempt to parody the excess that made Jerry Lee Lewis
great, tables and chairs were thrown across the stage while
Jerry Lee pounded out "Whole Lotta Shakin'." Elvis's early
music has drama because as he sang he was escaping limits,
testing them, working out their value; unlike Jerry Lee, he at
least knew the limits were there. With Southern power in his
music, Elvis had mainstream savvy in his soul.

The problem was that the shallowness of the poorest of
the music that captured Elvis's restraint, and the inoffen-
siveness of the best of it, opened up the I Walked Like a
Zombie saga that Elvis would act out in the long years before
his comeback in 1968—a saga that, in a much more extrava-
gant way, he acts out today.

Elvis was very comfortable with his country music, and
with the romantic ballads that were its mainstream equivalent; so were his first teenage fans. This was mother's milk;
the responses the music elicited were virtually automatic. Elvis's ability to sing this music and to like it—to put it across
without lying to himself or to anyone else—would never
have brought him fame nor burst any limits. But that ability
was crucial to his power to hold onto his success, and to keep
at least that part of his original audience (and to attract so
many more) who didn't grow with the musical culture Elvis
founded: those who, all through the sixties, lived in an
America that was ignored or damned by the Rolling Stones
and the counterculture; those who put the endless movies
into the black; who made the soundtrack to *Blue Hawaii* the
best-selling Elvis album of all (over 5 million copies at last
count); those who bought reassurance tinged with a memory
of excitement and independence. When all this proved too
dull and predictable even for Elvis—when he came roaring
out in the explosion of vitality and commitment that was his
comeback (returning, then, as a King of Rock 'n' Roll who
was also a definitive Middle American)—there were plenty
from every sort of white rock 'n' roll audience who were glad
to leave whatever they had made of the sixties behind and
join him in his pageant. Elvis's accommodations, all larger

than life, and brilliantly orchestrated on stage to preserve the
thrills that were once discovered in his blues, make a very
glamorous home for our own retreats.

The country sides, the later music that derived from
them, the shining acceptance of the great stage show, give us
the contradictions that have kept pace with rock 'n' roll from
the beginning (contradictions that are, of course, much bigger than the music): The desire of the rebel to conform; the
wish for quiet despite allegiance to an ideology of noise; the
need for rest after excitement; the retreat that replaces ambition, be that ambition personal, cultural, or political. But this
aesthetic—of rest, of quiet, of retreat—so convincing in those
first country records, grows easily into a riskless aesthetic of
smooth-it-away. This is really the last word of our mainstream; its last, most seductive trap: the illusion that the
American dream has fulfilled itself, the utopia is complete in
an America that replaces emotion with sentiment and novelty
with expectation. Elvis contained this aesthetic within himself—Tocqueville's bad dream, the aesthetics of playing it
safe. When he is ready to play it safe, that aesthetic contains
him, just as it usually contains most of us. Breaking loose
and starting over cost more every time, and in the America
that Elvis has come to symbolize so powerfully, in an
America that only wants to applaud, to say Yes and mean it,
the risks are hard to find.

MYSTERY TRAIN

It was the last record Elvis made at Sun; to me, it tells
the best tale of all.

Sam Phillips and Junior Parker wrote "Mystery Train"
together in 1953; the original, a slow, dark blues released
under the name of Little Junior's Blue Flames, was exquisite.
An odd, chopping beat carried the threat of the title; a sax
brought out the inevitable train sound with an unusually ominous flair. And Parker sang halfway from the grave, chasing
his lover through the gloom, giving just the slightest sugges-

tion that she had been kidnapped by a ghost. There was a feeling of being in the wrong place at the wrong time, a hint of a curse.

This was the blues realism of Robert Johnson: one of those tunes that says, This is the way the world is, and there's nothing you or anyone can do about it.

> *Train I riiide,*
> *Sixteen*
> *Coaches long*
> *Train I riiide,*
> *Sixteen*
> *Coaches long*
> *Well, that long black train*
> *Carry my baby and gone*

They may ride the same train—somehow, it runs away from itself.

To understand the strangeness of those lines, we have to go back to the place where Parker and Phillips found them: back to the Carter Family's "Worried Man Blues" of some twenty years before. It was a folk song, passed back and forth between the races, that in truth was older than any-one's memory.

"Worried Man" is the story of a man who lays down to sleep by a river and wakes up in chains. The Carters don't tell you if the man is black or white; if he killed someone, stole a horse, or did anything at all; and the man doesn't know either. You would have to go a long way to match that as an image of the devil in the dream, or as the plain symbol of a land whose profound optimism insures that disaster must be incomprehensible.

There is no protest in the song, no revolt, only an abso-lute, almost supernatural loneliness: a bewilderment that is all the more terrifying because it is so self-effacing and matter-of-fact. The emotion is there in the steady roll of the beat, in the resignation of Mother Maybelle's guitar, and in A. P. Carter's squeaky, toneless singing: the sound of a man who has told his story more times than he can remember,

and who hopes that one more telling will finally let him rest.
He rides a train to nowhere.

The train I ride is sixteen coaches long
The train I ride is sixteen coaches long
The girl I love is on that train and gone *

Like the rest of the song, it makes no sense; it simply
defines the singer's world, and there is no way out, save for
the death the man promises will someday save him from his
song.

Even without these details—the mystery behind their
train song—and even with a tacked-on happy ending that
gives the singer back his girl, Parker and Phillips recreated
this mood, or submitted to it. So, when Parker sings that his
baby will come home, that the train will surely bring her
back, you don't really believe him. He sounds as if he has already lost more than anyone can return.

The Carter Family was completely real to Elvis; the white
gospel culture they represented was implicitly *his* in a way that
no other culture, be it Hollywood or the blues, could ever quite
be. This was his inheritance and his birthright; the blues and
the movies were something he made real for himself. On the
earlier Sun records, Elvis had left home with the blues and
come back on the flipside; "Mystery Train" gave him a blues
that was rooted in his own community, and the context was not
so open.

EE #7. I had a dream one night, 4/25/73. In the dream, I am
looking into a carny peep-show machine, wherein tiny shots of Elvis,
Scotty Moore, and Bill Black, circa 1954, flicker in and out of view.
Naked, they are rehearsing their live act, kicking their legs in tandem like
the Rockettes. Slowly, the camera moves in on Elvis's penis. It is an accurate dream: I look to see if Elvis is circumcised, and of course he is not. In
close-up his member fills the screen. A message has been carved on his
penis in block letters. "ELVIS LIVE AT THE INTERNATIONAL HOTEL LAS
VEGAS," it reads.

There was the purely musical side; most of the material Elvis had used at Sun was weak or undeveloped in its original form, giving him plenty of freedom to exploit possibilities others had missed. With "Mystery Train," both originals were brilliant. They took the train as far as it could go—in one direction—and the hard meaning Junior Parker and the Carter Family gave to the song was also part of Elvis's inheritance. If that meaning was forcefully obscure, that uncertainty was the song's point: the uselessness of action, the helplessness of a man who cannot understand his world, let alone master it. The singer was to enter this world, suffer it, make that world real, and thus redeem it. Elvis had his job cut out for him if he was to make the song his own.

One more time, he found an opening and made it through. His attack on "Mystery Train" is as strong as Sly Stone's transformation of "Que Sera, Sera" from a little hymn to the benevolence of fate into a massive ode to dread. If the two performances go in different directions, maybe that tells us how far we have come; tells us that rock 'n' roll had to begin with an honest refusal of doubt and fatalism, and grow, along with its audience, to the point where it would have to absorb such things to survive.

Inspired by the feeling of going up against the old meaning of the tune, or determined to beat out Junior Parker, the black man, or simply thrilled by the music, Elvis sings this song with shock: he rebels against it. There is so much fire in his singing, so much personality and soul, that he changes the meaning of the song without smoothing it over. There is a tremendous violence to the record: "Train I ride," Elvis sings, but he sounds as if he's going to run it down. "It took my baby," Parker had moaned (riding us back to the days when a black locomotive was the symbol of a force no one could resist, of fate on wheels), "It's gone do it again." "Well," Elvis declares, "it took my baby—BUT IT NEVER WILL AGAIN—no, not again." His rhythm guitar seizes the music, forcing the changes; Scotty Moore, as he always did, lives up to Elvis's passion. Moore gives us one hard solo, which seems to hang the song between what it has always been and what Elvis is making of it, and then Elvis is back, and he turns the train around. As he speeds off into the night with the girl he has stolen off that mystery train, he cuts loose one more time. "Woo, woo—WOOOO!" he shouts, full of delight; he laughs out loud; and he's gone.

Elvis escaped the guilt of the blues—the guilt that is at the heart of the world the blues and country music give us— because he was able to replace the sense that men and women were trapped by fate and by their sins with a complex of emotions that was equally strong and distinctive. As he sang, Elvis changed the personae his songs originally offered his listeners. When the persona was one of anger, or delight, he outdistanced it. He didn't have to tell us that the blues is about displacement, about not being at home, about a brooding fear the music was meant to ease, but not resist. And if at its deepest the blues is hellfire music, worth the trouble of the black preachers who have damned it, that Elvis escaped this truth and still made his music ring true was precisely his genius.

FINALE

These days, Elvis is always singing. In his stage-show documentary, *Elvis on Tour*, we see him singing to himself, in limousines, backstage, running, walking, standing still, as his servant fits his cape to his shoulders, as he waits for his cue. He sings gospel music, mostly; in his private musical world, there is no distance at all from his deepest roots. Just as that personal culture of the Sun records was long ago blown up into something too big for Elvis to keep as his own, so the shared culture of country religion is now his private space within the greater America of which he has become a part.

And on stage? Well, there are those moments when Elvis Presley breaks through the public world he has made for himself, and only a fool or a liar would deny their power. Something entirely his, driven by two decades of history and myth, all live-in-person, is transformed into an energy that is

ecstatic—that is, to use the word in its old sense, illuminat-
ing. The overstated grandeur is suddenly authentic, and
Elvis brings a thrill different from and far beyond anything
else in our culture; like an old Phil Spector record, he
matches, for an instant, the bigness, the intensity, and the
unpredictability of America itself.

It might be that time when he sings "How Great Thou
Art" with all the faith of a backwoods Jonathan Edwards; it
might be at the very end of the night, when he closes his
show with "I Can't Help Falling in Love With You," and his
song takes on a glow that might make you feel his capacity
for affection is all but superhuman. Whatever it is, it will be
music that excludes no one, and still passes on something
valuable to everyone who is there. It is as if the America that
Elvis throws away for most of his performance can be given
life again at will.

At his best Elvis not only embodies but personalizes so
much of what is good about this place: a delight in sex that is
sometimes simple, sometimes complex, but always open; a
love of roots and a respect for the past; a rejection of the past
and a demand for novelty; the kind of racial harmony that for
Elvis, a white man, means a profound affinity with the most
subtle nuances of black culture combined with an equally
profound understanding of his own whiteness; a burning
desire to get rich, and to have fun; a natural affection for big
cars, flashy clothes, for the symbols of status that give pleasure both as symbols, and on their own terms. Elvis has long
since become one of those symbols himself.

Elvis has survived the contradictions of his career, perhaps because there is so much room and so much mystery in
Herman Melville's most telling comment on this country:
"The Declaration of Independence makes a difference." Elvis
takes his strength from the liberating arrogance, pride, and
the claim to be unique that grow out of a rich and commonplace understanding of what "democracy" and "equality"
are all about: no man is better than I am. He takes his
strength as well from the humility, the piety, and the open,
self-effacing good humor that spring from the same source: I

am better than no man. And so Elvis Presley's career defines success in a democracy that can perhaps recognize itself best in its popular culture: no limits, success so grand and complete it is nearly impossible for him to perceive anything more worth striving for. But there is a horror to this utopia— and one might think that the great moments Elvis still finds are his refusal of all that he can have without struggling. Elvis proves then that the myth of supremacy for which his audience will settle cannot contain him; he is, these moments show, far greater than that.

So perhaps that old rhythm of the Sun records does play itself out, even now. Along with Robert Johnson, Elvis is the grandest figure in the story I have tried to tell, because he has gone to the greatest extremes: he has given us an America that is dead, and an unmatched version of an America that is full of life.

All in all, there is only one remaining moment I want to see; one epiphany that would somehow bring his story home. Elvis would take the stage, as he always has; the roar of the audience would surround him, as it always will. After a time, he would begin a song by Bob Dylan. Singing slowly, Elvis would give it everything he has. "I must have been mad," he would cry, "I didn't know what I had—Until I threw it all away."

And then, with love in his heart, he would laugh.

EPILOGUE

ITINERANT SINGER REVEALS NAME ON TAIL OF SHIRT
'Disgusting,' Witnesses Claim

REPORT HUGE STONES BLOCK ALL ROADS

MAN WITH BLACK WHIP SEEN AGAIN IN CEMETERY—
ONLY COMES OUT AT NIGHT
Gravediggers Threaten Walkout

ALTERCATION OVER STETSON HAT ENDS IN DEATH

AFRICANS EAGER TO 'SEE THE USA' ASSERTS TRAVEL AGENT—
'BIG BUCKS IN NEW TOURIST MARKET'

MAN FOUND IN CHAINS HELD, DENIES ALL WRONGDOING
'Only Wanted Nap,' Claims Prisoner

FIANCEE DISAPPEARS ON TRAIN, REPORTS ASTONISHED PASSENGER—
'Old Story,' Says Stationmaster

MAN AND WOMAN ESCAPE TRAIN WRECK UNHARMED
'Line Hasn't Run For Thirty Years,' Babbles Rail Exec

Walt Whitman once wrote that he didn't want an art that could decide presidential elections; he wanted an art to make them irrelevant. He was interested in an artist's ability to determine the feel of American experience; to become a part of the instinctive response of the people to events; to affect the quality and the costs of daily life. Whitman cared less that he would be remembered (though he certainly cared about that) than that his beliefs in the promises of American life would be lived out by other Americans—those of his time, and those far beyond his time. He thought that his work might affect whether or not his country would grow, and die, and start over again; whether his country would, at the margins of change, maintain a soul and a vitality that could be recognized, loved, and feared far more easily than it could be defined.

I think few artists have come closer to these dreams than those whose stories make up this book. Harmonica Frank, known to no one; Elvis, known to all; and the others: each catch an America that has shape within an America that is seamless—and that, most likely, is the best one can really hope for.

But Whitman, like Elvis or the Beatles or any true pop original, wanted it all, a grand battle between art and politics pitched right here. "Did you too," he wrote in *Democratic Vistas*, "suppose democracy was only for elections, for politics, for a party name?" Whitman thought limits were undemocratic. As good democrats, we fight it out within the borders of his ambition.

NOTES AND DISCOGRAPHICS

This section, organized by chapter, deals with the records, books, and articles discussed in the rest of the book, along with others that seem relevant. I have included information of the year of release and *Billboard* chart positions of records whenever that was to the point; in many cases, I wouldn't have had that information without Joel Whitburn's Record Research compilation books, especially *Top Pop Records 1955–72*, *Top LP's 1945–72*, and *Top Rhythm & Blues Records 1949–71* (all available from Record Research, P.O. Box 82, Menomonee Falls, Wisconsin, 53051).

There is also a good deal of other material: a rock 'n' roll top five of Robert Johnson songs; quite a bit of discussion of unreleased and rare material by the Band; *The Truth About Staggerlee* (such as I have been able to put it together); and, in the Elvis section, the transcript of a furious argument between Sam Phillips and Jerry Lee Lewis—circa 1957—as to whether or not rock 'n' roll really is the devil's music. Jerry Lee takes a strictly orthodox position; Phillips falls back on Anne Hutchinson's doctrine of the Inner Light, and carries the day.

HARMONICA FRANK

After nearly thirty years as an entertainer, Harmonica Frank made his first recordings for Sam Phillips in 1951; seven songs were released. They were once very hard to come by, and I want to thank Greg Shaw for providing the tapes that sparked my interest in the first place.

All those 1951 sides, plus a dazzling 1958 single that featured Frank on "Rock a Little Baby," are included on *The Great Original Recordings of Harmonica Frank* (Puritan 3003). If you can't find the record in the stores, you can get it, for $6 postpaid, from the man himself: write Frank Floyd, Box 446, Amelia, Ohio, 45102. Along with the album come pictures of Frank in 1930, the late forties, and 1972—including one that shows how he plays two harmonicas simultaneously, one with his mouth, the other with his nose.

Frank's music does not lend itself to classification. He told blues collector Steve LaVere: "I spent a lot of time listening to the darkies in days gone by singing in the cottonfield down South, and I picked up their songs and speech. That is the reason people think I am a colored man, but I really am white." That seems to matter. "I never played with no blacks," Frank wrote me in response to a query, "but I was a fan of Blind Lemon Jefferson, Lonnie Johnson, and Fats Domino." And, he might have mentioned, a contemporary of all three.

Frank learned many styles so he could work for many different audiences. His music can be heard in the context of rock 'n' roll on *Put Your Cat Clothes On—Sun Rockabillies Vol. 1* (Sun/Phillips 6467, English),* a brilliant collection of Sun rarities. Frank's masterpiece, "Goin' Away Walkin'," can be heard in the context of Memphis blues on *Memphis and the Delta: The 1950s* (Blues Classics 15), as can his lovely "She Done Moved," on *Genesis Vol. 2— Memphis to Chicago* (Chess 6641, English), a monumental four-record reissue that contains many of the sides by Memphis R&B singers Sam Phillips recorded for Chess. "Train Whistle Boogie," written by Frank Floyd but recorded by Charles Dean & the Ron-

* This record, and the other English and Dutch albums mentioned in the Discography, can usually be obtained by mail from J&F Southern Records Sales, 4501 Risinghill Road, Altadena, California, 91001.

dells on the Benton label of Dyersburg, Tennessee, can be found on *Rare Rock-a-billy Vol. 2* (Collector Records 1020, Dutch); Frank never recorded the tune himself. He did cut a new album for Adelphi Records following his rediscovery in 1972; Adelphi, however, has yet to release it.

Frank has asked me to note that of all those who have reissued his music, only Chris Strachwitz, who handles the Blues Classics line, has ever paid him any money for it.

ROBERT JOHNSON

Before Columbia Records began their reissue of Johnson's songs in 1961, his tunes traveled by rare old 78's, an occasional blues bootleg, cover versions, tapes passing from hand to hand. Some of his finest compositions—"If I Had Possession Over Judgment Day," for one—had never been heard on record at all.

The sixteen tracks of *Robert Johnson: King of the Delta Blues Singers* (Columbia 1654) offer virtually all of Johnson's greatest songs: "Crossroads," "Terraplane," "Come on in My Kitchen," "Walking Blues," "Rambling," "When You Got a Good Friend," "Me and the Devil," "Hellhound on My Trail," "Stones in My Passway." There has not been a better album in the history of the recording industry.

A second LP—the remainder of Johnson's songs, plus some alternate takes—was issued in 1970; worth seeking out for Tom Wilson's magnificent cover paintings of Johnson making his first records, it has now been replaced by *The Complete Robert Johnson* (Columbia 1811). Produced and annotated by Steve La Vere, this is a three-record set of every Johnson performance extant, with each song and its alternates programed chronologically; the set includes a lyric sheet (arguments over *that* will be going on for a long time), a guide to song tunings, and an analysis of Johnson's sources and his impact on others. More important, it contains a biographical essay by LaVere based on conversations with Johnson's sister, whom LaVere found living in Washington, D.C. And there is, after all these years, a picture of Robert Johnson, taken professionally in Memphis around 1935—a formal pose, with Johnson dressed in a blue serge suit, hat, tie, holding his Gibson guitar on his lap. Before LaVere's discovery, the search by blues fans for such an item had been only slightly less intense than the quest of King Arthur's knights for the Holy Grail.

These records (and *King of the Delta Blues Singers* is definitely the one to buy first) do not take in the whole of Johnson's music. Versions of "Take a Little Walk With Me" and "Little Boy Blue," two songs apparently written but never recorded by Johnson, can be found on *Otis Spann Is the Blues* (Baranby 30246), vocals and guitar by Robert Jr. Lockwood. Both performances are lovely, perhaps too much so; they lack the fire Johnny Shines brought to another unrecorded Johnson tune, "Tell Me Mama" (on Shines's *Sitting on Top of the World*, Biograph 12044). Johnson loved church music, even if he could not rest with the gospel; like so many black bluesmen, he was partial to Jimmie Rodgers's blue yodels; as often as not, songs he heard on the radio in the morning found their way into his repertoire by nighttime.

There will be more to say about Bobby Bland in the Band discography, but for the moment, I want to mention that "Lead Me On," quoted at the beginning of the Johnson chapter, comes from Bland's finest album, *Two Steps from the Blues* (Duke 74). The cover shows us Bobby posed in front of a blue building, which does indeed have two steps. The songs include "I Pity the Fool," "St. James Infirmary," the title tune, and the ghostly "I'll Take Care of You," which opens with these lines: "I know you've been hurt, by somebody else/ I can tell by the way you carry yourself." Bobby Blue Bland and Robert Johnson would have had a lot to say to each other.

JOHNSON AND ROCK 'N' ROLL

In recent years, as Johnson's music has been recorded by more and more rock 'n' roll groups, someone called Woody Payne has taken to putting his name on Johnson's songs ("Love in Vain" on the Rolling Stones' *Let It Bleed*, and others; since the Stones know better, it makes you wonder what's going on). "Payne" is not the first to do so and he won't be the last, but he merely illustrates how wasteful some find it that such popular material is in the public domain. At any rate, I offer the top five rock 'n' roll versions of Johnson's songs—the greatest hits of, as he is usually known, P.D.:

1. The Rolling Stones, "Stop Breaking Down," from *Exile on Main Street* (Rolling Stones 0996). This was the fifth straight album on which the Stones included a classic country blues number, but the first time they approached the country blues as rock 'n' roll—

perhaps because in sound and spirit the rest of the album approached rock 'n' roll as country blues. *Exile* was a nice tour of
morgues, courts, sinking ships, claustrophobic rooms, deserted
highways; the whole album was a breakdown, one long night of
fear. Johnson's best bragging song gave the Stones a chance to blow
their fears away. With Mick squeaking his harmonica, calling for
chorus after chorus, this stands as one of the Stones' best.

2. Taj Mahal, "The Celebrated Walking Blues," from *Taj
Mahal* (Columbia 9579). Still *his* best. Not completely Johnson—
Taj re-creates the lyric with bits and pieces from Willie Brown's
"Future Blues" ("Minutes seem like hours/ Hours seem . . . just
like days"), Muddy Waters' songs, his own inventions. Taj's first
few guitar notes go right back to "Stones in My Passway," but he
doesn't take the song all that seriously; his "Walking Blues," like
Johnson's, is one cosmic joke life is playing on him, but no one can
say Taj doesn't get it.

3. Eric Clapton, "Ramblin'," from *John Mayhall's Blues Breakers*
(London 492). Early Clapton: peaceful, modest, absolutely convincing.

4. Cream, "Crossroads," from *Wheels of Fire* (Atco 2–7000).
Clapton calls Johnson his guru; he will likely be playing this song
as long as he can hold a guitar. In the seventies Clapton has made
"Crossroads" his statement of faith; back in the late sixties, when
this live version was cut, his singing conveyed pure excitement. As
for what the band does here, the album title is descriptive enough.

5. The Rolling Stones, "Love in Vain," from *Get Yer Ya-Yas
Out!* (London 5). The studio version on *Let It Bleed* is very stiff; on
stage, Mick Taylor's guitar and Charlie Watts' drumming said
whatever it might have been that Jagger left out.

Among the objects scattered across the cover of Bob Dylan's
Bringing It All Back Home is Johnson's first album; if one listens to
Dylan's "Pledging My Time," one will hear "Come on in my
Kitchen" in the background, and Johnson seems to be hovering
over "Visions of Johanna" as well. The finest pieces of guitar rock
'n' roll of the last few years—Paul Rodgers' "Wishing Well" (on
Free's *Heartbreaker*, Island 9324), Led Zeppelin's "Stairway to
Heaven" (on *Zo-So*, Atlantic 7208), Duane Allman's "Loan Me a
Dime" (on *Duane Allman: An Anthology*, Capricorn 0108, or *Boz
Scaggs*, Atlantic 8239)—would all be unthinkable without Robert
Johnson.

And one has to end with Clapton. Playing with Allman in
Derek & the Dominos, he made his greatest music with "Layla"
and "Any Day"—loud, fierce, and majestic (*Layla*, Atco 704); returning three years later in 1974, after kicking heroin, he made *461
Ocean Boulevard* (RSO 4801), and somehow managed to bring the
devils of country blues and the grace of gospel together. No one
else, as far as I know, has ever really done that.

JOHNSON AND POSTWAR BLUES

Johnson's impact—as a stylist—cut all across the board, but
within the Delta-to-Chicago tradition, Muddy Waters, Elmore
James, and Johnny Shines have been Johnson's chief inheritors.
Waters' initial Mississippi recordings, cut in 1941–1942 for the
Library of Congress (*Down on Stovall's Plantation*, Testament 2210)
were uncertain imitations; by 1948, in Chicago, Waters had taken
what he wanted from Johnson and made it his own, with his extraordinary recordings of "Rollin' Stone" (*Sail On*, Chess 1539) and
"Feel Like Going Home" (*Genesis, Vol. 1*, Chess 5541 047, English,
an excellent anthology). The spidery lines of Waters' guitar playing
are unparalleled for their tension; his singing is hard, unassuming,
and terrifying.

As Peter Guralnick has written, Elmore James took Johnson's
"Dust My Broom" and made a career out of it. Waters reached for
the distant margins of Johnson's music; James went for his sound,
his volume, and his flash. A contemporary of Johnson (and later
the idol of the early Rolling Stones, the Yardbirds, and many other
British bands), James did not record until 1953, when he emerged
with a wild, trebly electric guitar style and a slashing vocal attack
that traded subtlety for excitement. Of the many James LP's on the
market, my choice would be *The Best of Elmore James* (Sue 918, English), which collects powerful versions of "Dust My Broom,"
"Stranger Blues," "The Sky Is Crying," and the stunning "Done
Somebody Wrong"—all free of the horns and clumsy rhythm sec-
tions that marred much of his later work.

Johnny Shines tagged along when Robert Johnson hit the road
in the thirties. He moved to Chicago in 1941, but recorded only occasionally until the blues revival of the sixties; with James dead and
Waters committed to the Chicago band style, Shines remains the
one real master of Johnson's original form. In his best moments, he
doesn't simply add to Johnson's history, he makes his own: there is

a horror in Shines's "Tom Green's Farm" (*The Johnny Shines Band*, Testament 2212) that is fully the equal of and very different from anything Johnson ever conjured up. Shines finds evil in the white man's rule while Johnson found it in himself no less than in the world; but it is Shines's ambiguous acceptance of the horror—I mean the peculiar strength he assumes when he speaks *for* it—that makes the song so disquieting. Certainly no one has ever put more menace into a guitar solo or a lyric than Shines does on this song. He has many albums out, and all are good ones; *Johnny Shines* (Blue Horizon 4607) and *Standing at the Crossroads* (Testament 2221) are essential for anyone who has felt the attractions of the country blues.

A NOTE ON MISSISSIPPI COUNTRY BLUES

The Mississippi blues from the twenties and thirties make up an aesthetic world that is complete in itself. Sam Charters once wrote that only a black man, living in the Delta in the thirties, could possibly understand what Son House meant when he sang, "My black mama's face shines like the sun," but to say that the world of the country blues is complete is not to say that it is exclusive. There is a unique American language in the shared body of riffs and phrases that change in meaning from singer to singer— an attempt to deal with a landscape and a way of life that escapes both; there is something very old about this music, a distance that has little to do with dates, with the words "archaic" or "primitive." The music is old in the way that some of Faulkner's characters, black and white, seem to have been old before they were born. I cannot explain this, but it must have something to do with why the country blues do not wear out; the greatest songs do not really call up the years in which they are made. Listening, one feels out of time.

There are far too many good country blues collections to list here; the best place to start would be *Really! The Country Blues* (Origin Jazz Library 2), which brings together perhaps the supreme performances of Skip James ("Devil Got My Woman"), Garfield Akers ("Cottonfield Blues"), Tommy Johnson ("Maggie Campbell Blues"), and Son House ("My Black Mama"). Other Origin releases (*The Mississippi Blues 1927–1940*, OJL 5; *Country Blues Encores*, OJL 8; *The Mississippi Blues Transition*, OJL 17) are hardly less rich.

Charley Patton, a rough, fierce singer who had as much influence on Captain Beefheart as he had on Howlin' Wolf, is considered the original master of the music; *Charley Patton, Founder of the Delta Blues* (Yazoo 1020) contains twenty-eight of his sides.

Skip James was the most individualistic of the Mississippi singers (and guitarists, and piano players), and arguably the very greatest; *Skip James, King of the Delta Blues Singers* (Biograph 12029) (too bad James and Johnson can't have a battle of the bands) collects ten of James' performances from the late twenties and early thirties. The records James made after his rediscovery in the sixties, especially *Devil Got My Woman* (Vanguard 29237), capture him shortly before his death, and at the height of his powers.

Tommy Johnson made only a handful of records in 1928 and 1930, but played around Jackson until his death in the fifties; his songs are among the most beautiful and influential of all country blues, and his slurred, fading moans must be heard to be believed. *The Famous 1928 Tommy Johnson–Ishman Bracey Session* (Roots 330, English) is hard to find, but most of Tommy Johnson's work is scattered through the OJL anthologies and the excellent *Jackson Blues 1928–1938* (Yazoo 1007).

Paul Oliver's books are likely the best guides to the music, especially the beautifully illustrated *Story of the Blues* (Philadelphia: Chilton, 1969; Baltimore: Penguin, 1972), which traces the blues from Africa to Chuck Berry. Peter Guralnick's *Feel Like Going Home* (New York: Outerbridge and Dienstfrey/Dutton, 1971) gives a superb short history of the country blues, plus wonderful portraits of Skip James, Muddy Waters, Howlin' Wolf, and Johnny Shines, not to mention Jerry Lee Lewis, Charlie Rich, and Sam Phillips. Stanley Booth's "Even the Birds Were Blue" (in *The Rolling Stone Rock 'n' Roll Reader*, ed. Ben Fong-Torres [New York: Bantam, 1974]), from which I quoted in the Johnson chapter, is a moving, depressing account of black bluesmen suffering the good intentions of their white admirers—a piece that anyone who cares about the complexities of race and American music ought to read.

THE BAND

Music from Big Pink (Capitol 2955) came out late in the summer of 1968, and while it never rose higher than #30 on the charts, it stayed on for nearly a year, and a lot of people thought it was number one anyway. Al Kooper called the debut of the Band an event, and in youthful communities around the country, it was that and more. The day after the record first hit the stores you could hear people singing "The Weight"; before long, the music became part of the fabric of daily life.

The leitmotif of the record, I think, was obligation—a kind of secret theme, perhaps not all that conscious on anyone's part, but at the heart of the lyrics and the music too. What do men and women owe to each other, how do they keep faith, how far can that faith be pushed before it breaks? Those are problems community and friendship share. Such questions would rise naturally from the work of men who were preparing to present themselves to the public, and who, after all those years together, had to find out what the essence of their particular group identity was.

Certainly "Long Black Veil," the one song on the album written by neither the Band nor Dylan, takes obligation as far as it can go. A murder has been committed; a man is singled out of the crowd as the culprit, but he will not confess his alibi, because he "has been in the arms of his best friend's wife." She keeps silent as well. The singer owes something to his lover, and he owes as much to his friend; the woman will not injure her husband by revealing the secret, and she keeps faith with her lover even as he goes to the gallows—by allowing him to die with his friendship intact, and by haunting his grave.

Shortly before making *Big Pink* the Band put down several tunes they have never used (also left off was a mad Dixieland version of "Lonesome Suzie"); their sound wasn't there, but they were getting to it. "Ferdinand the Impostor," "Ruben Remus," "Katie's Been Gone," and "Blues for Breakfast" are clumsy and self-pitying, but "Yazoo Street Scandal" is a gas: stinging hard rock, all good-humored menace like a Bo Diddley number, with Levon shouting out his unique mixture of comic horror and helpless delight. The off-the-wall characters ("The Widow," "The Cotton King," "Breezy," "Liza"—or is it "Elijah"?) and the Biblical imagery ("I just started a flood, for forty days and forty nights") that later sail across *Big Pink* spur the tale of a man seduced by the town mystery woman—apparently at the urging of his girlfriend. What's he to make of that? "She rocked me kinda slow, and kinda easy" is all he can tell us.

The Band (Capitol 132), #9 in the fall of 1969, was the group's most popular album, as it deserved to be. The sound was clean and immediate; in every way, the record was easier to hear than *Big*

Pink. "Cripple Creek," the single, even got some airplay, though the Band has still never had much impact on AM radio (the closest they came was with Joan Baez's massacre of "The Night They Drove Old Dixie Down," #3 in 1971).

Around this time the first Band bootlegs appeared—rough stuff, but sometimes containing the only available versions of some of the Band's best on-stage performances: Dylan's "Dontcha Tell Henry," "Little Birdies," "No More Cane on the Brazos," and the great "Slipin' and Slidin'." All had disappeared from the Band's show by the time they started recording live.

Stage Fright (Capitol 425), out in the summer of 1970, climbed a little higher on the charts than *The Band*, but it was not really as popular, probably because, as a collection of songs rather than a complete world, it depicted so accurately the uncertainty and fragmentation that were its subject. It was hard to get a feel for this record, and a certain vibrancy was missing; the music was too worked out, too careful. "The Rumor," potentially the most compelling of all the songs, was somehow overarranged and at the same time unfinished. *"Stage Fright* needs one cut to really shake things up," Dave Marsh wrote; "The Shape I'm In," which held back in its lyrics just where it delivered in its music, wasn't the one; "Baby Don't Do It (Don't Break My Heart)," recorded as a studio tryout up in Bearsville, planned as a single but never released, was.

This was an extraordinary recording; hard rock beyond the reach of any band you'd care to name, including, as far as their official releases went, the Band itself. On stage, they sometimes risked going out of control to make music that can't be made any other way; on record, never. Here, with a Marvin Gaye tune they had worked into their act some time before (along with the Four Tops' "Loving You (Has Made My Life Sweeter Than Ever)," which Rick Danko liked to sing), the Band acknowledged their enormous debt to Motown (the Temptations in their vocals, James Jameson in Danko's bass, and perhaps the whole Motown aesthetic of controlled craftsmanship in their music as such); on this one song, the Band outdid Motown as well. They made most rock 'n' roll sound fragile.

What the Band do with Gaye's song is what white groups usually do with black material: they hold to the original arrangement, amplify the beat, turn up the volume, and yell. They delight in the technology of two or three electric guitars, an electric organ, super-miked drums. They don't worry about "worrying" a line into an elusive rendering of "soul"; they simply sing as hard as they can.

They hit everything hard. Robertson is all over the music; Levon sounds as if he has four hands. Danko is there like fuel injection on a Corvette. Hudson lets loose a mighty screech, while Manuel holds onto the song, hitting one key on his piano over and over again. "My biggest mistake was loving you too much"—Blam Blam—"And letting you know . . ."

Gaye's performance of "Baby Don't Do It" (on his *Super Hits*, Tamla S300) is perfectly adequate; it's thin, careful, much like "Ain't That Peculiar," to which it was the follow-up. Genre music, then, a play on the expectations of an audience that has already proved it will buy a given sound. Motown makes music incrementally, after all. The Band's version is every man at extremes, valuable partly because they rarely go so far. Gaye sings against a polite soul chorus, and you get the idea his girl really won't do it— Break His Heart—because after all, she and many of her sisters are right there singing along with him. The Band enlist their full arsenal of voices, each man coming in at his own pace and declaiming, "Oh, baby, don't do it, don't break my heart, *pleeeeze*, don't do it," marching across the battlefield of broken dreams like an army of men ready to give it all for love. They wail on until they reach that point where the song ought to end, and suddenly Robbie takes over and drives straight out of the music. His pals catch up, cut him off, and slam it to a close. There were, and are, moments like this in the Band's concerts—but there have never been enough of them.

Cahoots (Capitol 651), #26 in late 1971, was literal where the other records had been tantalizing, strained where they had rocked. There was a feeling of flatness to the music, the sense of good ideas forced through a banal, occasionally didactic mesh. The idea of "cahoots" was the soul of the group, but nothing on the record captured it.

The original cover *had* captured it. Robbie chose an Irving Penn photograph of two little Peruvian children (it can be found in *Photographing Children* [New York: Time-Life Books, 1971])— brother and sister, dressed in grownups' working clothes and posing formally for the camera. They held hands firmly, conceding nothing to the photographer, you, or the world; they weren't cute. The way they looked and held their small bodies told you they would stick to each other forever—that as long as their bond held, they were ready to take whatever life had in store for them. It was a picture of very strange beauty, and Capitol refused to allow it on the cover of *Cahoots* because they thought the little girl looked pregnant.

Rock of Ages (Capitol 11042), a two-record set recorded mainly on New Year's Eve, 1971, and released in the fall of 1972, hit #6, and it remains one of the two or three best live albums ever made. The sound is deep and full, the Band was blazing, and the hornmen—all first-class New York jazzmen on a busman's holiday with New Orleans Rockmaster Allan Toussaint's strong, witty horn charts—made the difference. It was not simply that the hornmen added to the music, but that they and the Band so obviously turned each other on.

On almost every song, they outran the original versions. With "Chest Fever" the Band and the horns fought for the tune, and it took on a new urgency as the hornmen slapped back at Levon's furious drumming near the end; Howard Johnson's absurd tuba solo on "Rag Mama Rag" ranks with anything King Curtis ever played with the Coasters.

Toussaint dug deeply into New Orleans traditions for his charts—Dixieland, blues, fifties and early sixties rock 'n' roll. There had always been a lot of New Orleans in the Band, perhaps especially the wild piano and general hilarity of Huey Smith, and Toussaint simply brought this to the surface. My favorite touch was the riff he used to kick off the encore, "Rock and Roll Shoes," which runs like this: "Dat *DAH* (boomp boomp)/ Dat *DAH* (boomp boomp)." The sound teases the memory, because it turns out to be one of those timeless fragments that can pop up anywhere, like an ancient blues line in a Top 40 hit, tying American music together, for a moment. This riff linked the Band to the first bars of Shirely and Lee's classic "Let the Good Times Roll"; likely to pre–jazz funeral marches of the 1880s; and to the music of a half-forgotten New Orleans blues singer named Rabbit Brown, who probably got more out of the riff than anyone else when he used it to open his 1928 "James Alley Blues." "I seen better days," he sang, "but I'm puttin' up with these."

Rock of Ages also documented Garth Hudson's crazy piano on "The Weight" (he seems to be coming in from another dimension, and I have yet to hear him play his part the same way twice); his long organ invention that originally grew out of the fanfare that begins "Chest Fever" (here Garth gives us a history of American music, from stovepipes to bandboxes, pausing neatly for "Auld Lang Syne"); a staggering "Don't Do It"; and a tune written years earlier but never released, "Get Up Jake." This last—about a man so lazy the whole town shows up to watch him get out of bed—was in some ways the best of all. "Me and Jake worked out on the river, on a ferry called the *Baltimore*," it began—one of those commonplace evocations of a hazy frontier that the Band has made their own. It's a very modest song, and perfect. Garth has never played so prettily.

Moondog Matinee (Capitol 11214) came out late in 1973 (named after Allan Freed's original rock 'n' roll radio show), with a finely detailed cover painting that pictured the men in the Band haunting a Toronto dive that had once known them as the Hawks. Made up of numbers they had liked and played in those days, the album went nowhere commercially, even though it coincided with the Band's 1974 tour with Bob Dylan, the most publicized outing in rock 'n' roll history.

Flop or not, *Moondog Matinee* contained some of the Band's best music, and I think "Third Man Theme" could have been the hit single they've never had. (The single that was released, "Ain't Got No Home," held a surprise; on the flipside the *Rock of Ages* version of "Get Up Jake" was listed, but instead of the live cut, it turned out to be the original studio take of the song, dating from *The Band* sessions—Capitol 45–3758.) "Share Your Love" far outclassed Bobby Bland's original; Manuel had more to give the song, and Garth's knack of making his Lowrey organ sound like a complete string section added enormous warmth. "Mystery Train" was almost entirely retooled by Robertson; he kept the first verse, added two of his own, and made up the chords from scratch. After a spooksy false start, the Band crept into the classic and took it over, their music dark and funny; when Robbie's new lines appeared, one would have thought they had been in the song since it was first sung, fifty years or twice as long ago. Levon cried,

Come down to the station meet my baby at the gate
Ask the station master if the train's runnin' late
He said, If you're a-waitin' on the old 44
I hate to tell ya son that train don't stop here anymore

"I tried to get to that old Robert Johnson–Arthur Crudup mood," Robbie said. Well, he did; those are the best lyrics he has written since *The Band*.

THE HAWKS

When Ronnie Hawkins made his first two albums (*Ronnie Hawkins*, Roulette R 25078, 1959; *Mr. Dynamo*, Roulette R 25102, 1960), the Hawks were Will Jones (piano), Kenny Ray Paulsen (guitar), James Evans (bass), and Levon Helm (drums)—country boys all, and a first-rate rock 'n' roll band, a tough combination of early Clyde McPhatter Drifters and rockabilly, bent on speed and flash. Paulsen sounded like Carl Perkins, Jones like Jerry Lee Lewis, and Levon sounded like himself. He was faster than most rock drummers and used a much heavier beat; at his best, he dominated the music, which, for a drummer, was unheard of at the time. The Hawks played brash and dirty; Hawkins himself sang like a lunatic when he could pull it off, which put him square into the tradition of the great rockers he longed to emulate.

Ronnie Hawkins produced two small hits: "Forty Days" and "Mary Lou" ("She took my Cadillac car"), plus "Odessa," a tribute to the band's favorite hooker (who likely reappears as Bessie in "Cripple Creek"). *Mr. Dynamo* is memorable for the very spooky "Southern Love" and for "Hey, Boba Lu," Robbie's first song— and also, I think, his first recording. The tune itself is a straight teenage lament, yet it is written around doomy twists and turns that make it stand out from everything else on the album.

Shortly thereafter, Robbie took over as lead guitarist, and Manuel, Danko, and Hudson joined up. The Hawks began to play blues, and two of the albums they treasured most were by Howlin' Wolf. *Moanin' in the Moonlight* (reissued as *Evil*, Chess 1540) collected Wolf's early sides and featured Willie Johnson's fiery guitar playing on "How Many More Years," recorded by Sam Phillips in Memphis in 1951, along with "Smokestack Lightning," "I Asked For Water" (Wolf's remake of Tommy Johnson's "Cool Drink of Water Blues"), and more. *Howlin' Wolf* (Chess 1469, with the rocking chair on the cover) was all Chicago, and Hubert Sumlin's album as much as Wolf's; he cut his crazed solo on "Wang Dang Doodle" plus stunning efforts on "Down in the Bottom," "Spoonful," "You'll Be Mine," and "Going Down Slow." This music, which was to have such an impact on the Rolling Stones, the Yardbirds, and the like, was at once rougher and more sophisticated than the rockers and ballads the Hawks were used to. It was music of drive *and* nuance.

Just as important as Wolf's music was an album split between Little Junior Parker and Bobby Blue Bland: *Blues Consolidated* (Duke 75), released in the late fifties, marking the first appearance on LP for either singer. Both had started out in the late forties in Memphis, singing with the Beale Streeters, a band that included Johnny Ace on piano. Recording in Memphis for Sam Phillips and others, and later for the Duke label in Houston, the three were to define a whole new kind of rhythm and blues—occasionally fierce, but usually stressing a kind of tragic sentimentality, very delicate, highly arranged, based in carefully written blues ballads. *Blues Consolidated* showcased Bland's first real hit, "Farther on Up the Road," and his incredible "It's My Life, Baby." (This was a much more exciting performance than "Farther On," which is probably why the Hawks didn't bother attempting it; they passed Bland when they cut "Farther On," but there was no way on earth they were going to touch him—or his guitar player—on "It's My Life.")

At first one of many Roy Brown imitators, Bland found his own style and went on to a string of hits that still continue; he remains the most sensitive and original blues singer of the last twenty years. Along with (to a lesser degree) Junior Parker and Johnny Ace, Bland mattered enormously to what the Hawks were and to what the Band became. The deceptively quiet, despairing moods of his most distinctive records shaped Richard Manuel's singing particularly, but the group as a whole absorbed this music—not merely the phrasing, or the style of arranging, but the sensibility.

See, for Bobby Bland, *Two Steps From the Blues* (Duke 74), *Best of* (Duke 84), *Best of, Vol. 2* (Duke 86); for Junior Parker, *Best of* (Duke 83—includes his classic "Drivin' Wheel"); for Johnny Ace, *Memorial Album* (Duke 71—includes "Pledging My Love").

While the Hawks were listening to Bland and Wolf—and early Motown, the New Orleans rock of Irma Thomas and Ernie K-Doe, and everything else—they and Hawkins slogged on together. During the folk boom Ronnie got so desperate he even recorded "The Ballad of Caryl Chessman" (who knows, maybe he thought it'd get him a spot on *Hootenanny*). They cut two more albums: *The Best of Ronnie Hawkins* (Canadian Roulette 252250), which featured the scarifying "Who Do You Love," and *Mojo Man* (Canadian Roulette 25390), which held Levon and the Hawks' brilliant versions of "Farther On" and "She's 19" (mistitled as "Have a Party"). Of the other tracks on these albums, one can only say that Hawkins' tired vocals made an interesting contrast with the sizzling blues guitar that crept out behind him.

"Who Do You Love," "Bo Diddley," "Odessa," "Mary Lou," and others less memorable are available on *The Best of Ronnie Hawkins* FEATURING HIS BAND (Roulette 42045). Hawkins gained new fame after the Band's success, and he went on to make two smooth, expert albums (*Ronnie Hawkins*, Cotillion 9019, and *The Hawk*, Cotillion 9038), followed by one drooling mess-around that finally told his story the way it was meant to be told: "Willie and the Hand Job," more or less (*Rock and Roll Resurection*, Monument 31330).

On their own in 1964–1965, Levon and the Hawks made three singles: "Leave Me Alone" (basically Chuck Berry's "Almost Grown" tightened up)/"Uh-Uh-Uh" (recorded under the name of the Canadian Squires, Ware 6002); "Go Go Liza Jane" (an attempt to catch the tail of the go-go craze?)/"He Don't Love You" (Atco 45-6625); and "The Stones I Throw (Will Free All Men)"/"He Don't Love You" (Atco 45–6383). All the ambitions, a bit of the sound, and none of the poetry of *Big Pink* and *The Band* are here: "Something makes me want to stand up and do what's right . . . and take my brother's hand," Richard Manuel sang. "I will show them by the stones that I throw." Anything this explicit would have sunk *Big Pink*; that was a drama of morals, but not moralism, and the difference is everything.

About this time Robbie and Rick Danko worked with John Hammond, Jr., on the sessions that later came out on Hammond's *I Can Tell* album (Atlantic 8152). Anyone who has the stamina to sit through Hammond's ludicrous blackface vocals can hear what Robbie still considers some of his best playing: all rough edges, jagged bits of metal ripping through the spare rhythm section.

WITH BOB DYLAN

Robbie and Levon, joined by Harvey Brooks on bass and Al Kooper on organ, backed Dylan at his 1965 Forest Hills concert, his first electric gig to follow the infamous Newport Folk Festival earlier that year. Dylan's tour with the Hawks began in the fall; Levon was replaced by Bobby Gregg and then by Mickey Jones. In December, in New York, they went into the studio to make a few singles. The first released was "Can You *Please* Crawl Out Your Window?" (Columbia 43477); it was a wild, carnival version of the song Dylan had earlier recorded (and accidentally released, and pulled) with the group he used on *Highway 61 Revisited*. I don't think either he or the Band have ever sounded as if they were having more fun. "You gotta lotta *nerve* to say you are my friend," Dylan croaked, parodying "Positively Fourth Street," his hit of a couple of months before, "if you won't crawl out your window!"

"Crawl Out" missed the Top 40, and next up was "One of Us Must Know," which didn't make the charts at all. Here the Hawks gave Dylan perhaps the richest sound he ever heard. The record was frenzied, yet somehow stately; Richard Manuel has never played with more soul, and Robbie closed out the tune with some stinging notes that are probably worth more than all the solos he never got to play. The tune was a highlight on Dylan's *Blonde on Blonde* (Columbia C2S 841), of course; Robbie also played on "Obviously Five Believers" and, I think, "Absolutely Sweet Marie."

Four other numbers from that singles session have never been released. "I Wanna Be Your Lover" is a straight rocker, with chains of images that seem to go nowhere in particular; "Number One" is the instrumental track for lyrics that were never written. Very much like "One of Us Must Know," it stands on its own, mostly because of the power of Garth Hudson's straining organ. "Seems Like a Freeze Out" is the first version of "Visions of Johanna," a song Dylan and the Hawks were doing on stage at the time. Garth's organ seems instantly to lift the song about twenty feet off the ground; with Manuel's piano on one side and Robbie's unobtrusive guitar on the other, the music just swirls, round and round, until Dylan ends it with a long, low moan. The performance is gorgeous before it is anything else; Dylan recut the song for *Blonde on Blonde*, perhaps because the cold, dark sound of the album version really was more appropriate to the story he was trying to put across. And then there is "She's Your Lover Now," very rough, no more than a work tape. Thanks to a guitar note here, a piano rumble there, Dylan's bitterest lyrics, and his unforgiving vocal, it is one of the most terrifying performances ever recorded. "You just sit around and ask for ashtrays," Bob Dylan sings. *"Can't you reach?"* And that doesn't touch it.

Many of the concerts Dylan and the Hawks played were re-corded; officially, only one song has ever been released: "Just Like Tom Thumb's Blues," taped in Liverpool (Columbia 43683). The Hawks outran themselves, as did Dylan—this was voodoo music, strong enough to make Dylan's other records sound like he was only kidding. "He didn't know anything about *music*," Robbie says. "He was all folk songs, Big Bill, and we were Jerry Lee. So it'd be, 'Down the streets the dogs are barking—WHAM!!' A huge noise. And Bob would say, 'Hey, that's great, let's do it again, that way.' We had no help; everyone who wasn't telling him the combination was wrong for him was telling us it was wrong for us."

I don't buy the idea that Dylan "knew nothing about music," but what he knew he knew in a different way than the Hawks did; the combination of his instincts and their ability took them both to places they could never have reached on their own. The music they made in the mid-sixties was hard, hard rock, surrealistic dandy's blues cut with moments of gentleness and wild humor. On stage they *moved:* Dylan and Robertson charged across the stage, playing head to head, while Rick Danko rocked back and forth as if, in Ralph Gleason's memorable line, he could swing Coit Tower. They reveled in melodrama. In Paris, to face a crowd of French students who idolized Bob Dylan as the definitive anti-American, Dylan wangled an enormous Stars-and-Stripes, hung it up behind the amps, and almost caused a riot; to open their numbers, Dylan, Robbie, and Danko would turn and face the drummer—he would raise his stick high, suddenly bring it down with a crash as the three guitarists leaped into the air, kicking the song off as they hit the ground.

This music is captured on the famous *Royal Albert Hall Concert 1966* bootleg (available through Moe's Books and Records, Berke-ley, California); it contains eight songs, beginning with the unre-leased elsewhere "Tell Me Mama" and ending with a mean fencing match between Dylan and his audience that leads into, and is resolved by, "Like a Rolling Stone." "Tell Me Mama" has some fine lines in it ("Your cemetery hips . . . your graveyard lips"), but what counts is that it is one of the most exciting pieces of rock 'n' roll ever made. The timing of the musicians—the way Robbie's careening solo falls perfectly into Mickey Jones's thump, the way Danko's bass flips into a cymbal smash—is unlike anything I have ever heard. "If I told you what our music is really about we'd prob-ably all get arrested," Dylan said to an interviewer in 1965. Listen-

ing to their fury on "Ballad of a Thin Man," to Hudson and
Robertson framing Dylan as he drops back, ever so slowly, into the
song's chorus, turning the question Mr. Jones is afraid to answer
into an epigram of unspeakable horror, that boast seems altogether
convincing.

In 1967, up in Woodstock after Dylan's motorcycle accident,
the Band and Dylan made the Basement Tape, most of which has
since been bootlegged or covered by other singers. The tape included about twenty-five songs, plus many alternate versions,
music of greater emotional depth and subtlety than any that either
Dylan or the Band had previously recorded. Danko and Manuel
often sang back-up (on "Get Yer Rocks Off" they sound quite like
the Coasters, with someone growling a bass "Get 'em *off!*" every
chorus); Robbie occasionally played drums, as on "Wheel's on
Fire." It was a much quieter, more funky sound that they had used
on stage; just right for songs that were divided about equally between the confessional and the bawdyhouse. This is not the place
to probe a session that produced music as satisfying and complex as
anything on *Blonde on Blonde* or *The Band*—merely Dylan's singing
and Robbie's calm, desolate guitar solo on "I Shall Be Released" are
enough to make it that—but that Dylan went on to *John Wesley
Harding* and the Band to *Big Pink* is not hard to understand.

In early 1968 Dylan and the Band showed up for the Woody
Guthrie memorial concert in New York; the album that resulted
was badly recorded, and most of the performers were maudlin.
Dylan and the Band ripped out a ragged, updated rockabilly
music, and with "Grand Coulee Dam," they came across (*A Tribute
to Woody Guthrie*, Columbia 31171). Their show at the Isle of
Wight Festival in 1969 did not fare as well; the recording was
atrociously produced, with the Band shoved far into the background and Dylan's muddled, unsure singing forced up front. The
planned live album was killed, but four numbers were mixed into
Dylan's *Self Portrait* album (Columbia C2X 30050). Most of the Isle
of Wight bootlegs that appeared were better, because they caught
what the performance actually sounded like—occasionally distracted, often tight and funny. On bootleg evidence, the highlight
was "Highway 61 Revisited," with Garth leading the Band around
supercharged twists and turns while Dylan, Helm, Danko, Robertson, and Manuel screamed "OUT ON HIGHWAY SIXTY-ONE!" like

Mexican tour guides hustling customers for a trip to the best whorehouse in Tijuana.

Late in 1973, preparatory to their joint nationwide comeback tour, Dylan and the Band cut *Planet Waves* (Asylum 1003), mostly first takes of songs the Band had not heard before they walked into the studio. Loose as street-singers, the six came up with a good, scrawny sound—"stray cat music," Bob Christgau called it— nothing like past music they had made together or solo, and definitely not slick. In some ways, the joys-and-sorrows-of-family-life tunes that dominated the album were ("Wedding Song," which Dylan recorded alone, was an exception), but the tour that followed made *Planet Waves* beside the point.

Before the Flood (Asylum 201), recorded almost entirely on February 14, 1974, the last night of the tour, in Los Angeles, collected the guts of the performance Dylan and the Band offered the country: proof that the best music of both had endured and changed along with the men who played it.

Separately, neither Dylan nor the Band did anything astounding; the Band's eight numbers on *Before the Flood* ("Apres moi le deluge?" Now, really) included an old, never before performed number called "Endless Highway," and in general their music was a lot more raucous than *Rock of Ages*—"Cripple Creek" was a drunken brawl. Together, they cut loose with music that made the Rolling Stones' live show sound polite, and yet within the storm was an emotional complexity that went beyond Dylan's lyrics. Roaring with fury and wit, riding Levon's enormous beat, and fusing all parts into a collective momentum, this was rock 'n' roll at its limits.

With Dylan there to take the heat, that side of the Band that is scared of the crowd, that seeks refuge in craftsmanship and arrangements, disappeared, replaced by the chaos and intensity of those old Howlin' Wolf records. With the Band around him (they were not a "backing group" on this tour), Dylan broke through the strictures of casualness and ease that had weakened his last few albums. He was forced to use most of what he had simply to keep up, and so he became that stray cat, howling at the moon.

The music, as I heard it in concert, was hard and angry, with Levon Helm (sometimes Richard Manuel joined him on a second set of drums) at the center. On record, I hear endless textures within the sound, and Garth Hudson seems like the star: shifting the rhythms, darting in and out of every song like a phantom horn section, sometimes wrestling the tunes away from the other five and tossing them back with all the strength he has. The music cracked open with a freedom few other records have even hinted at; the earlier versions of "All Along the Watchtower" and "Highway 61 Revisited" were trivialized as Dylan and the Band charged through their music, as if they had little idea what route they were traveling, let alone where they were going to come out, playing with the good-humored, nervy conviction that the trip would return in surprises whatever it cost in uncertainty.

The music was made in a particularly American spirit: big, loud, crude, and uncivilized. It was an old-fashioned, back-country big-city attack on all things genteel, an up-to-date version of Walt Whitman's YAWP.

And it is a standard rock 'n' rollers will be chasing as they can, the Band and Bob Dylan as much as anyone.

Despite their popularity with critics, not much of real merit has been written on the Band. An important exception is Ralph J. Gleason's work, particularly his superb review of *The Band* (*The Rolling Stone Record Review* [New York: Pocket Books, 1971]), his account of their disastrous/triumphant first nights in San Francisco ("The Band At Winterland," in *The Rolling Stone Rock 'n' Roll Reader*, ed. Ben Fong-Torres [New York: Bantam, 1974]), and his piece on the 1974 tour ("Like a Rolling Stone, Again," *Knockin' on Dylan's Door* [New York: Pocket Books, 1974]). My own "Heavy Breathing," also on the 1974 tour, appeared in *Creem* (May 1974); Bob Christgau wrote a brilliant review of *Before the Flood* for *Newsday* (July 7, 1974). My "Rock-A-Hula, Clarified" (*Creem*, June 1971) includes a long section on *Stage Fright;* that, and my piece on the Band's debut, from the old *Express-Times*, plus other commentary, will go into a book of songs, photos, filmscripts, and autobiographies the Band is planning to publish one of these days.

SLY STONE

STAGGERLEE

"Stack O'Lee" or "Stagolee" was one of several turn-of-the-century ballads about semilegendary characters (they were real, but their legends were more so)—figures like Tom Dula (Dooley), John Henry, Casey Jones, Railroad Bill, Frankie and Albert (later

"Johnny"). Endless variants were popular in the twenties, with whites and blacks, in versions by songsters John Hurt, Furry Lewis, Frank Hutchinson, Leadbelly, and others (see *Anthology of American Folk Music, Vol. 1, Ballads*, ed. Harry Smith, Folkways Records 2951); the tunes evolve today in the music of Tom T. Hall and especially Taj Mahal. These ballads seem to form a special genre; characters jump from song to song. Furry Lewis put Alice Fry (source of the trouble between Frankie and Albert) into his "Kassie Jones"; in Tom T. Hall's "More About John Henry" (on *The Storyteller*, Mercury 61368), John Henry meets up with Stackerlee, kills him, and throws his body into the river.

Yet while Frankie and Albert, Railroad Bill, and Casey Jones have been tracked down, and John Henry almost has been, Stackerlee remains a mystery. Almost all versions of the song share certain details: Stackerlee fought Billy Lyons over Stack's Stetson hat (in a version collected by John Lomax, Billy *spits* in it); Billy begs Stack not to kill him because he has a wife and children to support; Stack invariably kills him anyway. From that point on, the story, and Stackerlee's fate, were up to the singer.

Allan Lomax was the first to print the song; it was given to him by one Ella Scott Fisher, in 1910, as an account of a murder that had taken place in Memphis about ten years earlier. At the time, Memphis had the highest murder rate in the world; the daily carnage among blacks was almost unbelievable. It seemed odd to me that a single incident would be considered so memorable; that thought, plus the confusion in early versions as to whether Stack was black or white, made me wonder if a strange reversal might be hidden in the ambiguity of the song. Perhaps, I thought, a white man—Stackerlee—killed a black man—Billy Lyons. Stackerlee was doubtless never even charged, let alone hung. So blacks fought back through myth, first exacting justice in their songs; then, wishing for a freedom and mastery only a white man could possess, they identified with their oppressor, subsumed him into their own culture, took his name, and sent him out to terrorize the world as one of their own. Reversals of this sort are what myths are all about (Frankie, celebrated in every variant of her ballad for shooting her unfaithful lover, in fact died by *his* hand), but proof that the original Stackerlee was white would constitute as deep a subversion of cultural pride as Freud's claim that Moses was an Egyptian, and I had to find out.

I asked my friend Pat Thomas to go to Memphis and try to

dig out the truth; the truth seems to be that there were two original Stackerlees: one white, the other black.

Samuel Stacker Lee was born May 5, 1847; he died April 4, 1890. According to Paul Copock, a Memphis historian, Stacker Lee was the brother (others say the son) of James Lee, Sr., the man who founded the Lee Steamship Line that ruled the Mississippi from Cincinnati to New Orleans after the Civil War. Lee himself was born in 1808 and died in 1889; to my mind that makes him an unlikely brother for Stacker, but certainly not an impossible one.

James Lee was a good pal of Jefferson Davis and Nathan Bedford Forrest, later a Confederate hero; at the age of sixteen, in 1863, Stacker Lee went off to fight at Forrest's side, black manservant in tow. According to Shields McIlwaine's *Memphis Down in Dixie* (researched by William McCaskill [New York: Dutton, 1948]), Stacker Lee came out of the war a hell-raiser, a gambler, a rounder, an all-around ladies' man and tough guy, well-known up and down the river once James Lee gave him a ship of his own. James Lee liked the boy, McIlwaine reports; the rest of the family, perhaps developing a few pretensions toward gentility, spurned him, possibly because his women were mulatto as often as they were white. And the second Stacker Lee seems to have been Samuel Stacker Lee's mulatto son—to put it mildly, his father's son in every way.

That, at least, is what many older black residents of Memphis believe today. Stacker Lee, Pat Thomas was told by Thomas Pinkston (the last man alive to have played with W. C. Handy, author of "St. Louis Blues"), was a roustabout, a waterfront gambler, a legend in his own time; when someone threw a seven, the crowd called it a "Stacker Lee roll." McIlwaine hazily identifies him as a small, dark man with a bad eye, who worked the Anchor Steamship Line, but he gives no documentation and McCaskill's notes are gone; Pinkston remembers hearing his elders talk about Stacker Lee as tall, good looking, and mean.

A date of 1900 seems too early; Furry Lewis, who was already singing the song in the early twenties, recalls nothing of any specific incident. No one, in fact, remembers anything about a Billy Lyons, though, McCaskill says, Billy Lyons might have been a reflection of Sam de Lyon, alias Sandy Lyons, a Memphis cop who was famous for killing five men in one night. And that would turn my reversal on its head; here, in the song, at any rate, the black Stacker Lee kills Sam de Lyon, a white sheriff.

What happened to Stacker Lee, Pat Thomas asked Pinkston. "He just disintegrated; old [Sheriff] Joe Turner took him up . . . he took 'em all up." By that he meant to prison in Nashville; Sheriff Joe Turner ran black prisoners from Memphis to Nashville early in the century. In the words of an old song, "They tell me Joe Turner come to town, brought one thousand links of chain, gonna have a nigger for every link." But Thomas's search of prison records, birth, death, and cemetery records turned up nothing.

In 1902, twelve years after the first white Stacker Lee was buried, James Lee, Jr. put a boat called *The Stacker Lee* on the river. It was the crack boat of the Lee Line, 223 feet long, the most famous on the Mississippi; some called it "Stack O'Dollars," others "Bull of the Woods." In 1916, it dragged a landing and went down; the Lee Line was soon to be put out of business by land transport. James Lee, Jr., the last real riverboat man in the Lee family, had died in 1905. He left well over a million dollars, and the siblings of his prominent Memphis family fought over the money until the estate was finally settled, thirty years after his death. Blacks took possession of another descendant of the Lee family a long time ago, but the fight over his legacy is a fight over meaning, not money, and no settlement is in sight.

Frank Hutchinson, who was white, cut one of the earliest recorded versions of "Stackalee" in 1927; remarkably, its details (not merely the Stetson hat, but the barking bulldog, the fighting in the alley) seem to reappear more clearly in Lloyd Price's 1958 hit than they do in any of the many versions put down in the intervening thirty years. Hutchinson makes a good joke out of the story: "God bless your children, I'll take care of your wife," his Staggerlee says after Billy makes his plea; "They taken [Billy] to the cemetery," Hutchinson sings, "they failed to bring him back." But as the song ends we find Stack in jail—haunted by the phantoms of Billy Lyons that crawl around his bed (*Anthology of American Folk Music, Vol. 1, Ballads*).

Mississippi John Hurt's "Stack O'Lee Blues" (1929), featuring an irresistibly pretty guitar intro, is one of the loveliest of his many recordings (*The Mississippi Blues Transition*, Origin Jazz Library 17; also included on *The Story of the Blues*, Columbia 30008, but with very inferior sound quality). The most influential postwar version, before Lloyd Price's, was by the New Orleans singer Archibald (released in 1950 as "Stack-a' Lee," Parts 1 & 2, Imperial 5068, now out of print). Archibald offers the complete Staggerlee versus the Devil scenario, and here we find Stack not hounded by Billy's ghost, but Stack chasing the poor fool down to hell, where Billy must suffer still further tortures at the hands of his opponent. Dr. John covered Archibald on his tribute-to-New Orleans album, *Gumbo*, in 1972 (Atco 7006), retaining the words and adding the classic guitar solo from Guitar Slim's "The Things That I Used to Do," plus a horn introduction that can break your heart. It is said Dr. John can sing "Stagger Lee" for half an hour without repeating a lyric.

Lloyd Price also came out of New Orleans, and he put the tale on jukeboxes and car radios all across the country in 1958; "Stagger Lee" was his first and only number one hit, though he had topped the R&B charts back in 1952 with his magnificent "Lawdy Miss Clawdy." Judging strictly by lyrics, Price's version takes the prize, if only for his completely original intro—four lines, with the perfection of a haiku, that set the scene with extraordinary tension and grace.

> *The night was clear*
> *And the moon was yellow*
> *And the leaves . . . came . . . tumbling*
> *Down.*

Price's performance was hard saxophone rock, and in retrospect, his drive seems to be what many earlier versions lacked. However, an interesting thing happened. As "Stagger Lee" was rising up the charts, Dick Clark booked Price on *American Bandstand*, and then realized he could not possibly take the responsibility of exposing his millions of viewers to a song that celebrated gambling and murder. So, true to form, he had Price change the lyrics. Immediately, Price's label pulled the original, had Price record the *Bandstand* version, and the result was a tale wherein Stack and Billy "argue," not gamble, about a girl, not money and a hat. Staggerlee and Billy go home, feel very bad about all the mean things they've said to each other, and then *apologize*. "Staggerlee and Billy were no more sore," Price concludes. Paradoxically, Price sounded even more impassioned on this version than he had in the first place, and his band, perhaps to compensate for the change in lyrics, outdid themselves. The reformed Staggerlee can still be heard on a 45 (ABC-Paramount 9972); the X-rated cut is on *Lloyd Price's 16 Greatest Hits* (ABC 763).

Wilbert Harrison's version, which follows Price's original story line, is unique among modern treatments for its mournful, distressed tone; "That'll teach ya 'bout gamblin'," Harrison warns (*Let's Work Together*, Sue 8801). The Isley Brothers may have added to the tradition of Billy Lyons's "sickly" wife when they cut a raging stomp (withering guitar fire courtesy a young Jimi Hendrix) that Dave Marsh swears has Billy trying to talk Stack out of the inevitable by hinting, "I got four little children and a very *shapely* wife." I confess I don't hear it, but I do like the idea, and it's a great record anyway (*The Famous Isley Brothers Twisting and Shouting*, United Artists 6313).

These seem to me to be the most memorable Staggerlees; I've yet to find a version resembling Bobby Seale's, but I have hopes that someday he'll cut it himself.

As for the Staggerlee reflection in blues and rock 'n' roll, the records mentioned in the text are: "Crawling Kingsnake," John Lee Hooker (*I'm John Lee Hooker*, Vee Jay 1007, or *John Lee Hooker*, Everest FS 222); "Canned Heat Blues," Tommy Johnson, 1928 (*Blues Roots/Mississippi*, RBF 14); "Rollin' Stone," Muddy Waters, 1950 (*Sail On*, Chess 1539); "Brown-Eyed Handsome Man," Chuck Berry, 1959 (*Chuck Berry's Golden Decade, Vol. 1*, Chess 1514D); "Who Do You Love," Bo Diddley (*Got My Own Bag of Tricks*— a superb greatest hits package—Chess 2CH 60005); "Midnight Mover," Wilson Pickett, 1968 (*The Best of Wilson Pickett, Vol. 2*, Atlantic 8290); "Midnight Rambler," the Rolling Stones (the studio version on *Let It Bleed* is weak; the definitive performance is live, from *Get Yer Ya-Yas Out!*, recorded in 1969, London 5); "Back Door Man" and "Going Down Slow," Howlin' Wolf, 1960 and 1961 (*Howlin' Wolf*, Chess 1469); "There Is Something On Your Mind," Bobby Marchan, 1960 (originally Fire 1022, reissued as a 45 on Flashback FLB 2).

SLY & THE FAMILY STONE

Ben Fong-Torres' "Everybody Is a Star: The Travels of Sylvester Stewart" (in *The Rolling Stone Rock 'n' Roll Reader*, ed. Ben Fong-Torres [New York: Bantam, 1974]), a history of the Family Stone through 1970, is one of the finest rock profiles I have ever read; I relied on it for much of the biographical information, not to mention inspiration. Thanks, Ben.

Fong-Torres notes that Sly Stone's first record was "On the Battlefield for My Lord," cut with his siblings under the name of the Stewart Four. Sly played drums and guitar. He was five.

Early in his teens Sly began his apprenticeship with bands like Joey Piazza and the Continentals; "Long Time Away" b/w "Help Me With My Heart" came out in 1960 or 1961, under the name of Sylvester Stewart (G & P 45–901). In 1964 Sly co-authored Bobby Freeman's "C'mon and Swim" with Tom Donahue; it was a hit, but Sly's own "I Just Learned How to Swim" backed with "Scat Swim," out in 1964 (Autumn 45–3), and his "Buttermilk, Parts 1 & 2," from 1965 (Autumn 45–14) were not.

By this time, however, Sly had taken over as house producer for Donahue's Autumn and North Beach labels. His efforts are collected on *San Francisco Roots* (Vault 119). Here lie the hits and nonhits of the Beau Brummels, the Mojo Men, the Vejtables, the Tikis, and the Great Society (Grace Slick's original outfit). Legend has it that Sly drove the Great Society through more than two hundred takes of "Free Advice," the flipside of the first version of "Somebody to Love"; from the evidence of the record it certainly wasn't worth it, but then, maybe Sly just didn't like hippies.

Sly and the Family Stone (Sly, guitar, organ, other instruments; Rosie Stone, piano; Freddie Stone, guitar; Larry Graham, bass; Jerry Martini, sax; Greg Errico, drums) first released a single, "I Ain't Got Nobody" b/w "I Can't Turn You Loose" in 1966, on the local Loadstone label (45–3951). Their first album, *A Whole New Thing* (Epic 30333), came out in 1967. It missed the charts; 1968's *Dance to the Music* (Epic 26371) did little better, but the single of the same name made top ten. *Life* (Epic 26397) flopped, but the band broke through with "Everyday People," a completely new kind of rock 'n' roll and a number one single late in 1968. Then came the follow-up album *Stand!* (Epic 26456), a record that permanently changed black music. It rose to #13 in 1969, sold two million copies, and stayed on the charts for two solid years. From it came the songs that made the Family's name: "Stand!" "I Want to Take You Higher," the astonishing "Sex Machine." Live versions of "Higher" and "Dance" confirmed the Family's ability to set a crowd on fire—or, some said, to rouse a mob to quasi-fascist ecstasies (*Woodstock*, Cotillion 3-500).

Next up were "Hot Fun in the Summertime," #2 in 1969, and "Thank You falettinme be mice elf agin" b/w "Everybody Is a Star," number one in 1970. Sly announced his next album, *The*

Incredible and Unpredictable Sly and the Family Stone. Unpredictably, it did not materialize, and to fill the long dry spell that led to *Riot*, Epic put together *Greatest Hits* (Epic 30325) in late 1970, and it reached #2, selling over three million copies. A collection of the singles and crowd-pleasers, it is a stunning, absolutely essential album.

There's a riot goin' on (Epic 30986) reached back to the Robins/Coasters' 1955 "Riot in Cell Block #Nine" for its title ("Scarface Jones said it's too late to quit/ Pass the dynamite, uh, the fuse is lit—There's a riot goin' on"—on *The Coasters, The Early Years,* Atco 371); it shared the present with George Jackson's *Soledad Brother* (New York: Bantam, 1970), a book that had its influence on my ideas about Staggerlee and Sly. The album was an instant number one when it was released late in 1971, as was the first single taken from it, "Family Affair." Whether Sly's many white listeners were more open to this music than his white critics is a question the charts will not answer; by this time, the black record-buying public was big enough to put a disc over the top all by itself.

Fresh (Epic 32134), complete with Richard Avedon cover photo (the curse of rock—the Band's *Cahoots* had one too), arrived in 1973, and promptly settled in, along with "If You Want Me to Stay," its single, at number one. *Fresh* documented the conflicts within the group: Rusty Allen and Andy Newmark replaced Larry Graham and Greg Errico on bass and drums, respectively. Added were Pat Rizzo on Sax and Little Sister (a female vocal trio headed by Sly's sister Vanetta) on backing vocals. Rumors of Doris Day accompanying Sly on "Que Sera, Sera" did not pan out.

In 1974 Sly and Kathy Silva celebrated their marriage and their new son with a sold-out wedding at Madison Square Garden. Arriving about the same time was a new album, *Small Talk* (Epic 32930). Bill Lordan took over on drums; Little Sister was dropped; coming aboard were Vet Stewart on keyboards, and Sid Page, whose violin playing was a joy. But the album did not get off the ground, musically or commercially; there were no new hit singles. Though there were moments of emotion, the communal spirit of the band's music seemed gone for good; one got the sense that Sly, his wife, and his son were the only Family Stone that mattered. As the Orioles once put it, it's too soon to know.

RECORDS BEFORE AND AFTER RIOT

The tension between black movies and black records that emerged in the late sixties and early seventies brought a realistic necessity to the pop charts that will be felt for many years, just as the fantasies of the Staggerlee flicks revealed an untapped film audience and created a new cinematic genre. The imitations and sons and daughters of *Superfly*, *Black Caesar*, and *Cleopatra Jones* are now a regular, one might say essential, part of the Hollywood economy. It won't be too long before a black director makes a movie about a no-nonsense black director who offs his white producer after he catches the honky skimming profits to pay the dope and gambling bills the Mob holds on him. The picture, of course, will be financed with white money.

Social comment, however, has not been very common in black music. There have been the rare depression blues songs, a few about Korea (brought up to date for Vietnam), not much more. The Coasters' records—"Riot," "What About Us" ("He's got a car made a' suede/ . . . If we go out on dates, we go onna box on roller skates"), and the cryptic "Run Red Run" (a monkey, who may be the black man, pulls a gun on his master, who may be the white)—are notable partly because they are so anomalous; and all were strictly white inventions by Leiber and Stoller ("What About Us" and "Run Red Run" were two sides of a 1959 single, worth seeking out on *Coast Along With the Coasters*, Atco 135).

Usually, black voices have channeled the emotions of social despair into songs of sexual and romantic tragedy. It took the civil rights movement to make black protest acceptable on the radio, and certainly Sly's "Everyday People" was a turning point, along with Jerry Butler's deeply saddening "Only the Strong Survive," #4 in 1969 (on *The Best of Jerry Butler*, Mercury 61281), and the Temptations' brilliant "Cloud Nine," #6 in 1968, which was the first black record to hit dope head-on—as far as the singer was concerned, with arms open, though the irony of the song was hard to miss (on *The Temptations' Anthology*, Motown M782A3, a well-organized, low-price, three-record career survey, as are all the Motown, Tamla, and Gordy "Anthologies").

Butler's hard look at the world at large and the Tempts' tour of the streets let Paul Kelly into the church; his "Stealing in the Name of the Lord" (Happy Tiger 45–541), #49 in 1970, was a marvelously effective attack on shyster preachers preying on the

black community. "Step right up, drop a buck," Kelly chanted
over a fast blues guitar. Like most of the records mentioned here,
the music was even stronger and more inventive than the politics,
which only made the politics more convincing. Other seminal discs
were Edwin Starr's "War," a number one hit in 1970 (Gordy
45–7101), with its nicely understated chorus: "WAR! What is it
good for? ABSOLUTELY NUTHIN'!"; and the Chi-Lites' brooding "For
God's Sake Give More Power to the People," #26 (on *The Chi-
Lites Greatest Hits*, Brunswick 754184); Marvin Gaye's *What's Going
On* album, #6 (Tamla 310), his historic "Inner City Blues," #9
(*Anthology*, Motown M782A); the Undisputed Truth's "Smiling
Faces Sometimes (Tell Lies)," #3 (Gordy 7108); the Staple Singers'
occasionally ridiculous ("Put your hand over your mouth when you
cough") but mostly hard-nosed "Respect Yourself," #12 (Stax 45–
0104), all in 1971.

   If the breakthrough came with *Riot*, the takeover came with
Curtis Mayfield's soundtrack to *Superfly*. With the Impressions and
on his own, Mayfield had been exploring a somewhat bland Martin
Luther King-style progressivism for years, complete with sincere
heart, boundless optimism, tortured lyrics, and brotherhood
speeches to nightclub audiences; he sang buoyant numbers like
"We're a Winner", sticky ones like "Choice of Colors." With the
blasted truths of "Freddie's Dead," #4 in 1972, and the sardonic
yet sympathetic "Superfly," #8 later that year, Mayfield found a
completely new voice, and the post-Sly-of-the-sixties soul music to
go with it. His assault was complete when the soundtrack album
hit the top of the charts (*Superfly*, includes both singles, Curtom
8014).

   Along with *Superfly* came the deluge: the O'Jays' "Back Stabbers," #3 (on *Back Stabbers*, Philadelphia International 31712, also
includes "992 Arguments" and "Love Train"); War's "Slipping into
Darkness," #16 (United Artists 45–50867); Stevie Wonder's "Superstition," #1 (on *Talking Book*, Tamla 319); Johnny Nash's shimmering "I Can See Clearly Now," #1 (Epic 45–10902); the Staple
Singers' "I'll Take You There," #1 (Stax 45–0125); and the Temptations' "Papa Was a Rolling Stone," #1 (on *Anthology*)—most of
them crammed into the last few months of 1972.

   Part and parcel of this post-sixties resurgence were a few white
records: the Rolling Stones' "Gimmie Shelter" and "You Can't
Always Get What You Want," probably their two finest recordings
(*Let It Bleed*, 1969, London 4); their definitive *Exile On Main Street*

(1972, Rolling Stones 2900); and perhaps also Jim Croce's hits, "You Don't Mess Around With Jim" and "Bad, Bad Leroy Brown," two Staggerlee songs in which Billy comes out on top (*You Don't Mess Around With Jim*, ABC 756; *Life and Times*, ABC 769).

Contrasting most sharply with the heroes of the movies were the personae of Al Green and the Chi-Lites: vulnerable, open, searching for new ways to define what it meant to be a man. Green's string of hits began in 1970 with "Tired of Being Alone," #11; "Let's Stay Together" was quickly #1 in 1971; his best, "Look What You Done for Me," was among three top ten discs in 1972, and Green has hardly slowed down since. He makes good albums; *Call Me* (Hi 32077) is his best, while *I'm Still in Love with You* (Hi 32074) and *Livin' for You* (Hi 32082), which includes his wonderful "Let's Get Married," are only a cut below. The Chi-Lites' more extreme, and in some ways even more moving, music can best be heard on *Greatest Hits* (noted above); it collects "Have You Seen Her," #3 in 1971, "Oh Girl," #1 in 1972, plus "A Lonely Man" and "The Coldest Days of My Life," which might be their masterpiece.

The Chi-Lites' "We Need Order" (Brunswick 45-55489), which died at #61 in 1972, was joined in anti-Stack overcompensation by the Four Tops' "Keeper of the Castle," which linked street life with politics, and damned both—"while you're worryin' about society/ The leaves are witherin' on your family tree"—#10 in 1972 (Dunhill 45-4330). This retreat was matched in a completely idiotic way by Brighter Side of Darkness's "Love Jones" (20th Century 45-2002), and more subtly, for a time, by Gamble-Huff labels. The true social vision of the O'Jays' "Back Stabbers" was undercut by the bullshit social vision of "Love Train" (a great record, not withstanding); when the next few innocuous releases died, the group was back with *Ship Ahoy* (Philadelphia International 32408), which offered a song pegging money as the root of all evil. The killer, however, was the title tune: a ten-minute encapsulation of the voyage of a slave ship from Africa to America. It was pretentious, overblown, and powerful.

Most groups, writers, and producers retreated from the work of 1971–1972, or trivialized it with bad imitations; their music, like Sly's *Fresh*, lost much of its feeling. Still scoring were Marvin Gaye, who turned to pure sex with the unbelievably erotic "Let's Get It On," #1 in 1973 (on his fine album, *Let's Get It On*, Tamla 329—certainly the first Motown album to be introduced by a quote from T. S. Eliot); and Stevie Wonder, who continued his mastery of the charts with "Higher Ground" and the deathly "Livin' for the City," wherein the young hero of *Sounder* makes it to New York, is set up for a bust by a black brother, and emerges from prison years later, trying to remember the dream that brought him to the city streets he walks day and night. The hit single version stopped with the character's ambitions—you had to go to the album for his fate—but it was to Wonder's credit that the song worked either way (*Innervisions*, Tamla, 326V1).

Four other records deserve mention; they fall into no genre, but play in the gap between the imperatives of the movies and the music described above. First and most important is Diana Ross's much sneered at soundtrack for *Lady Sings the Blues* (Motown 758), #1 in 1972, a remarkably personal and vital piece of music that served as a backdrop, and a necessary historical anchor, for the other records of the period. It was also perhaps the first time the Staggerlee story was revised, and, more crucially, acted out, by a woman.

The Credibility Gap's comedy album, *A Great Gift Idea* (Warner Bros. 2154), featured a trailer for "Black Ivory Productions' " new release, *KingPin*, "the first movie that has dared to be suggested by the life of the late Dr. Martin Luther King, Jr.—a film of great importance not only to the Afro-American community, but to all Negroes." Opening with an uncanny imitation of Curtis Mayfield's *Superfly* music—"He's a king, he's a pin"—the piece confronts us with "Denver Deveroll, 8th-round draft choice of the New York Jets," who "*is* KingPin." "He's got a plan—to stick it to the Man/ They call him 'The Doctor'—and he's got a special treatment—*for Whitey!*" Executive producer "Samuel Hirschorn," natch. Also on the album was a rather strange "Evening With Sly Stone" in the form of an educational TV show, where we find Sly discussing the most subtle nuances of black culture with William Buckley, and then begging off because he has to get to bed by ten so as not to be late for the next day's "recital."

Taj Mahal's music for *Sounder* (Columbia 31944), variations on traditional themes played on traditional country instruments, was to me the finest black album of 1972; the movie, of course, could not have been more different from every other black film on the market. Taj's music and the performances of Cicely Tyson and Paul Winfield spoke for a kind of strength and pride that has every-

thing to do with love between a few who care about one another—
the mother, father, and children of *Sounder* did not stand for their
race, but for themselves. The movie was more painful than the big
city romances that outflanked it; Taj's music had more joy than the
records that were hits.

And finally, there is Lightnin' Rod's (I have no idea who
Lightnin' Rod is) *Hustler's Convention* (Douglas-United Artists UA-
LA 156). Bizarre, bizarre. *H.C.* is a two-record rap with music that
recounts the adventures of Sport, a black street kid who reaches the
top of the hustler's heap. About halfway into the opus, we move
into an incredibly detailed account of Sport's climactic poker game.
Sport is way ahead (about $100,000 ahead), but when an opponent
accuses him of cheating (he's not), he pulls his gun, grabs the pot,
and runs. The losers follow; Sport shoots two dead, but the rest
give chase, ducking out when cops pick up the gunfire. Sport is
shot, caught, sent up, and puts in twelve years on death row in
Sing Sing. "But I kept on coppin' a stay/ Till the death penalty was
done away/ And after a retrial they let me go." It cost him twelve
years, Sport says as the record ends, to discover that he has lived
exactly as the white man would have wished him to. Up to a point,
Sport's tale is a more sensational version of George Jackson's—
another man who put a new ending, or a new meaning, on the
story of Staggerlee.

RANDY NEWMAN

Randy Newman seems to have taken his first small step to-
ward fame in 1962, when the Fleetwoods recorded his "They Tell
Me It's Summer" as the flip of "Lovers by Night, Strangers by
Day." The Fleetwoods vanished from sight almost instantly.

Newman went on writing songs, cutting demos, and apparently released a few teenage discs under his own name, though I
haven't been able to find any of them. His first real notoriety came
with Judy Collins' recording of "I Think It's Going to Rain
Today" on her arty *In My Life* album (1966); with Van Dyke Parks'
fey version of the fabulous "Vine Street" (1967), a Hollywood-style
"On Broadway" that Newman has never recorded (on Parks' *Song
Cycle*, Warner Bros. 1727); and with Alan Price's *This Price Is Right*
(Parrot 71018), an album that featured five Newman songs, includ-
ing the perfect Sweet Sixteen fantasy, "The Biggest Night of Her
Life."

Randy Newman Creates Something New Under the Sun (Reprise 6286) was released in 1968, decked out in a cover that pictured Randy as a throwback to the thrilling days of, say, 1947; Reprise later substituted a photo of Randy with long hair, but it didn't do much good. Overproduced, occasionally musically cute, the album lived up to its title anyway. "Love Story," the first cut, was the clincher: here was an American romance, from proposal to the grave, with every warm promise vaguely undercut by a darker promise; when the kids are grown, Randy-the-Suitor pledges to his future bride, "they'll send us away"—but that's all part of the dream, isn't it? Also on the album were "So Long Dad" ("Love Story" sung from the point of view of Pop's grown-up son—"Drop by anytime," he assures his father, "Just be sure and call before you do"); "Living Without You"; "I Think It's Going to Rain Today"; "Davy the Fat Boy"; and "The Beehive State," a weird little masterpiece about the forgotten lands between New York and LA. At some grand All-American convention, the delegate from Utah rises. "We gotta tell this country about Utah," he says with all his courage, "Because nobody seems to know."

Twelve Songs (Reprise 6373), out in 1970, was a far better record; Randy's piano and voice were at the center, and the orchestration was muted. Where *Something New* was a show-music fantasia, *12 Songs* leaned on the blues and New Orleans piano rock. Newman's imagination went wild within his tight little structures; the album included "Let's Burn Down the Cornfield" ("And I'll make love to you, while it's burning"—an erotic image a lot of singers would have sold their souls to have created), "Suzanne," "Lucinda" (victim of the beach-cleaning machine), "Yellow Man," "Old Kentucky Home," "Underneath the Harlem Moon," and a few other works of genius. Three Dog Night got a number one hit out of a Stepin Fetchity version of "Mama Told Me Not to Come," later that year.

Randy Newman Live (Reprise 6459) was Newman's first chart entry, fading away at #191 in 1971. It's not a good record; the sound and the feeling are thin, and nothing of Newman's wonderful stage personality comes across. "Tickle Me" and "Maybe I'm Doing It Wrong," neither much more than one-line jokes, were thankfully left off other albums.

Sail Away (Reprise 2064) was issued in 1972, stopping at #163; it included "Lonely at the Top," "Burn On," "Political Science," and the best song about fatherhood I've ever heard, "Memo to My

Son." The title tune and "God's Song (That's Why I Love Mankind)" are really remarkable achievements. Like all Newman's best songs, they sneak up on a listener; float like a butterfly, sting like a bee.

"Sail Away" has been recorded by a lot of other people; Linda Ronstadt accomplished the dumbest version, and Salvation was responsible for altering the "little wog" reference to "little child". Newman's ironies were compounded geometrically when the tune was cut by veteran black songsters Sonny Terry and Brownie McGhee. They sang "Sail Away" as the song of two aging ex-slaves, reminiscing about the good old days before the Yankees came South to ruin their happy home, and it was not for the tenderhearted (on *Sonny & Brownie*, A&M 4397—an album that promoted some ironies of its own when it showcased archetypal British bluesman John Mayhall's harmonica on "White Boy Lost in the Blues").

In 1974 Newman unveiled a project he had been threatening for some time: *Good Old Boys* (Reprise 2193), nothing less than America from the twenties to the present, as seen through the eyes of a redneck. The ethos Newman aimed for was one of fierce pride undercut by terrible guilts, of guilt redeemed by pride. Included were drinking songs, love songs, political songs, a tune by Huey Long ("Every Man A King," unfortunately cut here as a sing-along instead of as the weird piece of soul music Newman singing alone could have made it), and a few strange adventures involving whites disguised as blacks, sexual impotence, exhibitionists, and other characters who seemed to have as much of a claim on the story as anyone else. One number, "Louisiana 1927," was more than one has a right to hope for even from Newman. A beautiful Stephen Fosterish string intro kicked it off, and then those familiar "Sail Away" piano notes were back again, guiding a first line that, in its simplicity and mystery—"art," to quote Kathleen Cleaver, "that conceals art"—is as pure an American language as any one will ever hear. To begin a song about a flood, Newman merely sang: "What has happened down here, is the wind have changed." And then, as one of the people that happened to, he tried, for two minutes or so, to tell you just how much that meant.

The album was not a complete success, perhaps because its ambitions were too great; often the orchestration is out of control, drowning Randy and his piano, and sometimes the feeling is just slightly off, as if Newman felt himself getting too close to home.

One suspects that that Newman was a little scared of his own work, and of his own talent. In 1974, not a very good year for rock 'n' roll, Randy Newman, Bob Dylan, and the Band were the only ones who took such chances.

Newman's only other recorded vocal work is a cut on the soundtrack to *Performance*, which he conducted—a dynamite rocker called (after an old King Solomon Hill blues) "Gone Dead Train" (Performance, Warner Bros. 2554). Of songs he has written for others but not recorded himself, Dusty Springfield's lovely "Just One Smile" and her "I Don't Want to Hear It Anymore" (both on *Dusty in Memphis*, Atlantic 8214—a great, great album) are likely the best.

I want to thank Susan Lydon for the help she gave me with this chapter; she gave me the benefit of her conversations with Randy Newman, and I have taken some quotes and much of my biographical information from her excellent piece, "Randy Newman—Out of Cole Porter, Hoagy Carmichael, Bob Dylan, Groucho Marx, Mark Twain, and Randy Newman" (*The New York Times Magazine*, November 5, 1972). We had a good time trading ideas one night at the Palace Theater in San Francisco, while Randy played God up on the stage and the audience gave him the cheers he deserves.

RAYMOND CHANDLER, NATHANAEL WEST, THE BEACH BOYS, & OTHERS

All of the quotes from Chandler come from *Raymond Chandler Speaking* (Four Square, 1962, English), a collection of letters, articles, and fiction fragments. His mysteries, especially *The Big Sleep* (1939), *Farewell, My Lovely* (1940), and his brilliant short story "Red Wind" have a good deal to do with my picture of Los Angeles, as do Ross MacDonald's books, especially *The Way Some People Die* (1951) and *The Chill* (1964). (Chandler's books are in various Pocket Books editions; ditto for MacDonald, published by Bantam.) I think West's *Day of the Locust* (1939), though in some ways inferior to Chandler's best, belongs to the same "There's nothing wrong with Southern California that a rise in the ocean level wouldn't cure" (MacDonald) genre, though each of these writers would expect to go under with everyone else *Miss Lonelyhearts and Day of the Locust* (New York: New Directions, 1962).

The other side of the Southern California story ("There's nothing wrong with surfing conditions a rise in the ocean level wouldn't cure") is best told by Jan and Dean and the Beach Boys. Jan and Dean's immortal "Surf City," written by Beach Boy Brian Wilson, is on their "Legendary Masters" *Anthology* (United Artists 9961), a crazed two-record set that comes with a concordance matching each of the duo's discs with the car and girlfriend each singer had at the time the records were released. The Beach Boys', mid-sixties stuff is collected on *The Best of the Beach Boys Vol. 2* (Capitol 2706), which includes "409," "Let Him Run Wild," the what-if-summer-doesn't-last-forever song "When I Grow Up to Be a Man," "California Girls," and their finest "I Get Around." Also worth seeking out are *Beach Boys Party* (Capitol 2364), to which Jan and Dean were luckily invited, and the marvelous *Wild Honey* (Capitol 2859). Avoid the *Endless Summer* reissue album, which presents lifeless stereo versions of songs that were never meant to be heard in anything but pure punchy mono; if the albums are unavailable, all the Beach Boys' sixties hits can be obtained as singles in Capitol's Star Line series.

The Beach Boys wanted more than cars and surf could give them; their vision had always been a passive one, and like many they went from easy questions to easy answers. When they recorded a song by Charles Manson—that drifting shaman who combined in equal parts the lumpenproletariat West found crusted beneath Hollywood and the Beverly Hills Dr. Feelgoods that Chandler hated above all others—the Beach Boys really did begin to grow up. Ed Sanders' brilliant account of Manson loose in post-surf rocker's Hollywood, *The Family* (New York: Dutton, 1971), lays out the facts of this Southern California synthesis of fun and horror, just as Randy Newman's songs capture its soul.

Unlike so many Hollywood groups that come from somewhere else, the Beach Boys have never been fakes. They celebrated the freedom of California hedonism, looked for its limits, owned up to its failures, but never lost the ability to delight in the sun and to share that delight with others. Their pleasures, as opposed to those claimed by such seventies inheritors as the Eagles and "America," have always radiated affection because those pleasures are rooted in friendship.

THE KINKS

The Kinks will likely be remembered as one of the strangest of all rock 'n' roll groups, and as one of the best. For crude, brutal hard rock, their early singles outclassed those of the Beatles and the Rolling Stones, probably because the spirit of resentment and rage such music communicates was exactly what Kinks' leader Ray Davies felt: he really doesn't like it here. He is genuinely at home only in his fantasies of a simpler time, when class lines were clear, when everyone knew their place, when, presumably, there would have been a place even for him. His search for a phantom paradise has taken him as deeply into the throes of nostalgia as anyone in popular music—thus his dull pleas for the preservation of village greens—and it has also given him the power to make records as disturbing and haunting as "The Way Love Used To Be," or as strong as "I'm Not Like Everybody Else," which is so honest it's frightening.

Those last are the highlights of *The Great Lost Kinks Album* (Warner Bros. 0598); the initial 1964–1966 smashes (the hard rockers, like "You Really Got Me," and Davies's first attempts at social comment, such as "A Well Respected Man") are on *The Kinks Greatest Hits* (Reprise 6217). Davies' sharpest work came in 1967 with *Fact to Face* (Reprise 6228), which included "Sunny Afternoon," and in 1968, with *Something Else* (Reprise 6279), an album that sings softly to a close with the Kinks' masterpiece, "Waterloo Sunset."

These records, however, sold hardly at all; *Arthur (Or, The Decline and Fall of the British Empire)* (Reprise 6366), released in 1969, and *Lola Versus Powerman and the Moneygoround* (Reprise 6423), from 1970, brought new fans even as Davies's songs grew more heavy-handed. The great "Lola" is perhaps better heard on *The Kink Kronikles* (Reprise 6454), a collection of later album cuts, nonhits, and unreleased tunes.

Ever campier, ever uncomfortable, Ray Davies and the Kinks roll on, but save for the occasional wonderful surprise like "Celluloid Heroes" or "20th Century Man," they roll downhill. Randy Newman is smarter than Davies, but whether his career will have a better ending remains to be seen.

ELVIS PRESLEY

ELVIS: AN INTRODUCTION

In 1974 RCA issued *Elvis, Vol. 1: A Legendary Performer* (RCA 0341), a single album that illustrates, both historically and aesthetically, virtually every side of the man's career. As an outline of my concerns, I could hardly have made a better selection myself.

Legendary Performer begins at Sun Records, in July of 1954, with "That's All Right (Mama)," E.P.'s first single, followed by "I Love You Because," the sentimental country-tune-with-narration that was in fact Elvis's very first professional recording (though Sam Phillips never released it, and this complete version was never previously released by RCA). Then immediately to "Heartbreak Hotel," completely unlike the Sun discs, number one on pop, country, and R&B charts early in 1956. A snatch of interview from that time: a reporter asks Elvis if his success is due to luck or talent, and Elvis, naturally, answers Luck. Without a pause we are into "Don't Be Cruel," also a three-chart number one, and it gives the lie to Elvis's modesty: no one has ever sung with such confidence.

We hear "Love Me Tender" from El's first movie, his first number one ballad; we hear "Peace in the Valley," from 1957, Elvis's first, and perhaps his best, gospel record. Then to "(Now and Then There's) A Fool Such As I," from 1958, where Elvis distances himself from his style with outrageous parody; then to "Tonight's All Right for Love," a ghastly number from the 1960 film *G.I. Blues*, where we find that the parody has become the style.

Scattered through the album are three songs, cut live with a studio audience, from the television comeback performance of late 1968: a joking "Are You Lonesome Tonight?"; a staggering version of "Love Me," with Elvis wavering between passion and parody until passion finally wins; and, finally, "Tryin' to Get to You," a song Elvis first recorded back in 1955. Thirteen years later Elvis sings it as if it is a message to his audience (directed not merely to those in the studio, but to all they represent): his way of telling us how hard it was to find his way back. His singing makes his early classics seem immature, unfocused, almost empty. They were not, of course; but this music—all glamour, fury, and drama—is quite beyond anything else in rock 'n' roll.

Legendary Performer ends, as it should, with "Can't Help Falling in Love," from the *Blue Hawaii* soundtrack of 1961, but now the theme song of Elvis-in-the-seventies. Elvis sings it as a hymn.

On this album, Elvis's long career makes sense, it has shape. One can see the artist grow, the god fail, the King return, and the man endure. As a version of American possibility and American limits, it is fully the equal of Robert Johnson's *King of the Delta Blues Singers*.

With *Legendary Performer* as a map, we can turn to Elvis's music in detail.

THE SUN SIDES, 1953–1955

Original Sun discs by Elvis now go for at least $100 each; RCA reissued all five singles in 1956, and reissues of *those* 45's are still available (and, because of the atrocious fake stereo now used on all Elvis albums made before 1960, the 45's are well worth ordering). Almost all the Sun material Sam Phillips put out is collected on two excellent albums. *For LP Fans Only* (RCA 1990) also includes brilliant early RCA cuts like "My Baby Left Me," "I Was the One," and "Lawdy Miss Clawdy." *A Date With Elvis* (RCA 2011), even in reprocessed stereo, is arguably the best Elvis album of all, combining Sun music with the great "Is It So Strange" and three wonderful tunes from *Jailhouse Rock*, El's finest movie: "Jailhouse Rock," "(You're So Square) Baby I Don't Care," and "Young and Beautiful."

Elvis's initial recordings were cut in June 1953, at the Memphis Recording Service, a make-your-own-record-for-two-bucks sideline that Sam Phillips had set up in order to supplement the uncertain income of the Sun label. Although according to legend Elvis showed up to sing a birthday song for his mother, I side with Hans Langbroek, author of the Dutch booklet *The Hillbilly Cat*, who suggests that since Gladys Presley's birthday fell in April, Elvis really made his record for himself: to find out if he was any good, or perhaps hoping someone would notice him. Whatever the motive, Elvis put down two standards: the Ink Spots' "My Happiness," and "That's When Your Heartaches Begin." A few months later he was back, to make "A Casual Love" and "I'll Never Stand in Your Way"; though the songs were ordinary, Marion Keisker, Phillips's secretary, heard something special in the voice and pushed Phillips to give the boy a formal audition. Phillips brought in Scotty Moore and Bill Black to help work out a distinctive sound;

on July 6, 1954, they began to record seriously. Elvis's Sun singles followed in this order:

"That's All Right (Mama)" b/w "Blue Moon of Kentucky," released August 1954 (Sun 209, RCA 45 447–0601). "That's All Right" is on *For LP Fans Only* as well as *Legendary Performer;* original version by Mississippi blues singer Arthur Crudup, 1946 (available on *Arthur Crudup Father of Rock and Roll*, RCA V–573; also included are original versions of "So Glad You're Mine" and "My Baby Left Me"). "Blue Moon of Kentucky" is on *A Date With Elvis;* the slow, early take of the song, with studio dialogue between Elvis, Phillips, and Scotty Moore, is on *Good Rocking Tonight*, Bopcat Records 100, Dutch); original version by Bill Monroe, 1948 (on *Bill Monroe's 16 Greatest Hits*, Columbia 1065).

"Good Rockin' Tonight" b/w "I Don't Care If the Sun Don't Shine," released October 1954 (Sun 210, RCA 45 447–0602). "Good Rockin' " is on *Date With;* original versions by Roy Brown and Wynonie Harris, 1949 (Harris's version available on his *Good Rockin' Blues*, King 1086). "I Don't Care" not available on LP as originally issued; alternate takes on *Good Rocking Tonight*.

"Milkcow Blues Boogie" b/w "You're a Heartbreaker," released January 1955 (Sun 215, RCA 45 447–0603). "Milkcow" is on *Date;* original versions by blues singer Kokomo Arnold, 1934 ("Milk Cow Blues," available on *Kokomo Arnold/Peetie Wheatstraw*, Blues Classics 4), and by Bob Wills & His Texas Playboys, 1946 ("Brain Cloudy Blues," available on *Bob Wills Anthology*, Columbia 32416). "You're a Heartbreaker" is on *For LP Fans*, first recorded by E.P.

"Baby Let's Play House" b/w "I'm Left, You're Right, She's Gone," released May 1955 (Sun 217, RCA 45 447–0604). "Baby, Let's Play House" is on *Date;* original version by R&B singer Arthur Gunter, 1955 (available on *Black & Blues*, Excello 8017). Buddy Holly's first clumsy attempt to turn himself into Elvis can be heard in his version of the tune, cut in 1955 as "I Wanna Play House With You" (on *Holly in the Hills*, Coral 757463). "I'm Left" is on *For LP Fans;* first recorded by E.P. "My Baby is Gone," the slow, torchy alternate of "I'm Left" that Sam Phillips pressed only for DJ's is on *Good Rocking Tonight*.

"Mystery Train" b/w "I Forgot to Remember to Forget," released August 1955 (Sun 223, RCA 45 447–6000). "Mystery Train" is on *For LP Fans;* original versions by Little Junior's Blue Flames

(Junior Parker), 1953 (no reissue, out of print), and by the Carter Family ("Worried Man Blues," A. P. Carter, lead vocal, available on *The Famous Carter Family* Harmony 11332; a much weaker version, with Sarah Carter on lead, is on *My Old Cottage Home*, RCA ACL1–0047). "I Forgot" is on *Date;* first recorded by E.P.

The following Sun recordings were sold, along with Elvis, to RCA Victor in 1955, and released on *Elvis Presley* (RCA 1254) in 1956: "I Love You Because," "Just Because," recorded 1954; "I'll Never Let You Go (Little Darlin')," "Blue Moon," and "Tryin' to Get to You," recorded 1955. The original of "Tryin' to Get to You" is interesting mainly because it was one of the first attempts at rockabilly after Elvis; it was cut in 1955 in Clovis, New Mexico, by Roy Orbison and the Teenkings, and produced by Norman Petty, who later guided Buddy Holly and the Crickets to fame. Orbison's initial treatment (he later recut the tune and its flipside, "Ooby Dooby," for Sam Phillips at Sun) is available on *Memphis Rocks the Country* (Redita 106, Dutch), a collection of sides that feature Sam Phillips's first attempts to teach rock 'n' roll to country singers like Malcom Yelvington and Hardrock Gunter.

In 1956, Elvis, already on top, returned to the Sun studios in Memphis and sat in with Carl Perkins, Johnny Cash, and Jerry Lee Lewis for a session of gospel and rock. Phillips recorded his "Million Dollar Quartet," but the tape has never come out; songs include "Big Boss Man," "Blueberry Hill," "I Won't Have to Cross Jordan Alone," "Island of Golden Dreams," "That Old Rugged Cross," and "Peace in the Valley."

THE TRIUMPH, 1956–1959

Elvis's first RCA recordings were made with Scotty Moore on guitar, Bill Black on bass, D. J. Fontana on drums, and (usually) the Jordinaires on backing vocals. Shorty Long, Chet Atkins, and many others were often brought in as well. In essence, Elvis served as his own producer.

Elvis' Golden Records (RCA 1707) collects the hits from 1956 and 1957: "Hound Dog" (Willie Mae Thornton's treatment, though not her original version, can be found on her *She's Back!* album, Backbeat 68), "Don't Be Cruel," the superb "Anyway You Want Me," "All Shook Up," and others. This is simply one of the basic, one can say founding, rock 'n' roll records.

Elvis' Christmas Album came out in 1957 and has since been reissued (RCA/Camden 2428) in original mono; along with the predictable standards was the funky "Blue Christmas," plus Jerry Leiber and Mike Stoller's "Santa Claus Is Back in Town," which gave El the chance to leer: "Santa Claus is coming in a big black Cadillac!" It was, in Charles Perry's phrase, like finding a hamburger in a medicine chest.

50,000,000 Elvis Fans Can't Be Wrong—Elvis' Gold Records, Vol. 2 (RCA 2075, with the historic gold lamé outfit on the cover) handled chart entries from 1957 through 1959. It was during this period, as a friend of mine put it, that Elvis "sold out to girls"; aside from "Don't," the music is hackneyed, and even the parodies sound like clichés. Elvis was already devoting most of his time to the movies. The soundtracks for *Love Me Tender, Love Me* and *King Creole* produced bad rock and bad ballads; *Jailhouse Rock* was another story, perhaps because Leiber and Stoller were helping out (see *A Date With Elvis*). Elvis left for the army still on top.

DECLINE AND FALL, 1960–1968

Elvis returned in 1960, and immediately made *Elvis Is Back*, his first stereo LP (RCA 2231); though the album is uneven, every minute of it screams release, freedom, and relief. And what better way to affirm that rules and regulations were behind him than to find the best band in the land and cut loose with the blues? The group Elvis used on this record is amazing; nothing like the country blues sound of the Sun singles, but full-blown Chicago menace, highlighted by El's own acoustic guitar, recorded up front, and by absolutely demonic sax work from Boots Randolph. Elvis's singing wasn't sexy, it was pornographic. "Dirty, Dirty Feeling" and "Such a Night" were standouts; the killer was "Reconsider Baby," a blues that Lowell Fulson had first recorded in 1954. Fulson meant the song as a plea; Elvis, driving the band hard, sang the tune as a slow, measured threat. Anyone who thinks the army took the rebellion out of Elvis would change his mind after listening to his performance.

With that burst of life out of the way, however, Elvis settled down to work. He made two, sometimes three movies a year, plus full soundtracks for each. He was more successful than ever: "It's Now or Never" (1960) sold 9 million copies; the soundtrack from *Blue Hawaii* sold 5 million straight off. He did his job. There were echoes of his genius, of humor and excitement, in his singles, but they were only echoes. *Elvis' Golden Records, Vol. 3* (RCA 2765) collected hits from 1960 through 1963, but there was a soullessness to the music that he escaped only with the beautiful "Fame and Fortune," and with a remake of Chuck Willis's "Feel So Bad," a wild, frenzied masterpiece that was in truth a cut left over from the sessions for *Elvis Is Back*.

One must look hard and long through *Roustabout*, *Girl Happy*, *Elvis for Everyone*, *Paradise Hawaiian Style*, and the like, for even a glimmer of style and feeling; one such moment comes on *Spinout* (RCA 3702), released in 1966, with El's version of Bob Dylan's "Tomorrow Is a Long Time." Invariably during this period, his best music was pure gospel. *His Hand in Mine* (RCA 2328), from 1960, was straightforward and convincing; *How Great Thou Art* (RCA 3758), from 1967, which included his really profound version of "Crying in the Chapel," was enough to make you convert. But that was about it; when *Elvis' Gold Records, Vol. 4* (RCA 3921) came out in 1968, it contained not a single interesting track.

But late in 1967 Elvis had begun to stir. In short order he cut "Big Boss Man" (RCA 45 9341), "Guitar Man" (RCA 45 9425), and "U.S. Male" (RCA 45 9465). They weren't big hits, but they made people wonder if something new wasn't happening, and something was.

THE COMEBACK, 1968–1969

Thanks to producer Steve Binder, Elvis reappeared in late 1968, before a national TV audience, and saved his career. *Elvis' TV Special* (RCA 4088) opened with "Trouble" and closed with "If I Can Dream," a stunning ballad; in between were the live performances that proved Elvis really was the King. "Lawdy Miss Clawdy," "Baby What You Want Me to Do," and "Blue Christmas" were first-rate; "One Night" was Elvis's greatest moment (Smiley Lewis's 1955 original version, the lyrics of which Elvis sang for the first time on this show, can be heard on Lewis's *Shame Shame Shame*, Liberty 83308, English). Another song from this night, "Tiger Man" (an old Rufus Thomas number for Sun), was issued on the otherwise throwaway LP, *Elvis Sings Flaming Star and Others* (RCA/Singer 279). RCA still has hours of this material in their vaults; I'm waiting.

In May 1969 came *From Elvis In Memphis* (RCA 4155), the first nonmovie, nongospel, nonrandom collection studio album since

Elvis Is Back. "Long Black Limousine" and "I'll Hold You in My Heart (Till I Can Hold You in My Arms)" were powerful, mature performances, but perhaps the best was "Any Day Now"—a Burt Bachrach tune that Elvis sang with a naked emotion I have not heard in his recordings before or since.

"Suspicious Minds" (RCA 45 9764) was number one in the fall of 1969; it was Elvis's first chart-topper in seven years, as it deserved to be. Along with it came *From Memphis to Vegas/From Vegas to Memphis* (RCA 6020), a two-record set. One disc was composed of decent but unexciting studio material from the sessions that produced *From Elvis in Memphis;* the other LP was the first of many, many, many live albums—this one drawn from his first comeback shows in Las Vegas—that in the seventies would serve the same function as the old soundtracks: blind product. This was, though, a good live album; the seven-minute "Suspicious Minds" was astonishing, and "Can't Help Falling in Love" was, well, it was "Can't Help Falling in Love."

THE APOTHEOSIS, 1970–?

With his comeback assured, Elvis settled into a state of grace; his only sin, as Bob Dylan once put it, was his lifelessness. In this era one confronts events more often than music. Elvis played New York City for the first time in 1972; the reviews were both ecstatic and convincing, and *Elvis as Recorded at Madison Square Garden* (RCA 4776) was in the stores a week after the concerts. Twenty songs were crammed onto one LP, including "American Trilogy"; clearly, though, one had to be there. A good part of the magic must have come from the fans, and they took most of it home with them. Elvis reversed field later that year with "Burning Love," a brilliant, aching single that fought past records by Chuck Berry and Rick Nelson on the way to number one. Some said the disc reached the top only because of a revival of interest in the fifties, but they couldn't have been listening. "Burning Love" was a very rare kind of record; it was a natural, unstoppable hit, on the order of "I Heard It Through the Grapevine," "You're So Vain," or "Don't Be Cruel". Typically, RCA put it out on a budget album called *Elvis Sings Burning Love (And Hits From His Movies)*. Get the single instead (RCA 45 74–0769).

With his rocker's dues paid up again, El floated on with various gruesome ballads, and, in 1973, with another live opus,

Aloha From Hawaii via Satellite (RCA 6089). This double album, issued to commemorate his planetwide TV special, featured a map of the world emblazoned with "We Love Elvis" in twenty-nine languages, if my count is accurate. There was one song for each tongue, more or less, though all were in English, save for "Kuiokalani Lee," which was in Hawaiian. *Aloha* was the King's first number one album in nine years; the last had been *Roustabout*, which is appropriate enough.

And they keep coming, album after album; occasionally the songs change, but not often. One is left to pour through the records for hidden gems, or to ignore the records altogether; obviously, given moments like "Burning Love," Elvis can be as exciting, or as dull, as he chooses. In some ways, then, an album Elvis put out in late 1971, *Elvis Sings the Wonderful World of Christmas* (RCA 4579), is the truest statement of all—for here, in the midst of ten painfully genteel Christmas songs, every one sung with appalling sincerity and humility, we find Elvis tom-catting his way through six blazing minutes of "Merry Christmas, Baby," a raunchy old Charles Brown blues. And that is what he has to tell us: if his sin is his lifelessness, it is his sinfulness that brings him to life. Thirty years from now, when RCA puts out its Deluxe Half-Century Elvis Retrospective album (with an ad for his latest movie pasted on the back), that story will still be worth hearing.

Elvis has inspired some of the very best rock writing. Jerry Hopkins' *Elvis* (New York: Simon & Shuster, 1971) is the standard biography; well-researched, clear, including a comprehensive discography of all singles, EP's, and albums from 1954 through 1971. The book lacks any real point of view, but I certainly couldn't have worked without it. Hans Langbroek's *The Hillbilly Cat* (self-published, available through J & F Southern Record Sales) is a short history of the Sun period; not entirely accurate, but always fun. Clive Anderson's "How Elvis Bleached the Blues: Black Roots" (*Let It Rock*, Special Elvis Issue, December 1973) is, despite its title, a fine survey of the scores of black records Elvis has covered and changed in the last twenty years.

These pieces, however, are the classics: Stanley Booth's "A Hound Dog, to the Manor Born" (in *Age of Rock*, ed. John Eisen [New York: Vintage, 1969]), a moving, personal account of Elvis's emergence in Memphis in 1954, contrasted with his sixties limbo; Jon Landau's "In Praise of Elvis Presley" (in Landau's *It's Too Late to Stop Now*, Straight Arrow, 1972), a report on a 1971 Boston concert; Stu Werbin's "Elvis and the A-Bomb" (*Creem*, March 1972), a cosmic attempt to place Elvis in a cosmic perspective, written following the same concert Landau saw; Robert Christgau's "Elvis Presley: Aging Rock" (in Christgau's *Any Old Way You Choose It* [Baltimore: Penguin, 1973]), an analysis of Elvis's career focused around his comeback shows in Vegas in 1969 and his Madison Square Garden concerts of 1972; Nik Cohn's chapter on Elvis in *Rock From the Beginning* (New York: Stein and Day, 1969; expanded version in the retitled second edition, *Wop Bop A Loo Bop Lop Bam Boom*, Paladin, 1972, English); and, likely best of all, Peter Guralnick's review of *From Elvis in Memphis* (collected in *Rolling Stone Record Review* [New York: Pocket Books, 1971]). I didn't completely agree with any of these essays, and I've learned from all of them.

THE CARTER FAMILY, JIMMIE RODGERS, AND HANK WILLIAMS

The Carter Family (A. P., his wife Sarah, and his sister-in-law "Mother" Maybelle Addington) came from the Clinch Mountains in Virginia, near the Tennessee border. Ralph Peer recorded both the Carters and Jimmie Rodgers for the first time in August 1927; they dominated country record sales and country radio for most of the next decade. Maybelle Carter's guitar and autoharp playing has influenced literally every first-rate white guitar player since the twenties, not to mention a good many of the black guitar players; the Carters' songs have gone all over the world. They sang traditional folk material, gospel, some blues, nineteenth-century sentimental standards; of the many albums on the market, *The Famous Carter Family* (Harmony 11332) is probably the best introduction, featuring "My Clinch Mountain Home," "Keep on the Sunny Side," "Can the Circle Be Unbroken," "Wildwood Flower," "Worried Man Blues," and their joyous "Gospel Ship." *The Original and Great Carter Family* (RCA/Camden 586) includes the mystical "Diamonds in the Rough," "Little Moses," and "Wabash Cannonball." Discs that do not say "The Original" usually indicate records made after World War II by Maybelle Carter and her daughters, without A. P. and Sarah; they bear little relation to the music cut in the twenties and thirties.

Jimmie Rodgers was one of the most important and creative

singers in American history. Born in Meridian, Mississippi, in 1897, he spent a good part of his youth on the railroad, listening to black minstrels and work gangs; when tuberculosis forced him to quit the rails in 1925, he turned to music. By the time he began to record in 1927 he had mastered a brilliant, completely unique blues style: the "blue yodel" that Howlin' Wolf claims showed him how to howl. Rodgers' most striking album is *My Rough and Rowdy Ways* (RCA 2112), which collects "Blue Yodel No. 1 (T for Texas)," Rodgers' first real hit; "Blue Yodel No. 9" (backing by Louis Armstrong and Earl Hines); and "Long Tall Mama Blues." *Never No Mo' Blues* (RCA 1232) includes the great "California Blues," Rodgers' ironic tribute to the dispossessed Okies who sang the song all the way to the coast.

Hank Williams was born in 1923; he left home to sing in 1937, and first recorded in 1946. He was the first country singer whose music reached into every corner of the United States; in terms of music and impact, he might be called the white Ray Charles. His career, dragged down by drinking, drugs, and divorce, was as chaotic as it was successful; by the end Williams had been expelled from the Grand Old Opry for his sins. He died in 1953, only twenty-nine years old; people still pay to see the death car, but they would do better to read Ralph Gleason's "Hank Williams, Roy Acuff, and Then God!"—an epitaph that is worth more than all the books, speeches, prayers, and songs H. W. has inspired over the last twenty years (in *The Rolling Stone Rock 'n' Roll Reader*, ed. Ben Fong-Torres [New York: Bantam, 1974]).

Hank Williams' Greatest Hits (MGM 4775) is the basic collection; *Lost Highway and Other Folk Ballads* (MGM 4524) is essential, if only for the title track, the song on which Bob Dylan based "Like a Rolling Stone." *I'm Blue Inside* (MGM 3926) is almost all blues, and great; *I Saw the Light* (MGM) is the best for spirituals. Avoid the sets that present Hank Williams, Jr., singing along with tapes of his dead father; morbidity and necrophilia, as logical extensions of rural nostalgia, have always been central to country music, but these albums are just a little too much.

CHARLIE RICH, "LOUIE, LOUIE," AND OTHERS

Charlie Rich's "Feel Like Going Home" was released in 1973 as the flipside of "The Most Beautiful Girl" (Epic 45 5-11040). This harmless version has nothing to do with the performance I

saw Rich dedicate to Richard Nixon; producer Billy Sherrill buried
the vocal in chorus singing and horns, and smoothed out the
strange melody and the confusing chord changes that gave the
music its unsettling power. Rich did record the tune as he meant it
to be heard—his piano was the only instrumentation, a strange
wedding of Skip James craziness and stately country gospel. Epic
still has the tape, and it may come out one of these days.

Possibly the most soulful of all white singers, Rich's late fifties
work for Sun is collected on *The Best of Charlie Rich* (Trip 8502); his
superb recordings of the mid-sixties are on *Fully Realized* (Mercury
7505), with notes by Peter Guralnick, whose chronicle of Rich's ca-
reer can be followed with "Lonely Weekends" (in Guralnick's *Feel
Like Going Home*), an account of Rich's failure, and with "Charlie
Rich In New York" (*Let It Rock*, September 1973), an account of
Rich's success. *The Best of Charlie Rich* (Epic 31933) contains music
Rich cut for Epic before "Behind Closed Doors" made him a star;
"Life's little Ups and Downs," "Sittin' and Thinkin'," "A
Woman Left Lonely," "I Take It on Home," and the magnificent
"Set Me Free" define how far a country singer whose soul comes
from the blues can go.

Dolly Parton's "My Blue Ridge Mountain Boy" is best heard
on *A Real Live Dolly Parton* (RCA 4387), an album that also features
"Bloody Bones," a little ditty about orphans who burn down their
orphanage. The Allman Brothers' "Blue Sky" is on *Eat a Peach*
(Capricorn 0102); their "Pony Boy" is on *Brothers and Sisters* (Capri-
corn 0111). William Moore's timeless 1928 celebration, "Old
Country Rock," can be found on *Really! The Country Blues* (Origin
Jazz Library 2)

As for the saga of "Louie, Louie," the records that tell the
story are: "Riot in Cellblock #9," by the Robins, lead vocal by
Richard Berry, 1954 (originally on Spark; available on *The Coasters,
The Early Years*, Atco 371); "The Big Break," by Richard Berry,
1955 (originally on Flair, out of print, no reissue); "Louie, Louie,"
by Richard Berry, 1957 (originally on Flip; out of print, no reissue);
"Louie, Louie," by the Kingsmen, 1963 (originally on Wand; available on *Best of the Kingsmen*, Scepter 18002); "Louie, Louie," by
Paul Revere & the Raiders, 1963 (originally on Gardena; available
on *Paul Revere & the Raiders' Greatest Hits*, Columbia 3164); and
"Brother Louie," by Stories, 1973 (Kama Sutra 45 577).

SAM PHILLIPS, SUN RECORDS
& ROCKABILLY MUSIC

Sam Phillips, for those who haven't yet guessed, is the secret hero of this book; I don't know if he was merely the right man in the right place at the right time, or much more than that, and I don't really care. The man's history is in the records he made.

Phillips first recorded Memphis blues singers in 1949; much of the best of that music is collected on *Genesis, Vol. 2—Memphis to Chicago* (Chess 6641 125, English), a four-record set that includes historic sides by Howlin' Wolf ("Moanin' at Midnight," "How Many More Years," 1951), Jackie Brenston ("Rocket 88," 1951, one of several "first rock 'n' roll records"), Doctor Ross, Joe Hill Louis, and Harmonica Frank. It's worth placing Wolf's music at Sun next to his Chess material; on *Evil* (Chess 1540), a reissue of his first LP, "How Many More Years" leaps off the record, one straight shot of anger; the cuts recorded in Chicago, classics all, seem self-effacing by comparison. Phillips wanted feeling, flair, and novelty in his music; his records weren't offerings, they were demands. See also, for these first pre-Sun years, *Dr. Ross His First Recordings* (Arhoolie 1065), and *The Great Original Recordings of Harmonica Frank* (Puritan 3003).

Sun was founded in 1952. *Memphis Blues at Sunshine* (Redita 105, Dutch) collects many of the blues sides Phillips put out: Rufus Thomas's "Tiger Man," 1953, covered fifteen years later by Elvis; songs by Walter Horton, Joe Hill Louis, Johnny London, and Billy the Kid Emerson. *The Sun Story* (Sun 6649 167, English), a two record survey of Sun releases of all sorts from 1953 through 1966, includes Rufus Thomas's "Bear Cat," an answer record to Willie Mae Thornton's original "Hound Dog," 1953; Junior Parker's sizzling "Feelin' Good," 1953; and the Prisonaires' "Just Walking in the Rain," 1953.

"She Cares No More," by Don Poindexter, a pre-Elvis white release from early 1954, was significant only in that Poindexter's band, the Starlight Wranglers, included Bill Black and Scotty Moore. Phillips seems to have made his few conventional country and western recordings solely to pay the rent; the sides by Poindexter and "Hardrock" Gunter (so named for his strength, not for his musical taste) reveal none of the ambition or the spirit of the blues discs, let alone of Presley's (see *Memphis Rocks the Country*, Redita 106, Dutch).

With Elvis, the label changed. Blues vanished almost completely; Phillips went for the main chance, which meant white boys who could sing country rock. After Elvis, Malcom Yelvington was the first to record; "Drinkin' Wine Spo-Dee-O-Dee" and "Just Rollin' Along," both 1954, neither very good, are on *Memphis Rocks the Country;* the funkier "It's Me Baby," 1956, is on *Carryin' on—Sun Rockabillies Vol. 2* (Sun 6467 027, English), an uneven collection that also includes Warren Smith's "Miss Froggie."

When Elvis left Sun in the fall of 1955, dozens of new singers were beginning to record in Texas, Nashville, and other Southern music centers; the rest were in Memphis, begging Phillips for auditions. The best were Carl Perkins, Roy Orbison, and Billy Lee Riley, all of whom first recorded in 1955, and Jerry Lee Lewis, who started in 1956.

Perkins made beautiful records with Sam Phillips; "Blue Suede Shoes," "Boppin' the Blues," his gentle re-creation of the Platters' "Only You," the jailhouse rocker "Dixie Fried," and his stomping "Matchbox" (Jerry Lee on piano) can be found on *Carl Perkins—Original Golden Hits* (Sun 111); "Put Your Cat Clothes On" is on *Put Your Cat Clothes On—Sun Rockabillies Vol. 1* (Sun Phillips 6467 025), which also includes delights like Sonny Burgess's "We Wanna Boogie," Ray Harris's "Come on Little Mama," and Hayden Thompson's "Love My Baby." Perkins made many more albums for Columbia, Mercury, and other labels; he never really had another hit, nor ever matched his first music.

Orbison, after the one single for Jewel in New Mexico, cut "Ooby Dooby" and "Go Go Go" for Phillips; the latter, available only on a reissued 45 (Sun #8), is one of the most exciting rockabilly records ever made. Outside of the searing "Domino," which presages almost everything surf music later came to mean (unreleased until it appeared on the *Cat Clothes* LP), Orbison's other Sun sides were less striking. Most are collected on *Roy Orbison—The Original Sound* (Sun 113). Orbison went on to have many wonderful psuedo-operatic hits right through 1965 (see *The All-Time Greatest Hits of Roy Orbison*, Monument 31484); he finally dropped into oblivion singing "A Place for Lovers" over the final credits to *Zabriskie Point.*

Billy Lee Riley first cut "Trouble Bound" for the Fernwood label in Memphis in 1955, playing all the instruments; he hit a dark, brooding tone that only Presley surpassed. Phillips leased the disc and put it out on Sun, and then recorded two scorching sides that still make most everyone else sound as if they're only fooling around: "My Gal Is Red Hot" and "Flying Saucers Rock 'n' Roll," the latter being one of the weirdest of early rock records (it is available on *The Sun Story;* the others are as yet unissued in their original versions). Riley drifted into session work and occasional 45's under other names; he's still around, looking for that hit.

Jerry Lee Lewis started off playing piano in church, and turned to rock 'n' roll full-time when the preacher canned him for sneaking too much boogie woogie into the hymns. Jerry Lee recorded far more extensively than any other Sun artist: blues, country, rock, schmaltz, gospel, and even a comedy paste-up celebrating, sort of, the scandal over his marriage to Cousin Myra. *Rockin' Up a Storm* (Sun 6641 162, English) is a two-record hard rock set; all the hits are here, along with the flourishing "Lewis Boogie," and the title song, which just may be Jerry Lee's finest. His dirtiest, "Big Legged Woman," is on *Rockin' Rhythm and Blues* (Sun 107). An even better album is *Ole Tyme Country Music* (Sun 121); I don't know who made up the title, but Jerry Lee transforms everything from "Deep Elem Blues" to "You Are My Sunshine" into one long roadhouse stomp.

Jerry Lee never changed his act, never slowed down, never quit. He left Sun in the sixties for the Smash label, and turned out *The Greatest Live Show on Earth* (Smash 67056); many first-rate country albums; a duet LP with his sister Gail that is raunchier than his legend (*Together,* Smash 67126); and even a supersession with British musicians (*The Session,* Smash 2–803) that featured a version of "Drinkin' Wine Spo–Dee–O–Dee" that cut a swath through most everything else on the radio in 1973. If the day ever comes when rock 'n' roll is just a memory, Jerry Lee will still be up on stage, playing it.

Those were the titans of rockabilly. The other singers, many of them deified by misty-eyed collectors, are far less impressive. Warren Smith and Malcom Yelvington had no real affinity for the black music rockabilly took off from, and little enough personality of their own; Charlie Feathers, despite his great "One Hand Loose" (on *Mac Curtis/Charlie Feathers,* Polydor 1234, English), cut for King in 1956, was just a rather odd country singer. Carl Mann and Carl McVoy were not much more than fakes; Sonny Burgess, though occasionally wild–eyed, huffed and puffed more than he rocked. Charlie Rich was always a soul singer. Outside of Sun, with the rare exception of an original like Buddy Holly, most rockabilly singers weren't even imitating blacks, they were imitating "All Shook Up." Collectors call the likes of Alvis Wayne and Johnny Burnette geniuses, but their aggressive stance is never convincing and the flash is always forced.

Rockabilly was a very special music. For all of its unchained energy and outrage, it demanded a fine balance between white impulses and black, between fantasies of freedom and the realities that produced those fantasies. The sound Phillips invented for Elvis proves how well he understood this; but sometimes, working for that next hit, Phillips ran into mysteries in the music not even he could have expected.

In 1957, Phillips, Billy Lee Riley, and Jerry Lee Lewis were setting up to make "Great Balls of Fire," the follow-up to the monumental "Whole Lotta Shakin'," Sun's biggest record. Suddenly, Jerry Lee objected. In 1949, as a kid in Ferriday, Louisiana, he had talked his way onto a bandstand for the chance to bang out "Drinkin' Wine Spo-Dee-O-Dee," but on the way to Sun he had also put in some time at the Southwest Bible School in Waxahachie, Texas; like all rockabilly ravers, he was raised on the gospel. Sitting in Phillips's studio, reading over the lead sheet for "Great Balls of Fire," the meaning of the image must have hit him. "Great balls of fire"—that was a Pentecostal image, that meant Judgment Day—and now Sam Phillips wanted Jerry Lee to make the image into a filthy joke, to *defile* the image. Jerry Lee rebelled.

JERRY LEE LEWIS: H—E—L—L!
SAM PHILLIPS: I don't believe it.
JLL: Great Godamighty, great balls of fire!
BILLY LEE RILEY: That's right!
SP: I don't believe it.
JLL: It says, WAKE MAN! To the Joy of God! Only!

But when it comes to *worldly music* [Jerry Lee is already high on a pulpit]—that's rock 'n' roll . . .

BLR: Rock it out!
JLL: —or anything like that, you have done brought yourself into the world, and you're in the world, and you hadn't come on out of the world, *and you're still a sinner.*
You're a sinner—and when you be saved—*and borned again*—and be made *as a little child*—

And walk before God—
And be holy—
And brother, I mean that you got to be so pure! No sin shall
enter there: *No Sin!*
For it says, *No Sin.* It don't say just a little bit, it says, NO SIN
SHALL ENTER THERE—brother, not one little bit! You've got to walk
and *talk* with God to go to Heaven. You've got to be *so* good.
BLR: Hallelujah.
SP: Alright. Now look, Jerry. Religious conviction—doesn't mean
anything—resembling extremism. [Phillips suddenly picks up
speed.] *Do you mean to tell me* that you're gonna take the Bible,
you're gonna take God's word, and you gonna revolutio*nize*
the *whole universe!* Now listen! Jesus Christ was sent here by
God Almighty. Did he convince, did he *save*, all the people in
the world?
JLL: Naw, but he tried to!
SP: *He sure did.* NOW WAIT JUST A MINUTE. Jesus Christ—
came into this world. He *tolerated* man. He didn't preach from
one pulpit. He went around, and he *did good.*
JLL: That's right! He preached *everywhere!*
SP: Everywhere!
JLL: He preached on land!
SP: Everywhere! That's right! That's right!
JLL: He preached on the water!
SP: That's right, that's exactly right! Now—
JLL: And then he done everything! He *healed!*
SP: Now, now—here's, *here's the difference—*
JLL [Speaking as if horns have sprouted on Phillips head]: *Are you
followin' Those That Heal?* Like Jesus Christ?
SP [Confused]: Whata you mean, I, I, what—
JLL [Triumphant]: Well, it's happening every day!
The *blind* had eyes opened.
The *lame* were made to walk.
SP: *Jerry—*
JLL: The *crippled* were made to walk.
SP: Alright now. Jesus Christ, in my opinion, is just as *real today,* as
He was when He came into this world.
JLL: Right, right, you're so right you don't know what you're
sayin'.
SP [Back on the offensive]: Now, then! I will say, *more so—*

BLR: Aw, let's *cut* it.

SP: Wait, wait, wait just a minute, we can't, we got to—Now, look. Now, listen. I'm tellin' you outa my heart. I have studied the Bible, a little bit—

JLL: Well, I have too.

SP: I've studied it through and through and through and through and Jerry, Jerry—If you think, that you can't, can't do good, if you're a rock 'n' roll exponent—

JLL: *You can do good,* Mr. Phillips, don't get me wrong—

SP: Now, wait, wait listen, when I say *do good*—

JLL: YOU CAN HAVE A KIND HEART!

SP [Suddenly angry]: I don't *mean,* I don't *mean* just—

JLL: You can help people!

SP: *You can save souls!*

JLL [Appalled]: No. NO! No, no!

SP: Yes!

JLL: How can the DEVIL save souls? *What are you talkin' about?*

SP: Lissen, lissen . . .

JLL: I have the Devil in me! If I didn't I'd be a Christian!

SP: Well, you may *have* him—

JLL [Fighting for his life]: JESUS! Heal this man! He cast the Devil out, the Devil says, Where can I go? He says, Can I go into this *swine?* He says, Yeah, go into him.
    Didn't he go into him?

SP: Jerry. The point I'm tryin' to make is—if you believe in what you're singin'—you got no alternative whatsoever—out of— LISTEN!—out of—

JLL: Mr. Phillips! I don't care, it ain't what you believe, it's [as if explaining to a child], *it's what's written in the Bible!*

SP: Well, wait a minute.

JLL: It's what is *there,* Mr. Phillips.

SP: No, no.

JLL: It's just what's there.

SP: No, by gosh, if it's not what you believe [and Phillips hits the clincher] *then how do you interpret the Bible!*

BLR: Man alive . . .

SP: Huh? How do you interpret the Bible if it's not what you believe!

JLL [Confused]: Well, it's just *not* what you believe, you just *can't*—

BLR: Let's *cut* it, man . . .

And so they did; *Good Rocking Tonight*, the rockabilly bootleg that includes this conversation, follows it with a furious take of "Great Balls of Fire"—a take that, one might say, outsins the version that Sam Phillips ultimately released to the public.

"Sam's crazy," Jerry Lee told John Grissim, many years later. "Nutty as a fox squirrel. He's just like me, he ain't got no sense. Birds of a feather flock together. It took all of us to screw up the world. We've done it."

INDEX

"Everybody Is a Star," 82, 83, 88, 106, 110
"Everyday People," 81, 106
Excello Records, 183
Exile on Main Street, 93

"Fame and Fortune," 196*n*
"Family Affair," 85, 87, 88-89
Faulkner, William, 33
Feathers, Charlie, 166
Feel Like Going Home, 179
Fiedler, Leslie, 6, 104, 114
"Fingertips," 81
Fitzgerald, F. Scott, 22, 26, 34
Floyd, Harmonica Frank, 5, 11-20, 24, 39, 53, 126, 155, 168*n*, 210
Flynn, Errol, 182
Fogerty, John, 48
"Fool," 196*n*
Ford, John, 51, 129
"(For God's Sake) Give More Power to the People," 95
Four Tops, 68, 102
"Four Until Late," 28
Franciosa, Tony, 99
Franklin, Aretha, 80
"Freddie's Dead," 93
Freewheelin', 13
Fresh, 105, 106, 107
Frith, Simon, 124
Frizzel, Lefty, 182
"Fun, Fun, Fun," 120
"Further on Up the Road," 47

Gamble, Kenny, 101, 102
Garson, Marvin, 43, 44
Gaye, Marvin, 54, 68, 93, 102
"George Jackson," 115
"Get a Job," 81
"Get Up Jake," 52
G.I. Blues, 193
Gillett, Charlie, 184-185
"Gimmie Shelter," 92
Godfather, The, 95, 129
"God's Song," 39, 117
"Go Go Liza Jane," 49
"Goin' Away Walkin'," 14
"Going Down Slow," 78
"Good Rockin' Tonight," 169, 171, 192*n*
"Great Medical Menagerist, The," 14
"Great Pretender, The," 71
Green, Al, 102
Grossman, Albert, 65
"Guitar Man," 143

Gunter, Hardrock Arthur, 163, 183, 184
Guralnick, Peter, 179

Halberstam, David, 17*n*
Haley, Bill, 174
Hammond, John, Jr., 48
Harder They Come, The, 187
Harmonica Frank, *see* Floyd, Harmonica Frank
Harris, Wynonie, 171
Haven Records, 124
"Have You Seen Her," 95
Hawkins, Ronnie, 45-48
Hawks (later the Band), 45, 46-49
"Hellhound on My Trail," 28, 40
Helm, Levon, 13, 45, 46, 47, 48-49, 52, 55, 56, 60, 62
"Helter Skelter," 125
Hendrix, Jimi, 31, 78, 87, 90
Henry, Clarence "Frogman," 13
"Heroin," 122
"Hey Boba Lu," 46
"Hey Good Lookin'," 151
Hit Man, 95
Holly, Charles "Buddy," 13, 167, 175, 183
"Honky Tonkin'," 151
Hopkins, Jerry, 173
"Hot Fun in the Summertime," 81
Hot Shot Love, 163
"Hound Dog," 20, 169, 173, 180, 184
House, Son, 23, 25, 30, 31-32, 168*n*
"How Great Thou Art," 204
Howlin' Wolf, 47, 67, 78, 116, 145, 163
"How Many More Years," 47
Hudson, Garth, 45, 48, 54, 55, 64, 67, 159
Huff, Leon, 101, 102
Hurt, Mississippi John, 77, 96, 110
Hyland, Brian, 174

"I Can See Clearly Now," 93
"I Can't Help Falling in Love with You," 204
"I Don't Care If the Sun Don't Shine," 190
"(I Don't Want To) Hang Up My Rock and Roll Shoes," 70
"If I Can Dream," 196*n*
"If I Had Possession Over Judgment Day," 23, 36
"I Forgot to Remember to Forget Her," 190
"If You Want Me to Stay," 106

About the Author

Greil Marcus was born in San Francisco in 1945. He received A.B. and M.A. degrees in American political thought from the University of California at Berkeley, and taught American Studies there in 1971–1972. Mr. Marcus has written for the San Francisco *Express-Times, Creem, The New York Times, Newsday, Let It Rock,* and other publications, and was record editor and associate editor of *Rolling Stone* in 1969–1970. He currently writes for *City* (San Francisco) and *The Village Voice.* His articles have appeared in *Rolling Stones—An Unauthorized Biography, The Rolling Stone Record Review, The Rolling Stone Rock 'n' Roll Reader,* and other books. Greil Marcus lives in Berkeley with his wife and two daughters.